DRIVING
U.S.A.

PRENTICE
HALL
PRESS

New York • London • Toronto • Sydney • Tokyo • Singapore

CONTENTS

Written by Eric Inglefield

Copy editor: Janet Tabinksi

Edited, designed and produced by AA Publishing. Maps © The Automobile Association 1991.

The contents of this publication are believed correct at the time of printing. Nevertheless, the publishers cannot accept responsibility for errors or omissions, nor for changes in details given.

ISBN 0–13–917667–5

Published in the United States by Prentice Hall Press. A division of Simon & Schuster Inc.,
15 Columbus Circle, New York, New York 10023.

Typesetting: Wyvern Typesetting, Bristol

Color Separation: Mullis Morgan Ltd, London

Printed and bound in Italy by Printers SRL

Front cover: *Yosemite National Park, California*

Title page: *Centrust Tower and Metromover, Miami*

Above: *Boston's JFK Library*

Opposite: *Amish buggy at dusk*

INTRODUCTION

This book is not only a practical touring guide for the independent traveler, but is also invaluable for those who would like to know more about the country.

It is divided into 10 regions, each containing between 2 and 5 tours. The tours start and finish in major cities which we consider to be the best centers for exploration.

Each tour has details of the most interesting places to visit *en route*. Side panels cater for special interests and requirements and cover a range of categories—for those whose interest is in history, wildlife or walking, and those who have children. There are also panels which highlight scenic stretches of road along the route and which give details of special events, crafts and customs. The numbers link them to the appropriate main text.

The simple route directions are accompanied by an easy-to-use map of the tour and there are addresses of local tourist information centers in some of the towns *en route* as well as in the start town.

Simple charts show how far it is from one town to the next in miles and kilometers. These can help you to decide where to take a break and stop overnight, for example. (All distances quoted are approximate.)

Before setting off it is advisable to check with the information center at the start of the tour for recommendations on where to break your journey and for additional information on what to see and do, and when best to visit.

Colorado's Rocky Mountains rise beyond fir-clad lower slopes

ENTRY REGULATIONS

British visitors need to hold a valid passport (not the visitors' kind) but in most cases do not now require a visa, providing they are staying in the US for less than 90 days, are holding a return or onward ticket, and are traveling with a carrier who has agreed to participate in the no-visa program. To ensure you will not be turned back at the port of entry, confirm with your airline prior to departure that no visa is required. However, rules at city gateways vary about transit stops and visitors may not be able to re-enter the US after a visit outside the country without a visa.

Other nationals (except for Canadians) will require a valid passport and visa.

CUSTOMS REGULATIONS

Adult visitors may bring into the US, duty free, any items meant for personal use, including cameras and tape recorders, up to one liter of alcohol, 200 cigarettes, 50 cigars or 3lb (1.4kg) of tobacco, or proportionate amounts of each. There is no limit on the amount of money, US or otherwise, brought into the country, although you must file a report with Customs if the amount exceeds $10,000.

Drugs (other than prescribed) are banned, and fresh meat, fruit, vegetables and plants are either prohibited from entering the US, or restricted.

EMERGENCY TELEPHONE NUMBERS

There is no nationwide emergency system in the US. There are emergency numbers you can call, and these are sometimes indicated on pay phones, but they vary from place to place. The best thing to do is call the operator by dialing '0' to connect you.

HEALTH

Health care in the US is of a very high standard but it is also 'private', so very expensive. It cannot be emphasized enough that international visitors should be covered by adequate health insurance before they set out and, if they are on prescribed medicines, should take a sufficient amount with them plus the actual prescription.

If you require a doctor or a dentist in a hurry, consult the Yellow Pages or your hotel.

Vaccinations are not required.

CURRENCY

The American monetary unit is the dollar ($) which is divided into 100 cents (¢). Coins are issued in cent denominations of 1 (a penny), 5 (a nickel), 10 (dime), 25 (quarter) and 50 (half-dollar). Notes (bills) are issued in denominations of 1, 2, 5, 10, 20, 50 and 100 dollars. All bills, regardless of denomination, are the same size and color. The

Chicago's dramatic skyline on the shores of Lake Michigan

amount of the bill is clearly shown in all corners and each bill has its own US statesman pictured in the center.

Always carry US dollar travelers' checks since they can be used as cash.

CREDIT CARDS

You can use credit cards almost anywhere. All the major credit cards are widely used and accepted.

BANKS

Banks are open from 09.00 to 15.00hrs, Monday to Friday and are closed on weekends and public holidays, although in some major towns and tourist areas, hours may be longer.

POST OFFICES

Some main post offices stay open 24 hours a day, but they are usually open between 08.00 and 18.00hrs Monday to Friday and 08.00 to 12.00hrs Saturdays.

Stamps are available from drug stores, hotels, motels and transport terminals.

TELEPHONES

Exact change in 5, 10 or 25 cent pieces is required to place a call. Phone cards can also be used. In the case of an emergency dial '0' for the operator if there is no obvious emergency number. To make a call, lift the receiver, listen for a tone, then deposit coin or card. If you want to make a reverse-charge call, dial the operator and ask for a 'collect' call, in which case your initial coin (25 cents) is refunded.

Country codes for international calls:
Australia 61
Canada 1
New Zealand 64
UK 44

TIME

The US has four major time zones. Eastern Standard Time is three hours ahead of Pacific Standard time, two hours ahead of Mountain Time and one hour ahead of Central Time. In April clocks are put forward one hour to take advantage of extra daylight, and they are put back again in late October. Eastern Standard Time is five hours behind Greenwich Mean Time (GMT), 17 hours behind Sydney and 19 hours behind New Zealand for most of the year.

MOTORING

Documents

You need only a valid driving licence from your country to rent a car, though an International Driver's Permit is required for visitors from certain countries.

Visitors wishing to enter Canada or Mexico should check documents needed, also passport and visa requirements.

USEFUL WORDS

British (and other visitors) may find it helpful to be reminded of some of the differences between American and British usage.
British American
autumn fall
bill check
biscuit cookie
bonnet hood (of car)
boot trunk (of car)
braces suspenders
caravan trailer
cupboard closet
dustbin garbage can
flat apartment
football soccer
gents men's room
lavatory rest room
lift elevator
lorry truck
pavement sidewalk
petrol gas, gasoline
post mail
tap faucet
tram streetcar
trousers pants

In multistory buildings, Americans begin counting the stories from street level, so the American first story is the British ground floor, and so on.

ELECTRICITY

The standard electricity supply in the US is 110 volts (60 cycles). You may have to bring an adaptor to convert. Sockets take plugs with two flat pins.

The performing killer whale, one of the main highlights of the show at San Diego's Sea World

Breakdowns

The American Automobile Association (AAA) is a member of a worldwide association of motoring organizations (AIT) and can make available its motoring/travel services to visitors who produce a valid membership certificate of a member organization. In case of a breakdown try the AAA nationwide emergency road service number, 1-800-336-HELP, and you will be told how to obtain emergency information. Help is also readily available from the efficient Highway Patrols. Just wait by the car. If it is a rented car, call the rental company and tell them about the breakdown.

Accidents

If you are involved in a traffic accident, you must report it to the police immediately and describe the nature of assistance needed.

Speed limits

The national speed limit in the US is 55mph (88kph), although a few states have upped the level to 65mph (104kph) on rural Interstate highways only. In cities and congested areas it is generally between 20–40mph (32–64kph). Road signs indicate specific limits and these are strictly enforced. The minimum speed limit posted on most Interstate highways or Expressways should be obeyed as rigidly as the maximum.

Driving conditions

Americans call motorways freeways, or interstate roads. Other roads are collectively known as highways. Toll roads also exist; they are known as superhighways and charge 2–3 cents a mile. Driving is on the right.

Driving tips

Two peculiarities to American driving are that it is permitted for a motorist to turn right at a red traffic light after stopping, and that traffic in both directions must stop while a school bus is loading or unloading.

Car rental and fly/drive

Most car rental agencies require the driver to be aged 21 or more, though some companies will rent to drivers of only 18 years. If a driving tour is planned, make sure that unlimited mileage is included (sometimes cars may only be driven in certain states).

Most of the national car rental companies will permit you to rent a car in one city and return it in another, but they may charge for this service.

Some operators feature fly/drive deals; sometimes the car is included in the cost of the holiday package.

Route directions

Throughout the book the following abbreviations are used for US roads:

I—Interstate Highway
US—US Highway
SR—State Route.

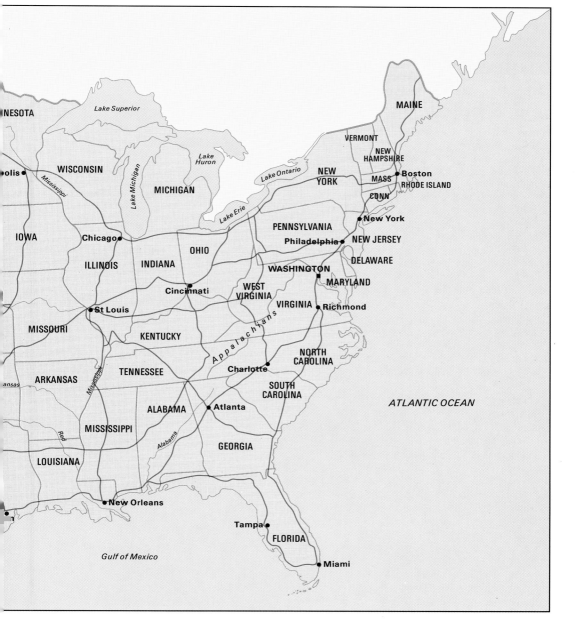

NEW ENGLAND & THE EMPIRE STATE

White clapboard churches with sharp-pointed spires, ripe yellow pumpkins piled against a red-painted barn, forested hillsides ablaze with fall foliage, quaint old whaling ports bobbing with sailboats, succulent lobsters and tasty clam chowder—the old, time-worn images of beautiful New England are still, thankfully, valid. Despite the ubiquitous automobile and tourist bus, the rural charm of this part of America—Maine, New Hampshire, Vermont, Massachusetts, Connecticut and Rhode Island—and of neighboring New York State has so far survived.

A third of the 30 million people who live in this Northeast region are concentrated in Boston and New York City, so the countryside still boasts considerable natural beauty. The land dips into the Atlantic Ocean along a deeply indented shoreline of rocky inlets, sandy bays, craggy headlands and offshore islands, with the long arm of Cape Cod jutting into the sea from Massachusetts' South Shore. Inland, the forest-clad ranges of the Appalachians—the White Mountains, Green Mountains, Berkshires and Catskills among them—form the region's rugged backbone, rising to 5,268 feet (1,606m) at Mount Katahdin in Maine. Ancient glaciers have left behind bare-rock summits, lake-filled hollows and vast deposits of rock debris on the lowlands and islands.

The Northeast's stony soil is not easy to cultivate, nor is it fertile, so farming is accompanied by forestry and fishing. Industry developed early along the region's coastal belt, where Boston, New York and other cities emerged as the powerhouses of economic activity. Although the cities are major centers of tourism, visitors also flock to such regional attractions as Niagara Falls, the Adirondacks, Newport, Cape Cod and the fall foliage display.

The first overseas visitors—the Vikings—appeared along the coast in the 10th century AD. Others followed later—John Cabot in the 1490s, Giovanni da Verrazano in 1524 and Henry Hudson in 1609. An English settlement was eventually established in 1620, when the Pilgrim Fathers landed from the *Mayflower* at Plymouth, Massachusetts. Less than 50 years later, the English ousted the Dutch from their colony of New Netherland, which included the Connecticut and Hudson valleys. A prize capture was the settlement of New Amsterdam on Manhattan Island, which the Dutch had acquired from local Indians for just a few trinkets in 1626. The English renamed it New York.

A century later, Boston became a hotbed of protest in the dispute with Britain over trade and taxation, which finally led to the Revolutionary War in 1776.

Boston:
The events and personalities of the Revolutionary War still figure prominently in the consciousness of this historic port city, founded in 1630. If you follow the marked $1\frac{1}{2}$ mile (2.5km) Freedom Trail on foot through the compact downtown and North End districts, you will find, tucked away among the modern glass skyscrapers, many of the historic buildings and sites associated with them. One such building, **Faneuil Hall**, is now the centerpiece of a bustling arcaded marketplace packed with colorful shops and food stalls.

With a population of nearly 3 million in its metropolitan area, Boston is New England's largest city and a major business center. Known as the 'Athens of America', it is a very civilized city, with fine shops, restaurants, entertainment and nightlife, a lively performing arts scene, and museums—like the renowned **Museum of Fine Arts**—with its international reputation. Although Boston suffers from frequent traffic congestion, there is a good subway system known as the 'T'.

Observation decks in the soaring **Prudential Tower** and **John Hancock Tower** offer spectacular views of the city and harbor and, across the Charles River, the neighboring city of Cambridge, home of prestigious Harvard University and the Massachusetts Institute of Technology (MIT).

Boston by night: the John Hancock Tower has a fine observatory

While in Boston don't miss a stroll around the old residential quarter of **Beacon Hill**, the beautiful **Public Garden**, with its lake and famous swan boats, and adjacent **Boston Common**.

New York:

Many of the immigrants who came to America around the turn of the century sailed into New York's great harbor past the welcoming Statue of Liberty. This beloved lady now gazes across the water at one of the most spectacular skylines in the world, the skyscrapers of Manhattan Island. From the roof-top observation decks of the 110-story **World Trade Center** and the old **Empire State Building**, there are stunning panoramas of this 12½-mile (20km) finger of land lying between the Hudson and East Rivers. Manhattan is one of the five boroughs—together with the Bronx, Queens, Brooklyn and Staten Island—that make up this magnetic city. It is the part that most visitors get to know best, a pulsating maelstrom of people and traffic. Here are the shops of **Fifth Avenue**, the theaters of **Broadway**, the bright lights of **Times Square**, elegant hotels and restaurants, opera and ballet at the **Lincoln Center**, world-famous museums, and the precious green space of **Central Park**. Here, too, are the colorful neighborhoods of **Greenwich Village**, **SoHo**, **Chinatown** and **Little Italy**, streets of brownstone houses, architectural gems side by side with demoralizing slums.

New York is fast-living, abrasive, noisy, dirty and dangerous; it is

The Romanesque-style Trinity Church (1877) in Boston

also exciting, stimulating and stylish. You can't be indifferent: it is the ultimate in big-city living. In the words of the city's own logo, it is the juicy 'Big Apple' at the top of the tree.

3 days – Approximately 324 miles (519km)

NEW ENGLAND'S HERITAGE

Boston ● Lexington ● Concord
Worcester ● Sturbridge ● Providence
Newport ● New Bedford ● Hyannis and
Cape Cod ● Plymouth ● Boston

This tour takes you back through nearly four centuries of American history to the landing of the first Pilgrims. On the way you will see the first battlegrounds of the Revolutionary War, a rural village as it was in the 1800s, an old whaling port straight out of *Moby Dick*, and the opulent summer mansions of America's super-rich. You will also experience the cultural and historic heritage of cities like Worcester and Providence, taste the unique tangy flavor of Cape Cod and enjoy a kaleidoscope of changing scenery.

ⓘ Prudential Plaza West, Boston

From downtown Boston follow Storrow Drive along the Charles River and pick up SR 2 northbound for about 10 miles (16km) through Cambridge. Turn north onto SR 4/225 for another 4 miles (6km) to Lexington.

Lexington, Massachusetts

1 In this small village just outside Boston, America's Revolutionary War against Britain began on April 19, 1775. The first clash took place on Lexington's grassy common, now called Battle Green, when someone—no one knows who—fired the first shot in a confrontation between local militiamen, or minutemen, and British Redcoats.

You can watch a dramatic re-enactment of the battle if you visit Lexington in mid-April. In any case, make your way to the Visitor Center by the Green for information and then take a walk to see the **Minuteman Statue** and other memorials on the Green, the **Buckman Tavern**, **Hancock-Clarke House** and other historic buildings in the surrounding area.

ⓘ near Buckman Tavern

Drive along SR 2A (the Battle Road) for 7 miles (11km) to Concord.

BACK TO NATURE

2 Nature is at its most spectacular in this region in early October, when the forested landscapes are ablaze with the reds, browns and yellows of the fall foliage. A favorite place for birdwatchers is the **Great Meadows National Wildlife Refuge** near Concord, while seabirds and shorebirds of all kinds can be seen anywhere along the coastal sections of the itinerary.

Cape Cod Highland Light strikes a solitary, evocative pose

Concord, Massachusetts

2 The Battle Road is the route used by the British to march to Concord. It is now part of the **Minute Man National Historical Park**, which also includes the site of the second clash on that fateful day. This occurred in Concord when 'the shot heard 'round the world' was fired at the Old North Bridge over the Concord River. It is a moving experience to walk down the quiet, tree-lined path to the reconstructed bridge and the **Minute Man Monument** that now commemorates the battle.

Concord also has other memories. Scattered about the area are the homes of such well-known writers as Louisa May Alcott, Ralph Waldo Emerson and Nathaniel Hawthorne, which you can visit. On the way out of town there is the tranquil beauty of **Walden Pond**, where Henry David Thoreau built his solitary cabin.

ⓘ Wright Tavern, Monument Square

From Concord follow SR 126 (Concord Road) south for about 8 miles (13km) to Wayland. Turn west onto US 20 and continue for 18 miles (29km) to Shrewsbury, then 7 miles (11km) on SR 9 to Worcester.

Worcester, Massachusetts

3 Worcester is New England's second largest city, a major industrial and commercial center with strong educational and cultural traditions. The city is known for its fine museums, the pick of which are the excellent **Worcester Art Museum**, whose exhibits include pre-Columbian, Asiatic, and ancient Greek and Roman art, and the **Higgins Armory Museum**, with outstanding collections of historic weapons and armor. For an evening out, there are the **Old Mechanics Hall**, a Victorian-style building, now an arena for concerts, and the **Centrum Civic Center**, which offers a range of entertainment in the downtown area.

ⓘ 33 Waldo Street

Leave downtown Worcester via I-290 southbound and after about 6 miles (10km) pick up I-90 westbound for another 12 miles (19km) to Sturbridge.

Sturbridge, Massachusetts

4 If you would like to see what life was like in rural New England in the early 1800s, a tour of **Old Sturbridge Village**, in Sturbridge, will turn back the clock for you. Here an entire village community of the 1830s has been re-created in a 200-acre (80-hectare) area, with restored houses, craft workshops, meeting houses, a working farm, gardens and woodlands. First go to the Visitor Center, then wander around and watch costumed performers demonstrating everyday tasks of the time. Be sure to see the **Freeman Farm** and to sample the New England fare served at the Bullard Tavern before you leave. And don't forget to see Sturbridge itself. In addition to the old **Publick House** and restaurant, there

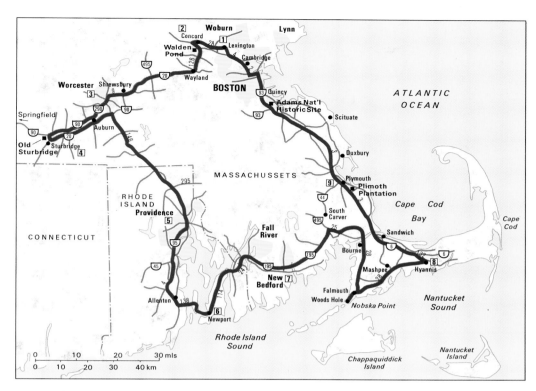

are two fascinating **museums**, one displaying cars, the other one dolls.

ℹ️ Old Sturbridge Village, 1 Old Sturbridge Village Road

*Take **US 20** east for 16 miles (25km) through Auburn, then turn south onto **SR 146** for the 33-mile (53km) drive along the Blackstone River valley to Providence.*

Providence, Rhode Island

5 Little Rhody's busy modern capital has come a long way since it was founded by religious dissenters in 1636 and named in gratitude for 'God's merciful Providence'. But its downtown area is still small enough to explore on foot—and there is plenty to see. Apart from the majestic **State Capitol** and **City Hall**, you will admire, as you wander along the streets, the old **Union Station** building and the Greek-style Arcade shopping center. But its greatest treasure, which Providence guards with pride, is the historic district centered on Benefit Street, the city's 'Mile of History'. Among the old buildings that line the streets here, there really is a house where George Washington once slept—the **Stephen Hopkins House**. Wander around and enjoy the atmosphere, then walk down to South Main Street for a browse among the boutiques and galleries that are now bringing life back to old waterfront buildings. And finally, hop into your car for a drive up Federal Hill

Concord's North Bridge, where in 1775 the citizen militia – Minute Men – drove off the British soldiers

RECOMMENDED WALK

6 Although it can be a little dangerous in places, the 3½-mile (6km) **Cliff Walk** at Newport, Rhode Island, is one of the finest trails on this tour. It follows the rugged east shoreline between Memorial Boulevard and Bailey's Beach and offers fine views of the sea and glimpses of Newport's great mansions along the way.

SCENIC ROUTES

If you can't manage the Cliff Walk around Newport's rugged peninsula, stay in your car and follow the 9½-mile (15km) **Ocean Drive** for an even more spectacular trip with ocean views and a sight of those great mansions. For a scenic drive back to Boston, take the alternative route via **SR 3A** along Massachusetts' South Shore through picturesque historic towns like Duxbury and Scituate.

FOR CHILDREN

8 Cape Cod has many attractions of special interest to children. Sandwich, for example, has the **Yesteryears Doll and Miniature Museum**, with its collection of antique dolls and miniature shops and houses, and the **Thornton W Burgess Museum**, containing mementos of the children's author best known for his Peter Rabbit and Briar Patch stories.

to explore the evocative neighborhood of **Little Italy**.

ℹ️ 30 Exchange Terrace

*For the 30-mile (48km) drive from Providence to Newport take **I-95** south to **Exit 9**, **SR 4** south to Allenton, and **SR 138** over the Jamestown and Newport bridges across Narragansett Bay.*

Newport, Rhode Island

6 When you catch your first glimpse of the bustling activity in the harbor at Newport, you will find it hard to imagine that the 'East Coast's Yachting Capital' dates back to 1639. When you have had your fill of state-of-the-art boutiques on the waterfront and enjoyed a one-hour cruise around the harbor, take a stroll through the charming back streets. Buildings dating from the Colonial era still stand here, like the famed **Hunter House** and the **White Horse Tavern**. But stealing the limelight in Newport are the extravagantly opulent mansions which the super-rich of the last century—the Vanderbilts, the Astors and others—built around the town as their summer 'cottages'. You will see most of them if you drive down Bellevue Avenue, but if you have time to visit only one, make it **The Breakers**, Cornelius Vanderbilt's Renaissance-style palace of 1895, which stands somewhat aloof on Ochre Point Avenue.

Overlooking the ocean, the aptly named Breakers is splendidly appointed in Renaissance style

ℹ️ 10 Americas Cup Avenue

*From Newport take **SR 114** and **SR 24** north for 19 miles (30km) to Fall River, then **I-195** east for 12 miles (19km) to New Bedford.*

New Bedford, Massachusetts

7 Now the home port for a large fishing fleet, New Bedford has a long seafaring history that goes back to its days as a whaling port. Here you can follow in the footsteps of Herman Melville, author of the whaling saga *Moby Dick*, as you walk down the gas-lit cobblestoned streets of Johnny Cake Hill to join in the excitement of the morning fish auction on the waterfront. The **Seamen's Bethel**, with its pulpit like a ship's prow, is where Melville once worshipped, and, across the street, the marvelous **Whaling Museum** has a half-size replica of the kind of whaler he once knew. Walk on through the town and you will find other places of interest, including the wonderful **Glass Museum** housed in a Federal-style mansion dating from 1821.

ℹ️ 70 North Second Street

*Continue east from New Bedford on **I-195** for 16 miles (26km) to **Exit 22**. Then follow **SR 25** east for 9 miles (14km) over the Cape Cod Canal to Bourne and Cape Cod. For the 50-mile (80km) tour of Cape Cod follow **SR 28** south to Falmouth and Woods Hole, then east through Mashpee to Hyannis. Return from Hyannis on **SR 132** and **US 6** to Sandwich.*

At Plimoth Plantation, a Thanksgiving repast is set out

Hyannis and Cape Cod, Massachusetts

8 Once you cross the Bourne Bridge into Cape Cod, you are in a year-round vacation playground that provides for every 20th-century need, and in summer it is very crowded. With its long sandy beaches, oceans of sea grass, wildlife preserves, fishing villages, yacht harbors, seafood restaurants and many other attractions, you can make it as busy or as quiet as you wish. This itinerary covers only the Upper Cape as far as Hyannis. Amid the rampant commercialism, especially on **Highway 28**, there are sightseeing attractions you should not miss. Along **Highway 28** are the replica **Aptuxcet Trading Post** at Bourne; the historic houses and **Historical Society Museum** around Falmouth's Village Green; the **aquarium** at the ferry port of Woods Hole; and the sea views from Nobska Point. At Mashpee you will see the **Old Indian Meeting House** of 1684 and the burial ground. And at the popular yachting port of Hyannis, the home of the Kennedy family, there is a one-hour harbor cruise that provides views of the Kennedy compound from the sea and also a memorial to John F Kennedy which is a popular place of pilgrimage. On the return journey along **US 6**, make a stop at **Sandwich**, the Cape's oldest town. It has many attractions, especially the **Glass Museum** and the fascinating **Heritage Plantation**, which portrays aspects of early American life.

Cross the Sagamore Bridge from Sandwich for the 17-mile (27km) drive along SR 3 to Plymouth.

Plymouth, Massachusetts

9 One of the best-known stories in American history tells of the storm-tossed voyage of the Protestant Pilgrims across the Atlantic Ocean on the *Mayflower* in 1620 and of their survival in the New World with the help of local Indians. If you turn off **Highway 3** just south of Plymouth, you can roll back the centuries at a convincing re-creation of the Pilgrim's **Plimoth Plantation**, as it was in 1627, and a Wampanoag Indian campsite. If you speak to the costumed 'villagers' as they go about their typical chores, don't be surprised if you hear strange 17th-century English dialects.

You will have a similar experience when you drive down to Plymouth's harbor and board the full-size replica of the *Mayflower* moored at the pier. As you leave, don't miss **Plymouth Rock**, the boulder on the nearby beach where the Pilgrims are said to have landed. In the streets around the harbor area you will find other points of interest, including several 17th-century houses and a burial ground and museums with exhibits related to the Pilgrims, especially **Pilgrim Hall** and **Plymouth National Wax Museum**. But don't leave town without visiting the unique **Cranberry World Visitors Center** on the waterfront, a fascinating museum dedicated to Massachusetts' foremost agricultural crop, cranberries.

ℹ 91 Samoset Street

From Plymouth continue north on SR 3 and I-93 for about 40 miles (64km) to Boston. Alternatively, take the longer shoreline route on SR 3A if you have time.

Boston – Lexington	14	(22)
Lexington – Concord	7	(11)
Concord – Worcester	33	(53)
Worcester – Sturbridge	18	(29)
Sturbridge – Providence	49	(78)
Providence – Newport	30	(49)
Newport – New Bedford	31	(50)
New Bedford – Hyannis	69	(110)
Hyannis – Plymouth	33	(53)
Plymouth – Boston	40	(64)

FOR HISTORY BUFFS

9 On a hill overlooking Plymouth, Massachusetts, you will see an imposing 81-foot (25m) tribute to the Pilgrim settlers, the **Forefathers' Monument**. Built between 1859 and 1889, the solid granite structure was a prototype for the Statue of Liberty in New York City.

Just south of Boston take **Exit 8** from **I-93** into Quincy, the 'City of Presidents'. Here you can take guided tours of the birthplaces of John Adams, the second president, and his son John Quincy Adams, the sixth president, at 133 and 141 Franklin Street. You can also visit the Adams family home and garden, now the **Adams National Historic Site**, at 135 Adams Street.

SPECIAL TO . . .

9 Plymouth County, Massachusetts, offers two memorable adventures if you have time. From Plymouth you can take an exciting whale-watching cruise to the waters off Cape Cod. And from South Carver, about 9 miles (14km) southwest of Plymouth, you can catch the **Edaville Railroad's** quaint old steam train for a pleasant 5½-mile (9km) ride through vast cranberry bogs.

3 days – Approximately 252 miles (403km)

THE MAJESTIC HUDSON VALLEY

New York City ● Yonkers ● Croton-on-Hudson
Garrison ● Poughkeepsie
Hyde Park ● Hudson ● Catskill
Kingston ● Newburgh ● West Point
New York City

Ever since Henry Hudson explored it in 1609, the Hudson River Valley has been admired for its spectacular scenic beauty. As a major waterway it was keenly fought for in the Revolutionary War, and many historic sites commemorate the old battles. Scattered among the wooded hillsides are historic riverfront towns, mansions built by the rich and famous, old inns, orchards and meadows and vineyards producing fine wines. 'America's Rhine' cuts through a land rich in folklore, alive with festivals and craft fairs and brimming with opportunities for outdoor recreation.

ℹ️ 2 Columbus Circle, Manhattan

Leaving from West Side Manhattan follow the Henry Hudson Parkway (SR 9A) northbound for about 12 miles (19km) to Exit 23. Take US 9 (Broadway), still heading north, to Yonkers.

Sunnyside, Washington Irving's home by the Hudson for 24 years

Yonkers, New York

1 You will barely have time to get settled in the car before you reach the first sightseeing attraction on the tour. It is **Philipse Manor Hall**, in Yonkers, now an art and history museum with fine paintings of US Presidents. 'Yonkers' comes from the Dutch word *jonkheer*, which means young nobility. Down the road, at Irvington, are **Sunnyside**, writer Washington Irving's pretty cottage and **Lyndhurst**, a 19th-century mansion in the flamboyant 'Hudson Gothic' style at Tarrytown is **Philipsburg Manor**, an 18th-century farm estate.

Continue north on US 9 for Croton-on-Hudson.

Croton-on-Hudson, New York

2 Van Cortlandt Manor, with its 20 acres (8 hectares) of period gardens, a tavern and other buildings, is a restored 18th-century Dutch-English manor, the home of Pierre Van Cortlandt, the first lieutenant governor of New York State. Further along, at Peekskill, the extraordinary **Dick's Hilltop Castle** is the nearest thing you will ever see to a replica of Spain's Alhambra Palace, but it remains unfinished because former owner Evans Dick lost his fortune in the stock market crash of 1911.

Continue north on US 9, SR 403 and SR 9D to Garrison.

Garrison, New York

3 By this point on the tour you will be aware of the spectacular scenery, so if you want a panoramic view of the Hudson Valley, a good place to stop is Garrison, perched high above the river. You can enjoy marvelous

The historic Hudson, flowing past verdant banks for 315 miles

views (and perhaps a summer concert) at the lovely gardens of luxurious **Boscobel** mansion before driving on to explore the antique shops of the nearby towns of Cold Spring and Nelsonville.

*Follow **SR 9D** for another 27 miles (43km) to Poughkeepsie.*

Poughkeepsie, New York

4 The town of Poughkeepsie, among its other claims to fame, is the place where Smith's cough drops come from. It is also the location of **Vassar**, the top women's college, which you can visit. The town has some fine old buildings, including **Clinton House**, which was the governor's home in 1777 when Poughkeepsie served briefly as state capital, and the 1853 Italian-style villa of Samuel F B Morse, who invented the telegraph. The house contains period furnishings, art, china and original telegraph equipment.

*Continue driving north on **US 9** for 6 miles (10km) to Hyde Park, then another 10 miles (16km) to Rhinebeck.*

Hyde Park, New York

5 At Hyde Park, the best place to eat well is unquestionably one of the gourmet restaurants at the Culinary Institute of America, the training school for great chefs. People generally come here, however, to tour the riverfront home of President Franklin D Roosevelt, its **Library** and **Museum**, his wife Eleanor's private retreat, called **Val-Kill**, and the elegant **Vanderbilt Mansion** nearby. All are National Historic Sites.

If you are still in the mood for house-visiting as you drive away, stop at Staatsburg to tour the opulent **Mills Mansion** and **State Park**. Otherwise, drive on to Rhinebeck, where a unique experience awaits you at the **Old Aerodrome**—a weekend air show, with a mock aerial battle and rides in vintage planes. Take a walk around the lovely old town and don't miss the historic **Beekman Arms Inn**.

*Continue north through the orchard country along **SR 9G** for 25 miles (40km) to Hudson.*

Hudson, New York

6 Along the highway to Hudson are two more impressive historic mansions that are worth a stop: first **Clermont**, the Livingston family home at Germantown, then **Olana**, the 'Oriental Gothic' home of landscape painter Frederic Edwin Church, just south of Hudson.

In Hudson, take a walking tour of the Warren Street Historic Restoration Area and see the old fire engines at the **American Museum of Fire Fighting**.

🛈 414 Union Street

*Cross the Rip Van Winkle Bridge on **SR 23** to Catskill.*

Catskill, New York

7 Catskill is a pleasant river town at the northern gateway to the scenic Catskill Mountains. When you have toured its marinas, antique shops and Court House, take a drive out of town

for a delightful encounter with animals from around the world at the **Catskill Game Farm**, just 12 miles (19km) west, off SR 32.

*Follow **SR 32** south from Catskill Game Farm for about 13 miles (21km) to pick up the New York State Thruway **(I-87)** at southbound **Entry 20** (Saugerties). Continue south for 10 miles (16km) and take **Exit 19** for Kingston.*

Kingston, New York

8 The old river port of Kingston was founded in 1652 as a Dutch trading settlement and became New York State's first capital in 1777. Many of its early buildings still survive, including the **Old Dutch Church** of 1659, the **Senate House** and the **Ulster County Court House**. Costumed guides will take you on a walking tour

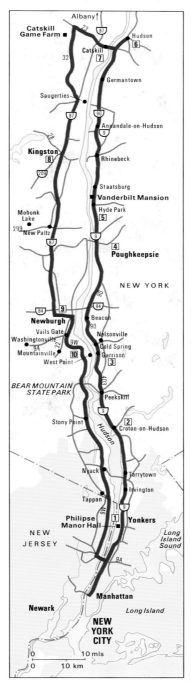

FOR CHILDREN

7 There is plenty for children to enjoy on this tour, but for a real bonanza of fun and excitement take them down **Highway 32** west of Catskill. In addition to the **Catskill Game Farm**, adventures on offer here include the Wild West town of **Carson City**, **Junior Speedway** and the fascinating **Reptile Institute**.

BACK TO NATURE

7 Slide Mountain is the highest peak in the Catskill Mountains and one of the best for wildlife. The forested slopes—a mixture of conifers and hardwoods—harbor mammals including white-tailed deer, squirrels, cottontail rabbits and raccoons. Birds include wild turkeys, ruffed grouse, pileated woodpeckers, yellow-bellied sapsuckers (a species of woodpecker), several species of thrushes and at least 12 species of warblers. To reach the trail head west out of Kingston on **I-87** and south on **SR 28** to Winisook Lodge.

RECOMMENDED WALKS

If you are not worn out by touring all those mansions, gardens and historic sites, then visit the Hudson Valley's state parks, such as **Hudson Highlands**, near Beacon; **Mills-Norrie**, at Staatsburg; and **Bear Mountain**, where you can enjoy spectacular views from the Appalachian Trail on Bear Mountain Bridge. There are also pleasant nature trails in the woods at **Montgomery Place**, Annandale-on-Hudson.

FOR HISTORY BUFFS

8 Leave the New York State Thruway **(I-87)** from Kingston at **Exit 18** to visit historic **New Paltz**, a French Huguenot settlement of 1678. Here you will see six of the original stone houses and a reconstructed church on Huguenot Street, one of the oldest streets in America and a National Historic Landmark (tours available). Then drive west out of town to visit the historic **Mohonk Mountain House** resort, which has panoramic views of Lake Mohonk, the Shawangunk Mountains and the Hudson Valley.

SPECIAL TO ...

9 The Hudson Valley has more than 30 operating wineries that are open for tours and tastings, many of them concentrated around Newburgh. A popular stop for visitors on **Route 94** southwest of town is the famous old **Brotherhood Winery** at Washingtonville.

SCENIC ROUTES

Every bend on this itinerary seems to open up marvelous new views of the Hudson Valley's scenic splendor. But there are extra-special sections of highway, including the drives between Peekskill and Beacon and between Newburgh and Stony Point, and the side-trips on **SR 32** to Mountainville and on the **Perkins Memorial Drive** up Bear Mountain.

of the original stockade area. On the historic waterfront you can ride an old trolley car, take a pleasant cruise and learn about life on the river in days gone by at the **Hudson River Maritime Center**. For good evening entertainment, you can choose a sailboat ride with food and music, or perhaps take in a show at the historic **Ulster Performing Arts Center**, on Broadway.

ℹ️ 7 Albany Avenue

*Continue south on **I-87** for 31 miles (50km) to Newburgh **(Exit 17)**.*

Newburgh, New York

9 Newburgh is another old riverport with surviving 18th- and 19th-century buildings open to visitors in its downtown area. Among them is the **Hasbrouck House** of 1750, which was George Washington's headquarters in the final days of the Revolutionary War and now has a museum relating to the conflict. South of town, in the Vails Gate area, you can tour the house used by General Knox and his staff and watch enactments of military life at that time at the **New Windsor Encampment**, the final campsite of Washington's Continental Army when hostilities ended.

If you like modern art, drive south on SR 32 to the **Storm King Art Center** in Mountainville. This 400-acre (160-hectare) sculpture park and museum has a permanent collection of more than 130 sculptures by over 90 contemporary artists, where you can also enjoy marvelous views of the Hudson River.

ℹ️ 72 Broadway

*From Newburgh take **US 9W** and **SR 218** south for a 23-mile (37km) drive that takes in West*

West Point holds parades in the spring and fall – visitors welcome

Point, Bear Mountain State Park and Stony Point.

West Point, New York

10 The country between Newburgh and Stony Point encompasses some of the finest mountain and river scenery on the tour. At West Point you can admire superb river vistas from historic **Fort Putnam** and **Trophy Point** and watch the cadets on parade as you tour the world-famous **US Military Academy**. A few miles south you will see the spectacular Bear Mountain Bridge, which carries the Appalachian Trail over the Hudson River into beautiful **Bear Mountain State Park**. In the park you will find many facilities for outdoor recreation (including swimming, boating and skating), the charming **Bear Mountain Inn**, a trailside **museum**, and a mountain-top **observation tower** offering spectacular views of the Hudson River below.

At Stony Point you can tour the battle site where General 'Mad Anthony' Wayne's army proved more than a match for the Redcoats in 1779. If you are here in mid-July you will see a rousing re-enactment of the fight.

ℹ️ Building 618, Thayer Gate (South Gate), US Military Academy, West Point (Academy only)

*Continue south on **US 9W** for 28 miles (45km) through Nyack and Tappan to the George Washington Bridge and Manhattan.*

New York City – Yonkers **15 (24)**
Yonkers – Croton-on-Hudson **20 (32)**
Croton-on-Hudson – Garrison **20 (32)**
Garrison – Poughkeepsie **27 (43)**
Poughkeepsie – Hyde Park **6 (10)**
Hyde Park – Hudson **30 (48)**
Hudson – Catskill **6 (10)**
Catskill – Kingston **35 (56)**
Kingston – Newburgh **31 (50)**
Newburgh – West Point **11 (18)**
West Point – New York City **51 (82)**

A light sea mist creeps inland at sunset on Long Island's coast, a haven of peace for city dwellers

ⓘ 2 Columbus Circle, Manhattan

*Take the Midtown Tunnel from Manhattan under the East River and follow the Long Island Expressway **(I-495)** east for about 32 miles (51km). At **Exit 48** follow Round Swamp Road to Old Bethpage.*

Old Bethpage, New York

1 Old Bethpage Village, one of Long Island's top visitor attractions, reminds you that this vacationer's paradise has a history. It is a re-created farm village of the pre–Civil War era, with buildings gathered here from other parts of the island, including a church, tavern and general store. The costumed 'villagers' will show you how to churn butter, bake bread, shear sheep and do many other everyday chores of bygone days.

*From Old Bethpage take **SR 110** south for 6 miles (10km). Turn west on Sunrise Highway **(SR 27)** for 4 miles (6km), then south for 6 miles (10km) on Wantagh State Parkway **(SR 105)** to reach Jones Beach.*

Jones Beach, New York

2 Thousands of sun worshippers flock to Jones Beach every summer to bake on the sparkling white sand that stretches for miles along this offshore barrier island.The many recreational and entertainment facilities include an outdoor roller-skating rink, court games and a pitch-and-putt golf course. There are also nightly concerts in the **Jones Beach Theatre** in summer. If the scene here is too busy for you, try Gilgo or Captree Beach farther east.

Follow Ocean Drive east along the island for 16 miles (26km) to Captree Beach for Fire Island.

Fire Island, New York

3 Drive across the sea inlet from Captree to Fire Island. You can go only as far as **Robert Moses State Park**, so if you want a closer look at this roadless wilderness island, a long slip of sand where pirates once buried their treasure, you will have to take a ferry from Sayville, Bay Shore or Patchogue, off **SR 27**. With its

AROUND LONG ISLAND

New York City ● Old Bethpage
Jones Beach ● Fire Island ● Westhampton and
The Hamptons ● Montauk ● Sag Harbor
Greenport ● Riverhead ● Stony Brook
Centerport and the Gold Coast ● New York City

If you need to wind down for a while after New York's frenetic pace, do what many New Yorkers do and take off for a change of scene amid the peace of Long Island. Leave behind the seething conurbation at the west end of the island and head east to sandy beaches, sheltered bays, rolling dunes, quaint fishing villages, farms, even a few windmills, and wildlife refuges, silent but for the breeze and the shrill call of seabirds. It is a place for enjoying outdoor activities, eating rich seafood, hunting for antiques and touring historic places, millionaires' estates, museums and wineries.

opportunities for walking, swimming, boating, wildlife-watching and other outdoor activities in unspoiled surroundings, this National Seashore island is a popular destination for New Yorkers.

ⓘ 120 Laurel Street, Patchogue

*Head north to join **SR 27**. Follow for 9 miles (14km) to the exit for Sayville. From Sayville and the other ferry ports, continue east on **SR 27** through the five towns known as 'The Hamptons'.*

Westhampton and The Hamptons, New York

4 Westhampton, Hampton Bays, Southampton, Bridgehampton and

RECOMMENDED WALKS

Apart from the beaches, good places for stretching your legs and sharpening your appetite are Long Island's many state parks. You will find pleasant trails in **Heckscher State Park**, near Bay Shore; **Hither Hills State Park**, near Montauk; and **Sunken Meadow State Park**, east of Centerport; not forgetting the nature trails on **Fire Island**.

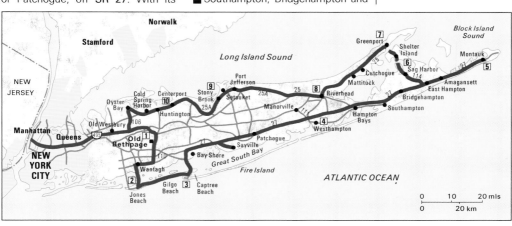

FOR CHILDREN

4 If you wish to add to all the exciting things for children on this tour, take **Exit 60** north from **SR 27** before you reach The Hamptons and see the animals and sealion shows at **Long Island Game Farm and Zoological Park**, Manorville.

7 Boys might be interested, too, in the armored vehicles and artillery displayed at the **American Armored Foundation Inc Tank Museum**, at Mattituck on the North Fork.

BACK TO NATURE

Long Island is renowned as a location for observing bird migration, especially in the autumn. **Robert Moses State Park** on Fire Island is good for land birds. 'Falls' occur in September and October. The Montauk Peninsula is excellent for seabirds, with **Montauk Point State Park** also being a 'hotspot' for landbirds. Shorebirds can be found almost anywhere around the Long Island coast, but **Orient Beach State Park** (near Montauk) and **Jones Beach State Park** (near Jones Inlet) are especially good.

SPECIAL TO . . .

Long Island's abundant opportunities for saltwater fishing—whether surf casting, open boat fishing or deep-sea charter fishing—make it a paradise for sports fishermen.

5 Montauk is a popular starting point for the big-fish hunters.

10 If oysters are your pleasure, come to Oyster Bay in early October, when you can join in the orgy of eating, cooking demonstrations and shucking (shelling) contests at the Annual Oyster Festival.

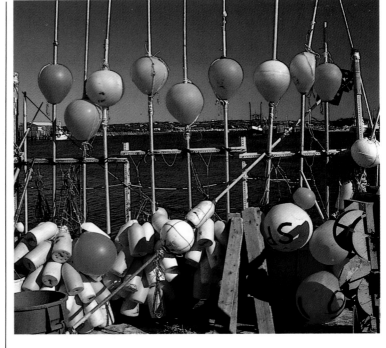

East Hampton—The Hamptons in the order in which you reach them—have long been a favorite haven for writers, artists and other celebrities. With their marvelous beaches, smart boutiques and fine restaurants, they are also a popular destination for summer visitors. Each has its own individual attractions. The **Parrish Art Museum**, at Southampton, has displays of Renaissance and 19th-century American art, while the old **Halsey Homestead** is of interest for its Colonial herb garden. There are automobile and motorcycle racing at Bridgehampton; and the boyhood home of theater man John Howard Payne, composer of *Home Sweet Home*, is at East Hampton.

ℹ 76 Main Street, Southampton

Follow the South Fork Peninsula east to Montauk.

Montauk, New York

5 You will be tempted to visit the **Town Marine Museum** at Amagansett, with its exhibits of shipwrecks and life on and under the sea. But eventually you will arrive at Montauk, a popular deep-sea-fishing port and whale-watching center lying amid the rocky bluffs, woodlands and sand dunes at the end of the peninsula. There is an excellent golf course here, but don't miss the 5-mile (8km) drive to Montauk Point to enjoy the sea views from the famous lighthouse built here in 1795 by order of George Washington.

*From Montauk return to East Hampton on **SR 27**, then follow **SR 114** north for 7 miles (11km) to Sag Harbor.*

Sag Harbor, New York

6 This little community, lying in a sheltered bay on the north shore of the South Fork, was a thriving whaling port in the 19th century, as you will discover if you visit its **Whaling Museum**. But its history goes back to 1707, and the town center has been

Where buoy meets gull: the fisherman's paradise of Montauk, a lively resort with many facilities

declared a National Historic District. You will see the historic **Custom House** and the **Fire Department Museum** as you walk around.

*Continue north on **SR 114** from Sag Harbor for the 8-mile (13km) journey to Greenport, on the North Fork which includes two ferry crossings and a drive across Shelter Island.*

Greenport, New York

7 There is plenty to see and do at Greenport, a lively, bustling old seaside town and fishing port which harvests especially good oysters. A well-known attraction is the **Museum of Childhood**, a special delight for children with its collection of antique dolls and other toys. At Cutchogue, southwest on **SR 25**, you can tour one of the area's many wineries and see the historic buildings on the village green.

*From Cutchogue follow **SR 25** west along the North Fork to Riverhead.*

Riverhead, New York

8 A few miles west you will come to Riverhead, which is known for its potatoes, annual **Polish Street Fair and Festival** and **Suffolk County Historical Museum**, which has whaling and local Indian exhibits in its collections. Strawberries, peaches and cauliflowers are also a major industry. Legend has it Captain Kidd landed on this part of the island to bury his treasure here.

*From Riverhead continue west on **SR 25**, then take **SR 25A** for 29 miles (46km) to Stony Brook.*

Stony Brook, New York

9 Drive on around the bay to see the 18th-century **Thompson House** in Setauket and the restored historic buildings and museum complex along Stony Brook's Main Street. Here you will enjoy the varied collections of the **Carriage Museum, Art Museum** and **History Museum** and see several period structures, including a grist mill and blacksmith's shop. On the state university campus you might also catch a show at one of the five theaters in the **Fine Arts Center**.

Follow SR 25A west from Stony Brook for about 19 miles (30km) (including a short stretch on SR 25 at The Branch) to Centerport and the Gold Coast.

Centerport, New York

10 At the turn of the century, anyone who was anyone— Vanderbilt, Woolworth, Roosevelt— had a luxurious mansion and estate on the fabled Gold Coast, Long Island's north shore. As you tour these houses today you can imagine the elegant lifestyle of their owners. Not to be missed is the **estate of William K Vanderbilt**, with its impressive planetarium and museum, at Centerport. More than 2,000 wildlife and marine specimens are on display in the mansion rooms and the Marine Museum, and the

The old whaling town of Greenport now offers antiques and oysters

planetarium features exhibits on astronomy and a sky theater with a 60-foot-diameter (18m) dome. Wonderful **Sagamore Hill**, Theodore Roosevelt's summer home is just outside Oyster Bay; and **Old Westbury Gardens**, the mansion and estate of John S Phipps, is further south near the Long Island Expressway.

In the north shore towns you will stumble across many other places of interest. Huntington, for example, has superb art collections in its **Heckscher Museum**; Cold Spring Harbor boasts its excellent **Whaling Museum**; and in Oyster Bay there are fine botanical displays in the **Planting Fields Arboretum** at the Coe Mansion.

From Oyster Bay follow SR 106 south for about 6 miles (10km), then take the Long Island Expressway heading west into Manhattan.

New York City – Old Bethpage	**36 (58)**
Old Bethpage – Jones Beach	**16 (26)**
Jones Beach – Fire Island	**16 (26)**
Fire Island – Westhampton	**38 (61)**
Westhampton – Montauk	**43 (70)**
Montauk – Sag Harbor	**22 (35)**
Sag Harbor – Greenport	**8 (13)**
Greenport – Riverhead	**22 (35)**
Riverhead – Stony Brook	**29 (46)**
Stony Brook – Centerport	**19 (30)**
Centerport – New York City	**43 (69)**

FOR HISTORY BUFFS

10 A must-see along the itinerary involves a short detour off **SR 25A** between Centerport and Huntington. A few miles south along **SR 110** you can see manuscripts, pictures, changing exhibits and other memorabilia of the poet Walt Whitman at his boyhood home at **Huntington Station**, a farmhouse furnished in period (*circa* 1810).

SCENIC ROUTES

Except for the spectacular Ocean Drive along the south shore from Jones Beach, the most scenically attractive highways are generally concentrated at the eastern end of Long Island. Especially enjoyable are the drive through rolling hills, woodlands and dunes from The Hamptons to Montauk on **SR 27**; the island-hopping trip from Sag Harbor to Greenport on **SR 114**; and the stretch of **SR 25** along the North Fork.

THE MID-ATLANTIC STATES

George Washington Country roughly corresponds to the Mid-Atlantic region of America's east coast and encompasses the states of New Jersey, Pennsylvania, Maryland, Virginia and Delaware, with the District of Columbia. It is a region in which momentous events forged the birth and destiny of the nation. Its territory saw the founding of Swedish, Dutch and English colonies in the 1600s, the long struggle for independence from Britain in the Revolutionary War (1776–83) and the painful conflict of the Civil War, which raged from 1861 to 1865. The epic story echoes with the names of the great—Thomas Jefferson, Benjamin Franklin, Abraham Lincoln and Robert E Lee to mention but a few—but it is the memory of that Colonial gentleman George Washington (1732–99) that gives this part of America its historic identity.

Today, nearly 34 million people live in this region, many of them in the industrial cities of Newark and Pittsburgh, historic Philadelphia and Richmond, the port of Baltimore, and Washington DC. Washington, Richmond and several other regional cities took root at the point where rivers, like the Potomac, plunge down falls or rapids at the head of navigation.

To the east of this fall line stretches the densely populated coastal plain, deeply indented by the great river estuaries known as Delaware and Chesapeake bays. Beyond the farmlands the tidewater marshes are the home of large numbers of waterfowl and shore-birds, while the bays yield blue crabs, oysters and clams to the watermen fishing from traditional skipjacks. Testimony to this coastline's diversity is the natural wilderness of New Jersey's Pine Barrens, the casinos and boardwalk of Atlantic City, the Colonial settlements and plantation homes along the James River, and the great naval base at Norfolk.

West of the fall line an irregular patchwork of fields, pastures, orchards and woodlands extends across the rolling country of the Piedmont region, scattered with historic towns such as York, Frederick, Alexandria and Fredericksburg, and now silent battlefields like Gettysburg. Further west are the beautiful forested ridges of the Appalachian Mountains, nowhere lovelier than in Shenandoah National Park. These hills and valleys are the home of hardy mountain folk, bred mostly from Scots-Irish stock, whose lifestyle is colored by country music, yarn-telling, shooting matches and simple traditional crafts.

Washington DC:
With its tree-lined boulevards, imposing public buildings, cultural institutions, monuments and park-lands, the nation's capital reflects the wish of its original designer, the French-born Pierre Charles L'Enfant, to create a city 'magnificent enough to grace a great nation'. Nearly 3½ million people now inhabit the metropolitan area, which occupies the 69-square-mile (179sq km) District of Columbia beside the Potomac River.

The city's focal point is the grassy expanse extending around the 555-foot (169m) **Washington Monument** to the **Capitol Building, White House, Lincoln Memorial** and **Jefferson Memorial**. Here, too, are world-famous cultural institutions, such as the **National Gallery of Art** and several museums that form part of the prestigious **Smithsonian Institution**.

Nearby, the downtown business district contains the **Old Post Office-Pavilion** shopping center and historic **Ford's Theater** where President Abraham Lincoln was assassinated in 1865. In the north-western districts are the elegant shops of Connecticut Avenue, the foreign missions along 'Embassy Row', and the lovely old town-houses, boutiques, restaurants and nightspots of historic Georgetown. And across the Potomac, **Arlington Cemetery** guards the last resting places of many of the nation's great figures.

Philadelphia:
The historic port city of Philadelphia, founded on the Delaware River in 1682 by the English Quaker William Penn, played a leading role in America's struggle for independence. Preserved in the heart of the city are some of the nation's most revered historic treasures, including **Independence Hall**, where the Declaration of Independence and the Constitution were agreed, and the hallowed **Liberty Bell**, protected inside in a glass pavilion.

The sign of refreshment outside a Colonial Williamsburg tavern

Washington DC, a verdant setting for its handsome monuments

Nearby are the historic riverfront area of **Penn's Landing** and the Old City district, containing **Elfreth's Alley** and the **house of Betsy Ross**, who reputedly sewed together the first Stars and Stripes. Several of the city's major cultural institutions, including the **Philadelphia Museum of Art, the Rodin Museum**, and the **Franklin Institute Science Museum**, line Benjamin Franklin Parkway on the way to magnificent Fairmount Park.

Richmond:

The **City Hall skydeck**, on Broad Street, affords striking views of Virginia's state capital, an old Colonial tobacco port laid out by the James River in 1737. Buildings and monuments reflecting over three centuries of history are scattered around its old streets. Among them are the beautiful **State Capitol** designed by Thomas Jefferson in 1785, the **Old Stone House** of 1737, and **St John's Church** of 1741, where patriot Patrick Henry made his famous 'Give me liberty or give me death' speech. Echoes of the Civil War, when the city served as the Confederate capital, remain at old **St Paul's Church**, the **Museum and White House of the Confederacy**, and **Richmond National Battlefield Park**. Fine 19th-century homes still grace the historic Fan district, Monument Avenue and Jackson Ward, while busy shops, restaurants and night spots brighten the old commercial Shockoe Slip district by the river.

3 days – Approximately 288 miles (461km)

SCENIC SHENANDOAH & HISTORIC VIRGINIA

Washington DC • Manassas National Battlefield Park • Front Royal and Shenandoah National Park • Chancellorsville Fredericksburg • Mount Vernon Alexandria • Washington DC

War and peace, you could say, are the theme of this tour of northern Virginia, a land that bears the scars of great conflict across its serenely beautiful face. You can follow George Washington's footsteps in historic Fredericksburg and Alexandria and at his beloved Mount Vernon estate. You can relive the pain and the glory of the Civil War as you tread the now-silent battlefields of Manassas and Fredericksburg. And all around you, as you travel the highways, is the breathtaking natural beauty of the Virginia countryside, nowhere more captivating than in the mountains of Shenandoah National Park.

FOR HISTORY BUFFS

2 In addition to the battlefields, another interesting source of information about the Civil War is the **Warren Rifles Confederate Museum** at Front Royal. Here you will see military uniforms, weapons, battle flags and various other relics of the conflict. About 4 miles (6km) west of Orange on **SR 20**, look out for **Montpelier**, the stately mansion built by the father of America's fourth president, James Madison, between 1755 and 1765. You can tour the house and garden before going on to visit the **James Madison Museum** in Orange, which is dedicated to his memory.

ⓘ 1445 Pennsylvania Avenue, Washington DC

*From downtown Washington DC cross the Potomac River to Arlington and drive 30 miles (48km) along **I-66** to Manassas National Battlefield Park.*

Manassas National Battlefield Park, Virginia

1 Two major Civil War battles were fought along the creek known as Bull Run, in July 1861 and in August a year later. Both were Confederate victories. Start your tour of the site at the Visitor Center and see the audio-visual presentation explaining the battle maneuvers. Then take the 1½-hour driving tour of the main scenes of the fighting. Don't miss a walk up Henry Hill, a key position in both battles, where you will have a panoramic view of the whole battle area. It was here that Confederate General Thomas J Jackson's calm courage earned him the nickname Stonewall and where an equestrian statue now stands in his memory.

ⓘ Park Visitor Center on **SR 234** between **I-66** and **US 29**

*Continue west on **I-66** for 45 miles (72km) to the town of Front Royal, Shenandoah National Park.*

Front Royal and Shenandoah National Park, Virginia

2 Just south of Front Royal is the start of the famed Skyline Drive, the scenic highway that meanders

---

Virginia's verdant tranquility, the scene of many bitter battles

---

for 105 miles (169km) through Shenandoah National Park and along the forested crests of the Blue Ridge Mountains—a land the Indians poetically called 'Daughter of the Stars'. Unless you want to explore the underground sights of the **Skyline Caverns** at the start of the drive, go straight to the Dickey Ridge Visitor Center and arm yourself with useful maps and information about the park. Along the highway from here, you will find many overlooks that offer quite outstanding views of legendary Shenandoah Valley to the west and the rolling hills to the east. There are also many picnic spots, campsites and walking trails to let you enjoy the forest scenery and see the abundant wildlife. You can join guided hikes conducted to the main points of interest in the summer, or just take off on your own along the recommended trails. This is an invigorating place, so do get out of your car and enjoy the tangy fresh air of the woods.

When you reach Thornton Gap, turn right onto **US 211** for a 25-mile (40km) round trip to **Luray Caverns**, where you can marvel at the fantastic underground rock formations and listen to 'music' made on the famed 'stalactite organ'. While here, you can also take a look at the old vehicles exhibited at the **Car and Carriage Caravan**.

Complete your drive along Skyline Drive at Swift Run Gap, exiting east onto **US 33**.

*Follow **US 33** for 21 miles (34km) to Barboursville. Turn left (north) onto **SR 20** and continue through Orange for 34 miles (56 km) to Wilderness. Turn right (east) onto **SR 3** for 5 miles (8km) to Chancellorsville.*

Chancellorsville, Virginia

3 At the Visitor Center at Chancellorsville you can get information and see an audiovisual presentation before touring the countryside where more than 100,000 soldiers fell during four tremendous Civil War battles. At Fredericksburg in December 1862 and Chancellorsville in May 1863, the Confederacy won the day, but at the **Wilderness and Spotsylvania Court House** in May 1864, Grant's Yankees came out on top.

Before driving into Fredericksburg you can, if you wish, tour one, two or all three of the battlefields outside the city, either by car or on foot along the trails to the main landmarks of the fighting.

Continue into Fredericksburg.

Fredericksburg, Virginia

4 Even without its reminders of the Civil War—'that terrible stone wall' on Marye's Heights in particular—it is easy to see why Fredericksburg is often called 'America's most historic city'. When you tour its picturesque streets, you will find buildings that were once lived in or frequented by members of George Washington's family or by other notables of colonial times. You will see the **Masonic Lodge** where, in 1752, Washington

was initiated; the charming 'in-town' cottage he bought for his mother, Mary; his sister Betty's stately **Kenmore mansion**, where, incidentally, you should sample the gingerbread made to Mary's recipe; and the celebrated **Rising Sun Tavern** built by his youngest brother, Charles (you will get only colonial spiced tea here now, as this fine old hostelry lost its liquor license back in 1827). Also in the town you can visit the quaint **apothecary shop** run by Washington's friend Hugh Mercer, and the law office and library of America's fifth president, James Monroe. In the **Historic Fredericksburg Museum**, a

The Blue Ridge Mountains, whose foothills project into the broad Shenandoah Valley

treasure trove of colonial and Civil War exhibits, you can recapture the atmosphere of the city's early days.

ⓘ 706 Caroline Street

*Leave Fredericksburg on **I-95** and drive north for about 34 miles (55km) through Woodbridge to **Exit 54**. Continue north on **US 1** for about 5 miles (8km), turn right (east) at the **SR 235** intersection and continue for 2 miles (3km) to Mount Vernon.*

FOR CHILDREN

2 If the children have had enough of the scenery, George Washington and the Civil War, you might arouse some enthusiasm with a tour of **Dinosaur Land** at White Post, just 9 miles (14km) north of Front Royal on **US 522**. Here they will see the monsters displayed realistically in a replica prehistoric forest.

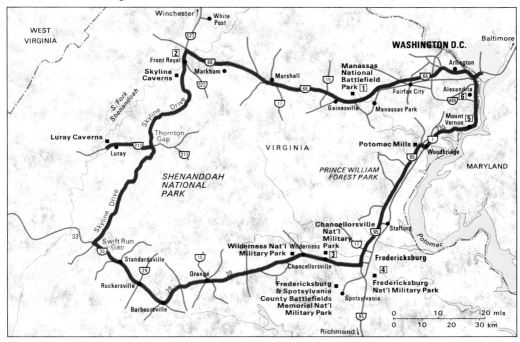

BACK TO NATURE

2 Highlight of the tour for nature lovers is **Shenandoah National Park**. Along the trails you might see black bear, deer, raccoon, skunk, gray fox, chipmunk and many other animals, and catch a glimpse of all kinds of birds, including ravens, hawks, turkey vultures and wild turkeys. You will also hear a chorus of songbirds and perhaps the tapping of woodpeckers. Wildflowers abound in the meadows in spring, but later in the year the great deciduous trees steal the limelight with their spectacular displays of fall foliage.

RECOMMENDED WALKS

If you enjoy walking in the woods, take **Exit 50** from **I-95** at Triangle north of Fredericksburg and drive west on **SR 619** to **Prince William Forest Park**, which has dozens of pleasant walking and nature trails. If you prefer visiting gardens, you can tour the beautifully landscaped grounds at **Woodlawn Plantation**, near Mount Vernon, or the gardens of the **American Horticultural Society** at River Farm, on East Boulevard Drive, Alexandria, which is open only on weekdays.

SCENIC ROUTES

The Skyline Drive through **Shenandoah National Park** stands out as the crowning glory of the itinerary, but you will enjoy many other stretches of the route, such as the road (**SR 20**) between Barboursville and Orange.

SPECIAL TO . . .

5 Potomac Mills is a mecca for the adventurous shopper. With around 200 stores under one roof it is the largest mall in America selling name brand merchandise at outlet prices. Take Exit 52 from northbound **I-95**.

Fredericksburg, a prosperous river port that grew from a 1676 fort, has often played host to history

Mount Vernon, Virginia

5 Overlooking the Potomac River, this beautiful mansion—the beloved home of George and Martha Washington—is the most visited historic estate in America. When Washington acquired the family property in 1754, he enlarged the smaller house built by his father and developed the estate as a working plantation. The house has since been authentically restored and still contains many of the original furnishings. After touring the buildings, take a stroll through the grounds and visit George and Martha's tomb at the foot of the hill.

Follow the Mount Vernon Memorial Highway north along the Potomac River for 9 miles (14km) to Alexandria.

Alexandria, Virginia

6 Less than 7 miles (11km) from the White House, Alexandria has all the trappings of a prosperous suburb of Washington DC, with the usual modern buildings, fine shops, fashionable restaurants and art and antique galleries. But it is, in fact, much older than the capital and has considerable historic charm and interest. Once a thriving tobacco port, it has a walkable 7-by-11-block downtown area called the **Old Town** which has gaslit, cobblestoned streets and buildings that were known to George Washington and Robert E Lee. After stopping for information at the Ramsay House Visitor Center, wander around adjacent Market Square. Here you will see the historic **City Hall**; the elegant **Carlyle House** of 1752; the **Stabler-Leadbeater Apothecary Shop** of 1792, where Martha Washington bought her medicines; and **Gadsby's Tavern**, where George met with other revolutionaries and danced with Martha during his birthnight celebrations (now an annual city event). A few blocks away, you will find **Christ Church**, where the Washingtons and, later, the Lees worshipped. The Lee family home (the **Lee-Fendall House**) and Robert's boyhood home are some blocks north, on Oronoco Street.

Before leaving Alexandria, don't miss a tour of the artists' studios in the rather unattractive **Torpedo Factory Art Center**. The Center is divided into 83 studios and five galleries where you can watch artists and craftsmen painting, sculpting, and making pottery, stained glass and jewelry. You should also make time to stroll through **Waterfront Park** on the Potomac River to see the schooner *Alexandria*.

ⓘ 221 King Street

Leave Alexandria via North Washington Street for the 7-mile (11km) drive to downtown Washington DC.

Washington DC – Manassas **30 (48)**
Manassas – Front Royal **45 (72)**
Front Royal – Chancellorsville **148 (237)**
Chancellorsville – Fredericksburg **8 (13)**
Fredericksburg – Mount Vernon **41 (66)**
Mount Vernon – Alexandria **9 (14)**
Alexandria – Washington DC **7 (11)**

Oatlands, built in 1804, combines Federal and Greek Revival styles

ℹ 1445 Pennsylvania Avenue, Washington DC

*From downtown Washington cross the Potomac River and drive north on George Washington Parkway to enter southbound Capital Beltway (**I-495**). At **Exit 13** take the Georgetown Pike (**SR 193**) west for about 4½ miles (7km), then turn onto **SR 738** to Great Falls Park.*

Great Falls Park, Virginia

1 This pleasant wooded park, just 15 miles (24km) from Washington, offers spectacular views of the falls and rocky gorge where the Potomac River tumbles over the edge of the Piedmont Plateau. A favorite escape for city dwellers, it has good walking trails and picnic sites, but stay on the trails and observe the signs as there are some hazardous spots.

*Continue along **SR 193** for about 5 miles (7km) through the town of Great Falls and join **SR 7** northbound at Dranesville. Continue for about 14 miles (23km) to Leesburg.*

Leesburg and Hunt Country, Virginia

2 With a history that goes back more than two centuries, Leesburg is an attractive old town with a Historic District packed with lovely colonial homes, fine antique shops and restaurants. Stop by the **Loudoun Museum** and **Visitor Center** for brochures and a slide presentation before taking a walking tour around its streets. Then drive out into the surrounding country, where you will find quaint old villages, like Waterford on SR 662, charming country inns, horse farms, wineries and perhaps even a craft fair or a meet of the local hunt. Fox hunting and other equestrian activities are a strong tradition here, for this is Virginia's 'Hunt Country'. Horses feature prominently at two of the area's leading visitor attractions. **Oatlands Plantation**, south of Leesburg, hosts equestrian events throughout the year, while **Morven Park**, to the north, has a fox-hunting museum and a marvelous carriage collection. Both are beautiful places to visit, even if you have never been on a saddle.

ℹ 108 South Street SE

*From Leesburg follow **SR 9** and **SR 671** north for 21 miles (34km) to Harpers Ferry.*

Harpers Ferry, West Virginia

3 This historic town lies at the junction of the Potomac and the Shenandoah rivers amid the wooded slopes of the Blue Ridge, a spectacular setting best viewed from the hillside overlook at Jefferson Rock. With its strategic position, the town changed hands several times in the Civil War. It was here that, in 1859, just before the war, the antislavery campaigner John Brown made his ill-fated raid on the Federal Arsenal and became a folk hero through the old battle song 'John Brown's Body Lies

FOUR STATES HISTORIC TOUR

Washington DC ● Great Falls Park ● Leesburg and Hunt Country ● Harpers Ferry Sharpsburg● Emmitsburg and the Blue Ridge Mountains ● Gettysburg ● Frederick Washington DC

A taste of the scenic beauty and historic heritage of four states—Virginia, West Virginia, Pennsylvania and Maryland—awaits you on this varied tour. Less than an hour's drive at the start will take you from the bustle of the nation's capital to the rural tranquility of Virginia's 'Hunt Country'. Then, driving north through the lovely Appalachian ridges, where the first Irish and German settlers put down their roots, you will come face to face with the Civil War in places whose names are forever etched on the pages of history—Harpers Ferry, Sharpsburg, Gettysburg and Frederick.

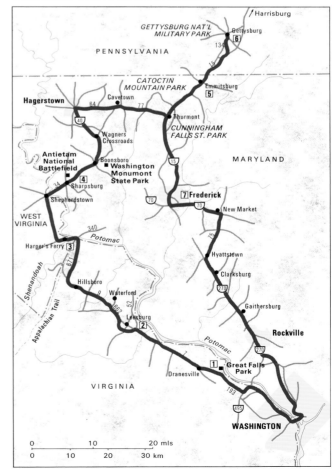

FOR HISTORY BUFFS

4 Just south of Thurmont, the Catoctin Furnace Historic District contains the ruins of a 17th-century iron-making village including the workers' stone cottages. The furnace, which continued operating until 1905, made iron for the Civil War battleship *Monitor.*

7 Rockville's West Montgomery Avenue Historic District contains more than 100 old buildings of architectural and historic interest. In the **Beall-Dawson House**, the strong-of-stomach can pore over a collection of gruesome 19th-century medical instruments. Also in the town is the grave of writer F Scott Fitzgerald and his wife, Zelda.

FOR CHILDREN

4 Near Thurmont, kids can get close to animals in the petting area at the **Catoctin Mountain Zoological Park.**

7 At Frederick, they can explore the log cabin, blacksmith shop, carriages and other farm objects at the **Rose Hill Manor Children's Museum**, with its many interesting hands-on displays.

BACK TO NATURE

3 Although it is difficult to single out any one location for wildlife, the Appalachian Trail provides the best opportunities for seeing the birds and mammals of upland forest. Look for deer, squirrels and raccoons and birds such as black-capped chickadees, ravens, ruffed grouse and chestnut-sided warblers.

5 The First Monument to George Washington in Washington Monument State Park is the best spot for observing migrating birds of prey in October and September.

RECOMMENDED WALKS

Opportunities for walking abound on this tour, but there are some places where stretching your legs is especially enjoyable. They include the towpath of the historic **Chesapeake and Ohio Canal** at Harpers Ferry **(3)**; the **Appalachian Trail** near Harpers Ferry and Boonsboro **(3)**; and trails in **Cunningham Falls State Park** and **Catoctin Mountain Park**, near Thurmont **(4).**

Amoldering in the Grave'. You will see the fort where he was captured on a tour of the **National Historical Park** which encompasses the town.

ⓘ Shenandoah Street

Follow **US 340** *west for 2 miles (3km), then* **SR 230** *north for 8 miles (13km) to Shepherdstown. Cross the Potomac into Maryland and follow* **SR 34** *for 4 miles (6km) to Sharpsburg.*

Sharpsburg, Maryland

4 John Brown's activities took him to Sharpsburg, and you can follow in his footsteps to the **Kennedy Farmhouse**, which was used by his band before the Harpers Ferry raid. Most people come here, however, to visit the site of the battle of Antietam (or Sharpsburg). At **Antietam Creek**, just north of the town, more than 23,000 men fell on September 17, 1862. It was the Civil War's bloodiest single day of fighting. The battle ended in a stalemate, but it halted the Confederate invasion of Maryland. After stopping at the Visitor Center you can take a self-guided auto tour of the main landmarks in the battle.

Take **SR 34** *from Sharpsburg for 7 miles (11km) to Boonsboro, then* **SR 66** *north for 4 miles (6km) to Wagners Crossroads. Continue north on* **US 40** *for 8 miles (13km) to Hagerstown. From here follow* **SR 64** *and* **SR 77** *east for 19 miles (31km) to Thurmont, then turn north on* **US 15** *for the 9-mile (14km) drive to Emmitsburg.*

Emmitsburg and the Blue Ridge Mountains, Maryland

5 If you enjoy mountain scenery with thick forests, crystal-clear streams and green valleys, you will love Maryland's scenic Blue Ridge region. Among the wooded ridges of South Mountain, once the scene of Civil War conflict, and the Catoctin Mountains farther east, you will find opportunities for fishing, hunting, boating, canoeing, cross-country skiing and hiking or just strolling along stretches of the Appalachian Trail and other designated pathways.

The Potomac cascades in a series of rugged falls and turbulent rapids at Great Falls Park

Virginia's memorial at Gettysburg, a poignant tableau of defeat

Places of interest abound along the route. Boonsboro has its **Museum of History**, and nearby are the **Crystal Grottoes**, **Old South Mountain Inn** and **Washington Monument State Park**. Hagerstown's attractions include historic buildings like the **Jonathan Hager House** and **Miller House**. But for beautiful mountain scenery take a walk in **Cunningham Falls Park** and adjoining **Catoctin Mountain Park**, the location not only of the presidential retreat at Camp David but also of the historic **Blue Blazes Whiskey Still**. If you want to learn how to make liquor, this is the place. Other places of interest await you along the lovely drive to Emmitsburg. Among them are the Roddy Road covered bridge; **Our Lady of Lourdes Grotto**, the beautiful replica of the Grotto of Lourdes in southern France; and the Shrine of Elizabeth Ann Seton, the first American-born saint.

*From Emmitsburg drive north for 9 miles (14km) on **US 15** and **SR 134** across the Mason-Dixon Line into Gettysburg.*

Gettysburg, Pennsylvania

6 Although the Gettysburg area has plenty of interesting things to see and do, people come here mainly to visit the **Gettysburg National Military Park**, where the bloodiest and most crucial battle of the Civil War was fought between July 1–3, 1863, resulting in 51,000 casualties and defeat for the Confederate army under General Lee, turning the tide against the South. Before touring the battlefield, stop at the Visitor Center and ride up the **National Tower** for a panoramic view of the area. Then take the shuttle bus for a tour

of President Dwight D Eisenhower's home (a National Historic Site) and stroll around the downtown Historic District.

ⓘ 35 Carlisle Steet

*From Gettysburg follow the same route back to Thurmont, Maryland, then continue south on **US 15** for another 17 miles (27km) to Frederick.*

Frederick, Maryland

7 This charming old colonial town lies in rolling farmland and orchard country in the shadow of the Catoctin Mountains. Known as the 'City of Clustered Spires', Frederick boasts many historic buildings in its downtown National Historic District. Every visitor wants to see the **house of Barbara Fritchie**, that redoubtable old lady who reputedly confronted Confederate General Stonewall Jackson with a union flag as he rode by. You can see her grave in Mount Olivet Cemetery, the last resting place also of Francis Scott Key, author of *The Star Spangled Banner*, who lived in Frederick for a time. Worth a visit is the old German farmhouse called **Schifferstadt**.

ⓘ 19 East Church Street

*From Frederick follow **I-70** east for 7 miles (11km) for a brief tour of New Market, then take **SR 75** south and join **I-270** southbound at Hyattstown for the 46-mile (74km) drive through Rockville back to Washington DC.*

Washington DC – Great Falls Park	**19 (30)**
Great Falls Park – Leesburg	**19 (30)**
Leesburg – Harpers Ferry	**21 (34)**
Harpers Ferry – Sharpsburg	**14 (22)**
Sharpsburg – Emmitsburg	**47 (75)**
Emmitsburg – Gettysburg	**9 (14)**
Gettysburg – Frederick	**35 (56)**
Frederick – Washington DC	**46 (74)**

SCENIC ROUTES

In addition to the pleasant drive to Great Falls at the start of the tour, the most scenic stretches of highway are in the Blue Ridge region; **SR 671**, Hillsboro to Harpers Ferry; **SR 66**, Boonsboro to Wagners Crossroads; **SR 77**, Cavetown to Thurmont; and **US 15**, Thurmont to Emmitsburg.

SPECIAL TO . . .

7 The town of New Market, east of Frederick, is the place to go for bargains in bric-a-brac and special antique treasures. The 'Antiques Capital of Maryland' is packed with more than 50 stores where you are sure to find something you like.

3 days – Approximately 287 miles (459km)

PENNSYLVANIA DUTCH COUNTRY

Philadelphia ● Chadds Ford and the Brandywine Valley ● Wilmington Strasburg and Lancaster County ● York Harrisburg ● Hershey ● Reading Hopewell Furnace ● Valley Forge Philadelphia

No matter what your interests and tastes, you will find much to enjoy on this tour of Pennsylvania's southeastern counties. Above all, you will experience the unique way of life of the Pennsylvania Dutch people who pioneered this land. You will see traces, too, of Delaware's Scandinavian heritage and feel the birth pangs of American nationhood at famous Revolutionary War sites. You will tour Pennsylvania's state capital and other cities of differing personalities, inspect pioneer homesteads, admire the great mansions and estates of the du Ponts and enjoy the fun—and the chocolate—at Hershey.

FOR HISTORY BUFFS

2 Of historic interest on this tour are the industrial exhibits at **Hagley Museum**. It is situated 3 miles (5km) north of Wilmington on **SR 141** in 230 acres (110 hectares) of the original Du Pont Mills site along the Brandywine River. Many of the mills have been restored to full working order, and there are exhibits and demonstrations, including an operating steam engine, a wooden water wheel and a restored machine shop from the 1870's.

🛈 1525 John F Kennedy Boulevard, Philadelphia

*Cross the Schuylkill River from downtown Philadelphia and pick up the northbound Schuylkill Expressway. After about 4 miles (6km) take **Exit 33** west onto **US 1** and continue for about 25 miles (40km) to Chadds Ford. West of town follow **SR 52** south down the Brandywine Valley.*

Chadds Ford and the Brandywine Valley, Pennsylvania and Delaware

1 At Chadds Ford **US1** crosses Brandywine Creek as it flows down its beautiful valley to Wilmington, Delaware. The Chadds Ford area boasts several early 18th-century houses; a winery; the **Brandywine Battlefield Park**, site of a 1777 British victory in the Revolutionary War; and the attractive **Brandywine River Museum**, which has paintings by the Wyeths and other American artists. Not to be missed to the west of town are the beautiful landscaped grounds and conservatories of **Longwood Gardens**, the country estate of industrialist Pierre S du Pont. Down

Decorative arts in America, 1640 to 1840, at the Winterthur Museum

the Brandywine Valley on **Route 52** are more impressive Du Pont mansions and fine museums, highlighted by the magnificent **Winterthur Museum and Gardens**, which contains Henry Francis du Pont's world-famous collection of antique furniture, paintings and other art treasures.

🛈 Longwood Gardens, Route 1, Kennett Square

*Continue driving south on **US 52** into Wilmington.*

Wilmington, Delaware

2 Delaware's largest city is a major center of the chemical industry and the headquarters of many US companies and banks. At the foot of 7th Street are historic reminders of the city's first Scandinavian settlers of 1638, including the **Old Swedes Church**, the **Hendrickson House** and the site of Fort Christina. Among the shops along Market Street are other sightseeing treasures, such as the **Old Town Hall**, the **Grand Opera House** and the restored 18th-century houses at Willingtown Square. At the foot of King Street you can tour the 1934 cutter *Mohawk* and take a cruise on the Christina River. Don't miss the **Delaware Art Museum**, in the north part of the city, where you can see fine American works as well as English pre-Raphaelite paintings among the collections.

🛈 1300 Market Street

*From Wilmington drive northwest on Lancaster Avenue **(SR 48)** and **SR 41** for about 34 miles (55km), then take **SR 741** west for about 9 miles (14km) to Strasburg and Lancaster County.*

Strasburg and Lancaster County, Pennsylvania

3 The rich, rolling farmlands of Lancaster County are the heartland of Pennsylvania Dutch Country. The plain lifestyle of the local orthodox Amish and Mennonite people, traditionally averse to modern gadgets and attitudes (including visitors' cameras), has ironically become a tourist attraction. So you can tour their farms and homes, sample their excellent home cooking, ride their horse-drawn buggies and buy their beautiful handmade crafts. You will get advice on suitable places at the Visitor Center on Greenfield Road just outside Lancaster.

Quaint Strasburg is the site of the famed **Railroad Museum**, which traces the history of railroads in Pennsylvania through memorabilia and restored locomotives, and many other attractions.

On the road from Strasburg to Lancaster you can detour on to **Route 340** to the varied attractions of Bird-in-Hand and Intercourse, where you can visit the craft shops of **Kitchen Kettle Village** and see beautiful quilts at the **Quilt Museum**; northwards on **Routes 772** and **272** to the historic **Ephrata Cloister** religious community site; then south on **Route 272** to Lancaster, with a stop just north of town to learn something of the

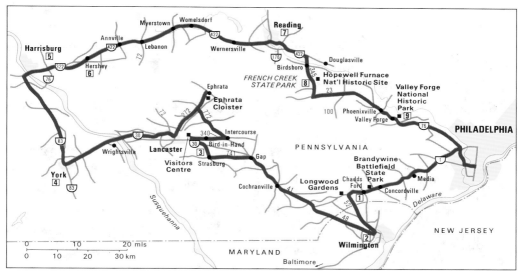

state's German rural heritage at the excellent **Landis Valley Museum**, set in 100 acres (40 hectares).

In Lancaster take a walking tour of the downtown area to see the colorful old **Central Market**; the **Heritage Center**, with its art and craft exhibits; and the **Demuth Tobacco Shop** of 1770, the oldest in America. And further out of town, visit the 1792 **Rock Ford Plantation** and President James Buchanan's elegant Federal-style **Wheatland Mansion** of 1828.

ℹ 501 Greenfield Road, Lancaster

*From Lancaster take **US 30** west for 24 miles (39km) across the Susquehanna River to York.*

York, Pennsylvania

4 The manufacturing city of York is known today for its motorcycles, shopping outlets and markets, cultural activities and events like the York Interstate Fair and Halloween Parade, and historic buildings. But for

Farmland yields bounteous harvests for Pennsylvania's 'Plain People'

several months in 1777 to 78 it was, in effect, America's first capital, after the Continental Congress fled here following the British occupation of Philadelphia. While touring the Historic District around Market Street, be sure to visit the reconstruction of the original 1755 **York County Colonial Courthouse** where the Congress met and hear dramatic sound-and-light re-enactments of the delegates' debates.

ℹ One Market Way East

*From York follow **I-83** north for 25 miles (40km) to Harrisburg.*

Harrisburg, Pennsylvania

5 It was in the late 1700s that John Harris Jr laid out the town that was to become Pennsylvania's state capital, and you can still see the mansion he built by the Susquehanna River in 1766 as you tour the historic district along South Front Street. Be sure to visit also the imposing domed **Capitol**, in the complex of public buildings in the Midtown district; the **State Museum of Pennsylvania** nearby, with its historic and other

FOR CHILDREN

3 The exciting **Toy Train Museum and Choo Choo Barn**, in Strasburg, is a 1,700-square-foot (160 sq m) miniature display of Lancaster County and Pennsylvania Dutch Country. It has 13 operating toy trains with over 135 animated and automated figures and vehicles, and there are miniatures of many of the area's landmarks.

BACK TO NATURE

7 Nature takes second place to other sightseeing attractions on this tour. But if you have time, drive 20 miles (32km) on **Route 61** north of Reading to see migrating hawks and eagles—best in September and October—and resident birds and mammals at the famed **Hawk Mountain Sanctuary**.

9 Be sure to visit **Mill Grove**, naturalist John James Audubon's home near Valley Forge, and walk through the wildlife sanctuary there.

RECOMMENDED WALKS

When you have seen the pictures at the Brandywine River Museum **(1)**, enjoy a pleasant stroll down the trails through the woodland nearby. There are more enjoyable walks at **Longwood Gardens (1)**; along the **Union Canal towpath** west of Reading **(7)**; and at **French Creek State Park**, near Hopewell Furnace **(8)**, where you can follow part of the lengthy **Horse Shoe Trail**.

SCENIC ROUTES

Get away from the main highways for the most enjoyable rides through southeast Pennsylvania's lovely countryside. The pleasantest stretches of road include **Route 52** down the Brandywine Valley; **Routes 722** and **272** through Lancaster County's farmlands between Intercourse and Ephrata; and the 3-mile (5km) Skyline Drive to the mountaintop Pagoda at Reading.

SPECIAL TO . . .

3 Special experiences at various points along the tour include the fun-packed **Renaissance Faire** at the Mount Hope Estate on **Route 72** north of Lancaster. It takes place at weekends from July to mid-October, including Mondays up to August, and is a fantasy recreation of a 16th-century English Tudor village with costumed performers juggling, jousting, conjuring and dragon-slaying.

collections; the fine **Governor's Mansion**; and **Strawberry Square**, a shopping and restaurant showplace. Walk, too, along 5-mile (8km) River Park, site of summer events, and take a leisurely riverboat cruise from City Island.

ⓘ 114 Walnut Street

Head east on I-83, US 322/422 and Hershey Park Drive (SR 39 north) to Hershey.

Hershey, Pennsylvania

6 A short distance from Harrisburg is 'Chocolate Town USA', a paradise for children. The town of Hershey, founded in 1903 by Milton S Hershey, is one of the largest chocolate and cocoa plants in the world. Stop first at the **Chocolate World Visitors Center** and take the short simulated tour of the chocolate-making process. You will then have to choose from the many other attractions on offer. For fun-seekers, old and young, there are 87 acres (35 hectares) of exciting rides, roller coasters, water attractions and shows on the Hersheypark complex. The less energetic might prefer a quiet tour of the **Museum of American Life**, to see the native wild animals and plants at the **ZooAmerica North American Wildlife Park**, or to stroll

Washington's headquarters as reconstructed at Valley Forge

around the superb seasonal flower displays in the 23-acre (9-hectare) **Hershey Gardens**.

ⓘ See Harrisburg

Continue east on US 422 for 38 miles (61km) through the Lebanon Valley to Reading.

Reading, Pennsylvania

7 While in Reading, don't miss a drive up to the oriental **Pagoda** that overlooks the city from its perch on top of nearby Mount Penn, where you can enjoy magnificent panoramic views of the surrounding area. Down in the city, take a walk around the Callowhill Historical District to see the fine 19th-century buildings in the Penn Square and 5th Street areas. Then go and hunt for bargains in Reading's numerous shopping outlets, many of them housed in the city's six major complexes.

Follow US 422 east for 10 miles (16km) from Reading to Birdsboro, then take SR 345 south for 5 miles (8km) to Hopewell Furnace.

Hopewell Furnace, Pennsylvania

8 Nestled in the quiet countryside around French Creek State Park is the **Hopewell Furnace National Historic Site**, a restored village that operated between 1771 and 1883 and one of the finest examples of an Early American iron-making community. On a tour of the buildings you will see demonstrations of iron-molding, blacksmithing, and open-hearth cooking and metal casting as well as re-enactments of village life by period-costumed interpreters.

ⓘ The Superintendent, Hopewell Furnace National Historic Site

About 2 miles (3km) south of Hopewell take SR 23 east for about 18 miles (29km) to the village of Valley Forge.

Valley Forge, Pennsylvania

9 The 3,000-acre (1,214 hectare) Valley Forge National Historical Park commemorates one of the most moving episodes of America's Revolution. Following defeat by the British at Brandywine in September 1777, George Washington's dispirited Continental Army encamped here and heroically recuperated during a winter of terrible privation. Call at the Visitor Center and take a self-guided tour of the fortifications and other park landmarks.

ⓘ The Superintendent, Valley Forge National Historical Park

Pick up I-76 (Schuylkill Expressway) eastbound from Valley Forge at Interchange 24 and continue for about 22 miles (35km) to downtown Philadelphia.

Philadelphia – Chadds Ford **29 (46)**
Chadds Ford – Wilmington **14 (22)**
Wilmington – Strasburg **43 (69)**
Strasburg – York **66 (106)**
York – Harrisburg **25 (40)**
Harrisburg – Hershey **15 (24)**
Hershey – Reading **38 (61)**
Reading – Hopewell Furnace **15 (24)**
Hopewell Furnace – Valley Forge **20 (32)**
Valley Forge – Philadelphia **22 (35)**

Tobacco, Colonial Virginia's earliest export, still a major crop

ℹ 1700 Robin Hood Road, Richmond

*From downtown Richmond follow East Broad Street to Richmond National Battlefield Park headquarters in Chimborazo Park. Retrace Broad Street to 25th Street and drive south to New Market Road (**SR 5**). Continue east for a few miles to either the Fort Harrison or Malvern Hill battle site.*

Richmond National Battlefield Park, Virginia

1 As capital of the Confederacy, Richmond was the Union forces' prime objective throughout the Civil War, and several major battles were fought east and south of the city in 1862 and 1864. These battle sites are now encompassed in the 10 units of **Richmond National Battlefield Park**. Get information and see the audiovisual presentation at the Chimborazo Park Visitor Center. Then visit one of the battlefields, off of Route 5; either **Fort Harrison**, which fell to Grant's Union forces in 1864, or **Malvern Hill**, where the Confederates stopped the first advance on Richmond in 1862.

ℹ 3215 East Broad Street

*Take **SR 5** southeast, then turn right onto **SR 156** and follow it to Shirley Plantation.*

Shirley Plantation and the James River Plantations, Virginia

2 The Virginia Peninsula, east of Richmond, is probably the most historic stretch of real estate in all America. Along the north shore of the James River, **Route 5** links a string of old plantation homes and stately mansions whose owners include several early US presidents and signers of the Declaration of Independence. Some are open only by prior appointment, but you should try to visit at least one. In the order in which you will reach them after leaving Richmond, they are: **Shirley Plantation** (circa 1613), **Edgewood** (1849), **Berkeley** (1726), **Westover** (grounds only, 1730), **Evelynton** (1930s), **Belle Air** (circa 1670) and **Sherwood Forest** (grounds only, circa 1730).

*Continue driving along **SR 5** to Jamestown.*

Jamestown, Virginia

3 At Jamestown, beside the James River, the first permanent English settlement in America was established in 1607. You can still see the ruins of the original site as you drive around what is now Jamestown Island (it was then connected by an isthmus). But to get an idea of what that first community was really like, spend some time soaking up the atmosphere at the nearby re-created **Jamestown Settlement** (formerly Jamestown Festival Park). Costumed interpreters re-enacting the life of the early settlers take you back centuries as you tour the reconstructed **James Fort** stockade, the **Indian Village**, the **Glasshouse** used for making glass objects, and one of the three

THE BIRTHPLACE OF COLONIAL VIRGINIA

Richmond • Richmond National Battlefield Park • Shirley Plantation and the James River Plantations • Jamestown • Williamsburg Newport News and Hampton • Yorktown Stratford Hall • Kings Dominion • Richmond

On this tour from Richmond around Virginia's Tidewater region, the natural scenery, lush, green and pleasant though it is, takes a back seat to the places of historic importance, especially along the Virginia Peninsula. At the forefront are Civil War battlefields around Confederate Richmond; plantations along the James River; major Colonial sites in the 'Historic Triangle' of Jamestown, Williamsburg and Yorktown; and fascinating museums at Newport News and Hampton. There are also places for fun and relaxation along the route and things for the children to enjoy.

Within Jameston Settlement are 18 primitive wattle-and-daub structures, including a church

ships which are replicas of the ones that braved the Atlantic voyage in 1607, bringing the first settlers to Virginia.

Take the Colonial Parkway north for 9 miles (14km) to Williamsburg, second capital of the United States.

FOR HISTORY BUFFS

4 If you enjoy touring
stately homes and
plantations, there are two
more important historic
houses which are
conveniently close to the
route for a visit. Lovely
Carter's Grove Plantation,
off **US 60** near Williamsburg,
was built in the 1750s, and
in its grounds are
reconstructions of slave
cabins and the archae-
ological site of 17th-century
Wolstenholme Towne.

8 West of **I-95**, near Kings
Dominion, is **Scotchtown**,
the white clapboard
mansion bought in 1771 by
the firebrand patriot Patrick
Henry, who gained fame for
his 'Give me liberty or give
me death' speech shortly
before the Revolution.

FOR CHILDREN

5 Youngsters are well
provided for on this tour,
but two additional places
that should prove fun for
animal lovers are: **Bluebird
Gap Farm**, at Hampton, a
sort of combined farm, park
and zoo with native Virginia
wild animals and farm
animals; and **Virginia Living
Museum**, at Newport News,
which has exciting exhibits
featuring wild creatures.

BACK TO NATURE

7 If you have never seen a
bald eagle in a natural
setting, make for **Caledon
Natural Area** on **Route 218**
by the Potomac River, just 4
miles (6km) west of Owens
from **US 301**. Large numbers
of these majestic birds
congregate here in summer
and can be seen from the
walking trails.
  Byrd Park in Richmond is
good for sighting wintering
wildfowl, which are usually
quite tame.

RECOMMENDED WALK

7 You will do a lot of
walking around plantation
estates, battlefields and
other historic places on this
tour, but to get away from
the crowds spend some time
in **Westmoreland State Park**,
near Stratford Hall, where
you will find hiking trails and
picnic spots overlooking the
Potomac River.

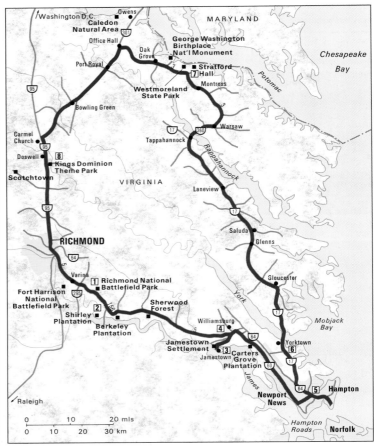

Williamsburg, Virginia

4 Though some might regard it as a
stage set, this tremendous restoration of the 18th-century Historic
Area—Colonial Williamsburg—is
quite remarkable, not only for the
colossal scale of the enterprise but
also for its historic authenticity. As
you stroll around the streets and
mingle with the 'citizens' in period
dress who are re-enacting the life of
those early days, you can almost
believe you have entered a time
warp. Take a special look at the
Governor's Palace, the **Capitol**, the
College of William and Mary, and
two of the town's lively old
hostelries, both conveniently on
Duke of Gloucester Street—the
famous **Raleigh Tavern** and
Wetherburn's Tavern.
  In the Williamsburg area are two
popular entertainment parks—**Water
Country USA** and **Busch Gardens/
The Old Country**—where you can
have a little relaxing fun.

ⓘ 901 Richmond Road

  *Take either **I-64** or **US 60** for the
  23-mile (37km) drive to Newport
  News and Hampton.*

Newport News and Hampton, Virginia

5 These two adjoining cities overlook
the immense natural harbor of
Hampton Roads from the tip of the
Virginia Peninsula. To get a good look
at this great port area and the ships
anchored at Norfolk Naval Base
across the water, take an exhilarating
boat cruise from the Newport News
waterfront. With its long tradition of
shipbuilding, Newport News is the
location of the world-famous

Mariners' Museum, which tells the
story of mankind's eventful relation-
ship with the sea. Not far away the
excellent **War Memorial Museum**
portrays American military history
since independence, complete with
marvelous war posters. At Hampton
are the **NASA Langley Visitor Center
Museum**, with displays on flight and
space exploration, and the **Casemate
Museum**, at historic Fort Monroe,
which traces American history since
independence.

ⓘ 13 San Jose Drive, Suite 3-B,
Newport News

  *Take **I-64** north from Hampton to
  Exit 62, then **US 17** north to
  Yorktown, a journey of about 15
  miles (24km).*

Yorktown, Virginia

6 In colonial times, Yorktown was a
thriving tobacco port on the York
River which, on October 19, 1781,
saw the dramatic surrender of British
forces under Cornwallis that brought
the Revolutionary War to an end. You
can relive the momentous events at
the **Colonial National Historical
Park**, which contains the battle site.
Watch a stirring film about the battle
at the **Victory Center**, then tour the
battlefield landmarks and the **Moore
House**, where the surrender terms
were negotiated.

  *Follow **US 17** across the York
  River and through Gloucester for
  59 miles (95km) to
  Tappahannock. Take **US 360** for
  7 miles (11km) to Warsaw, then
  take the **SR 3** north for 17 miles
  (28km) to Stratford Hall and
  George Washington's Birthplace.*

Stratford Hall, Virginia

7 Stratford Hall, the ancestral home of the Lee family, was built between 1729 and 1730 on the southern shore of the Potomac River, in Virginia's lovely Northern Neck region. It was here that the most illustrious member of the family, General Robert E Lee, was born in 1807. The imposing brick-built mansion is open to visitors year round.

A few miles west, on Route 204, is **George Washington's Birthplace National Monument**. Despite the name, you cannot tour the original house in which George was born in 1732, because it was destroyed by fire in 1779. However, you can visit the pretty **Memorial House** built near the site and tour the gardens, the colonial farm and the family burial ground.

Continue west on SR 3 for about 9 miles (14km) to Oak Grove, then a further 10 miles (16km) to pick up US 301 at Office Hall.

Colonial Williamsburg, a living restoration of a prosperous past

Continue for 29 miles (47km) to Carmel Church and pick up I-95 southbound for 7 miles (11km) to Exit 40 for Kings Dominion theme park.

Kings Dominion, Virginia

8 One way to end a tour of Virginia's impressive historic sites is with a little fun and entertainment at popular **Kings Dominion theme park** at Doswell, north of Richmond. Open daily in the summer months and weekends in the spring and fall, this 400-acre (160-hectare) park has rides and live shows in four theme areas: Safari Village, Candy Apple Grove, White Water Canyon and Old Virginia.

Continue south on I-95 for 22 miles (35km) to Richmond.

Richmond – Battlefield Park	**14 (22)**
Battlefield Park – Shirley Plantation	**7 (11)**
Shirley Plantation – Jamestown	**44 (70)**
Jamestown – Williamsburg	**9 (14)**
Williamsburg – Newport News	**23 (37)**
Newport News – Yorktown	**15 (24)**
Yorktown – Stratford Hall	**83 (134)**
Stratford Hall – Kings Dominion	**55 (88)**
Kings Dominion – Richmond	**22 (35)**

SCENIC ROUTES

Although this is not an itinerary with spectacular hill scenery, there are sections of highway that pass through lovely countryside and offer fine views over water. Most notable are **Route 5**, with its views of the James River; along **US 17**, across the farmlands and marshes of the Tidewater region; and along **Route 3**, up the Northern Neck.

SPECIAL TO . . .

Tidewater Virginia has as much to please the palate as the eye. Don't finish your tour without sampling the succulent seafood from Chesapeake Bay or Virginia's famed Smithfield ham, accompanied, of course, by excellent native-grown wines. You can taste some of these on a tour of the **Ingleside Winery**, near Oak Grove on the Northern Neck.

THE ATLANTIC SOUTHEAST

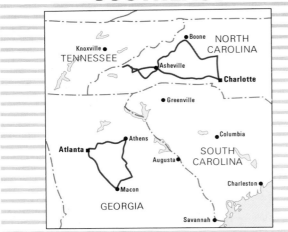

The last of the 13 original English Colonies to be established along America's Atlantic seaboard were founded in North and South Carolina in the late 1600s and in neighboring Georgia in 1733. Historically and culturally the region is part of the Old South. Here a genteel white plantation society developed during the Colonial era, in which black slaves provided labor for fields and mansions. But, as Margaret Mitchell described in her epic story *Gone with the Wind*, this way of life was to be brusquely swept away by bitter defeat in the War Between the States of 1861–65.

The Confederate flag is still often seen, a nostalgic symbol of Southern pride. Other reminders of the past survive too. There are Revolutionary War battle sites, old forts and plantation homes; the site of Sir Walter Raleigh's two ill-fated attempts to found England's first New World colony on Roanoke Island in the 1580s; and the North Carolina Colonial Governor's residence at restored Tryon Palace. Dotted throughout the region are historic small towns, like Old Salem, York, Camden and Madison. And the beautiful port cities of Charleston and Savannah preserve atmospheric old streets and gracious town mansions that transport you back to a more elegant age.

The land is similar to the Mid-Atlantic states further north: flat coastal plain and marshes, fall line, rolling Piedmont Plateau, and Appalachian Mountains. Of these, it is the 600-mile (965km) shoreline that shows greatest diversity. In North Carolina there is a maze of tidal inlets and marshes, broad river estuaries, and excellent offshore barrier islands, known as the Outer Banks; in South Carolina, beaches, including the 55-mile (88km) Grand Strand, and resort sea islands such as Hilton Head; and in Georgia, the moss-draped, pine-clad Golden Isles of the Colonial Coast and, inland, the eery Okefenokee Swamp.

Woodlands and farm country, extending across the broad coastal plain and the more populated Piedmont, contrast with important manufacturing cities, among them Raleigh and Charlotte in North Carolina, Columbia in South Carolina, and Atlanta in Georgia.

The region's most beautiful scenery is packed into the forested ridges and valleys of the Appalachian Mountains, land of the hillbilly, log cabin and moonshine. Here, too, on a small reservation beside the Great Smokies, live the descendants of the proud Cherokee nation whose land this once was.

Charlotte:
Named after Queen Charlotte, George III's German-born consort, North Carolina's largest city is a financial, transportation and textile-manufacturing center at the hub of the 'Carolinas Crescent' industrial region. A pleasant, livable city of over 300,000 people, it sprawls across the wooded Piedmont, surrounded by tree-shaded residential districts like the attractive Fourth Ward; shopping malls, outlets and trade marts; sports and entertainment arenas; country clubs, golf courses and recreational lakes; and many other places of interest to visitors.

Modern glass towers rise from the uptown business district, location of the **Civic Center** exhibit complex, the performing arts center of **Spirit Square**, and the hands-on science and natural history museum of **Discovery Place**. South of town are the **Mint Museum of Art**, with art collections housed in a re-sited 1835 building dating from Charlotte's gold-producing era; the log cabins at the 1795 **birthsite of President James K Polk**; and the exciting **Carowinds theme park**. On the east side of town you will find the area's oldest dwelling, the 1774 **Rock House** at the Hezekiah Alexander Homesite, and, further north, the **Reed Gold Mine**, where gold was discovered in 1799 by a 12-year-old boy, and the exciting **Charlotte Motor Speedway** with its stock car races.

Atlanta:
Atlanta is probably best known as the Southern city burned to the ground by the Yankees in the Civil War movie *Gone with the Wind*. Since then Georgia's capital has risen from the ashes like the mythical phoenix to become the main

Prosperous and cultured, Charlotte is a 'City of Trees'

Milledgeville escaped Sherman's wrath

business, financial and industrial hub of the Southeast. A vibrant modern city of almost $2\frac{1}{2}$ million people, Atlanta boasts a flourishing cultural scene, with fine museums, galleries and performing arts events. Amid the glittering glass towers that dominate the downtown skyline is the elegant **Peachtree Center**, a complex of hotels, offices restaurants and shops. Its sleek modern architecture contrasts with the classic 1889 gold-domed **State Capitol** and other government buildings.

Among the many other places of interest to visit around the city are the shops and night spots of Underground Atlanta; the **Martin Luther King Jr Historic Site** along revitalized Auburn Avenue, which includes Dr King's birthplace and grave; the renovated **zoo** and the famous **Cyclorama** in Grant Park that tells the story of the Civil War battle of Atlanta; and the **Wren's Nest**, the home of writer Joel Chandler Harris, the creator of the beloved Uncle Remus tales. North along Peachtree Street are the Art Deco-style **Fox Theatre**; the **Atlanta Botanical Garden** in Piedmont Park; and the impressive **Swan House** in the smart residential neighborhood of Buckhead.

For a final touch of nostalgia, drive out to Newnan, southwest of the city, to see **Tara**, Hollywood's version of the famous fictional plantation home of Scarlett O'Hara in *Gone with the Wind*.

3 days – Approximately 489 miles (782km)

JOURNEY TO THE LAND OF THE SKY

Charlotte • Gastonia • Lake Lure and Chimney Rock Park • Asheville • Cherokee • Great Smoky Mountains National Park • Blue Ridge Parkway • Charlotte

This is a journey through some of the most strikingly beautiful scenery in eastern America. You start with a drive across the green rolling country of central North Carolina to the pleasant town of Asheville, site of the Vanderbilts' famed Biltmore mansion, and enter the wild landscapes of the 'Land of the Sky', the Great Smoky Mountains, home of the proud Cherokee Indians. The Blue Ridge Parkway, one of America's great scenic highways, then leads you along the forested crests of the lovely Blue Ridge Mountains, past a succession of natural wonders, manmade attractions and unforgettable views.

FOR HISTORY BUFFS

1 In South Carolina, just 15 miles (24km) southwest of Gastonia via **I-85**, you can tour **Kings Mountain National Military Park**, site of a battle in 1780 that was a turning point in the Revolutionary War. Another reminder of Colonial times open for tours is **Fort Dobbs**, a State Historic Site near Statesville, built in 1756 to protect settlers during the French and Indian wars.

ⓘ 129 West Trade Street, Charlotte

*Leave uptown Charlotte by Freedom Drive or Wilkinson Boulevard and enter **I-85** westbound for the 20-mile (32km) drive to Gastonia.*

Gastonia, North Carolina

1 One good reason to stop at Gastonia is to visit the **Schiele Museum of Natural History**, a 30-acre (12-hectare) showcase of the natural world. Featuring a large collection of North American animals in habitat settings, it includes exhibits on minerals, fossils, archaeology and

Charlotte's skyline belies its Colonial origins, for it was once a 'hornet's nest of rebellion'

local history. The museum also has a fine planetarium, a pioneer settlement, a nature trail and special events throughout the year.

ⓘ Schiele Museum of Natural History, 1500 E Garrison Boulevard

*From Gastonia continue west on **I-85** for 8 miles (13km), then **US 74** for 57 miles (91km) through Shelby and Forest City to Lake Lure and Chimney Rock Park.*

Lake Lure and Chimney Rock Park, North Carolina

2 Lake Lure lies in majestic forest country on the edge of the Blue Ridge Mountains, its shores a popular recreational area with facilities for swimming, boating, fishing and golf. Nearby you can see the waterfalls of **Bottomless Pools**. For breathtaking views of the surrounding countryside follow the picturesque 3-mile (5km) road from quaint Chimney Rock village, nestled between the cliffs of Hickory Nut Gorge, as far as the base of Chimney Rock itself. From here, either take the elevator inside the rock or follow the exciting, but more strenuous, trail up to the viewing platform at the top. If you wish to explore further, you can follow one of the trails along the cliffs to 400-foot (122m) **Hickory Nut Falls**, one of the highest waterfalls in this part of the eastern United States.

*Continue west along **US 74** for 30 miles (48km) to Asheville.*

Asheville, North Carolina

3 Asheville is the gateway to North Carolina's scenic Appalachian high country region. It is also the location of one of the state's greatest visitor attractions, **Biltmore House**. Constructed for George Vanderbilt in the 1890s, this colossal, luxuriously furnished 250-room mansion was designed in the grand style of a French château and set in exquisite gardens laid out by Frederick Law Olmsted. Around it is a working estate that contains a winery (open to visitors) and a picturesque English-style village. Other places of interest you can visit include the **Botanical Gardens** on the University of North

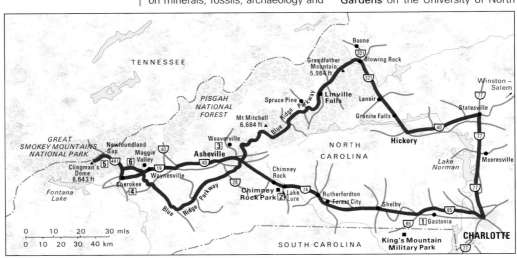

Carolina campus; the boyhood home of novelist Thomas Wolfe; and the **Antique Car Museum**, next door to the **Biltmore Homespun Shop**, where you can see wool being carded, spun and dyed.

ⓘ 151 Haywood Street

From Asheville follow I-40 heading west for 23 miles (37km). Just before Waynesville, take US 19 west for 27 miles (43km) through Maggie Valley to the Cherokee Indian Reservation at Cherokee.

Cherokee, North Carolina

4 Enclosed in lush forest at the foot of the Great Smoky Mountains is the home of the eastern band of Cherokee Indians. These are the descendants of the Cherokee who remained in this region after the majority were forced into exile in what is now Oklahoma in 1838. The

These Hills, which tells the exciting and moving history of the great Cherokee people.

ⓘ Main Street

From Cherokee it is just a few miles further north on US 441 to the Southern entrance of Great Smoky Mountains National Park.

Great Smoky Mountains National Park, North Carolina and Tennessee

5 Shrouded in the permanent blue haze that inspired its name, this 800-square-mile (2,072 sq km) jumble of worn-down, ancient mountains, dense forests, sparkling creeks and silvery waterfalls is one of America's most popular national parks. More than 9 million visitors come here each year to enjoy its unspoiled beauty, rich wildlife and recreational opportunities. As you enter the park, stop

Palatial Biltmore House: self-guiding tours take 3 to 4 hours

center of the reservation is the lively town of Cherokee, which is packed with visitor attractions, fun places for children, shops, restaurants and motels, so drop by the Visitor Center on Main Street for useful advice. But don't miss the **Oconaluftee Indian Village**, where you can see the traditional Cherokee way of life as it was in the 1700s; the **Museum of the Cherokee Indian**, which depicts Cherokee culture and history; and the enticing **Qualla Arts and Crafts Shop**. One of the highlights of a visit here, however, is a summer's evening performance of the drama *Unto*

for information at the Visitor Center and see the log buildings and exhibits at the **Pioneer Farmstead**. You can then follow self-guiding trails, which include the famed **Appalachian Trail**, for a walk in the park. But if you prefer a less strenuous visit, follow the 16-mile (26km) scenic drive up Newfound Gap Road (**US 441**), then a 7-mile (11-km) spur road and a ½-mile (1km) trail to **Clingmans Dome**, the Smokies' highest point. From the observation tower at the 6,643-foot (2,025m) summit, you will get marvelous views of the surrounding mountains, if there are no clouds.

ⓘ The Superintendent, Great Smoky Mountains National Park, Gatlinburg

FOR CHILDREN

3 At Maggie Valley, a town devoted to family entertainment west of Waynesville, take the kids up the chair lift to **Ghost Town in the Sky** on the mountain-top, where they will enjoy the fun and the stagecoach rides at the Wild West frontier village.

4 There is more entertainment and a big zoo at **Santa's Land Theme Park** at Cherokee, where they say Santa spends his summer vacations.

6 Another favorite with children is the **Tweetsie Railroad**, near Blowing Rock, which offers a delightful ride through spectacular scenery

BACK TO NATURE

North Carolina's mountain region is a year-round paradise for nature lovers. Spring begins the year here with a riot of color as wildflowers, dogwood and redbud burst into bloom, followed by mountain laurel, flame azaleas and rhododendrons; while the fall produces an extravaganza of red and gold foliage. Among the abundant wildlife you may see are black bears, cougars, white-tailed deer, bald and golden eagles and wild turkeys. You will certainly see some of these at the **Environmental Habitat Area** on Grandfather Mountain, in the Blue Ridge Mountains.

RECOMMENDED WALKS

Countless opportunities for a pleasant stroll are available on this tour. Be sure to get out of the car for a walk along the trails in **Chimney Rock Park** (2) and the **Great Smoky Mountains** (5) and at the many sightseeing points along the **Blue Ridge Parkway** (6), like Linville Falls, Peaks of Otter and Mount Pisgah.

SCENIC ROUTES

Most of the itinerary between Chimney Rock and Blowing Rock is extremely scenic. The highlights include the Newfound Gap Road (**US 441**) north of Cherokee and the entire length of the Blue Ridge Parkway, which is a riot of color with wildflowers from mid-May through mid-June and spectacular fall foliage.

SPECIAL TO . . .

5 Boone, 9 miles (14km) north of Blowing Rock on **US 321**, offers nightly outdoor performances in midsummer of the historical drama *Horn in the West*, which tells how mountain folk led by Daniel Boone rebelled against the British and moved over the Appalachians to start a new life in the West. The outdoor amphitheater is in a lovely mountain setting.

The ancient contours of the Blue Ridge Mountains converge with the Greak Smokies in dreamlike beauty

As you return from the Great Smoky Mountains on US 441, pick up the Blue Ridge Parkway on the left just before Cherokee for the 100-mile (160km) drive east as far as Blowing Rock.

Blue Ridge Parkway, North Carolina

6 A continuation of the Skyline Drive in neighboring Virginia, this marvelous road is one of America's finest scenic highways. Off-limits to commercial vehicles, it is used only for vacation travel. As it meanders at an average elevation of around 3,000 feet (914m) along the Blue Ridge Mountains, unfolding panoramas of forested mountain scenery can be viewed from many points. The Parkway also provides access to a wide range of visitor attractions.

On the first stretch of the parkway as far as Asheville, you can enjoy especially fine views of the wild **Pisgah National Forest**, an area of dramatic waterfalls and hiking trails. Just beyond Asheville you can watch demonstrations of handicrafts at the **Folk Art Center**; visit the pioneer farmstead where Zebulon B Vance, governor of the state during the Civil War, was born (north at Weaverville); and tour lovely **Craggy Gardens**, famous for displays of blooming rhododendrons and flame azaleas in mid-June.

A few miles east you can drive almost to the top of 6,684-foot (2,037m) Mount Mitchell, eastern America's highest peak, for panoramic views from the lookout tower at the summit, before driving on to visit the fascinating **Museum of North Carolina Minerals**, near Spruce Pine. On this stretch of the parkway be sure to see the double-level **Linville Falls**, where the Linville River plunges into a deep, rugged gorge (a challenge for rock climbers), and the **Linville Caverns** nearby on US 221.

Continue to Grandfather Mountain, at 5,964 feet (1,818m) the highest point in the Blue Ridge Mountains. Here you can enjoy the breathtaking scenery, walk the mile-high swinging suspension bridge and watch daring displays by hang-gliding experts. Leave the parkway at Blowing Rock and visit the famed cliff-top viewpoint 3,000 feet (914m) above the John's River Gorge, where strong up-draughts make light objects seem to fall upwards!

From Blowing Rock take US 321 south for 40 miles (64km) through Lenoir to Hickory, then go east on I-40 for 28 miles (45km) to Statesville. Pick up I-77 southbound for 42 miles (67km) to Charlotte.

Charlotte – Gastonia **20 (32)**
Gastonia – Lake Lure **65 (104)**
Lake Lure – Asheville **30 (48)**
Asheville – Cherokee **50 (80)**
Cherokee – Great Smoky Mtns **19 (30)**
Great Smoky Mtns – Blue Ridge Parkway **16 (26)**
Blue Ridge Parkway – Charlotte **289 (462)**

Many of Madison's historic homes can be toured in May and December

ℹ Omni Building, Marietta Street, Atlanta

*From downtown Atlanta follow **I-20** eastbound for about 10 miles (16km), then **I-285** north for 8 miles (13km) to **Interchange 30**. Take **US 78** east for 6 miles (10km) to Georgia's Stone Mountain Park.*

Georgia's Stone Mountain Park, Georgia

1 The unmistakable rounded outline of Stone Mountain, an 825-foot (251m) bare granite monolith, looms over the vast family entertainment and recreational park at its foot. Along its side is carved a colossal relief sculpture of Confederate heroes: Jefferson Davis, Robert E Lee and 'Stonewall' Jackson. Kids love spending their 'Mountain Money' enjoying the many attractions, which include an exciting skylift up the mountain, a steam train, a paddlewheel riverboat, an **antebellum** (pre-Civil War) plantation and a summer laser show. There are also facilities for camping, fishing, swimming, ice skating, golf and tennis. Just west of the park, **Stone Mountain Village** has a range of enticements for shoppers.

*Continue east on **US 78** for 49 miles (78km) through Monroe to Athens and the Antebellum Trail.*

Athens, Georgia

2 The 'Classic City' of Athens, set in the green hills of northern Georgia, grew as a cultural center around the University of Georgia, chartered in 1785. Fine mansions built in the antebellum years still stand in magnolia-shaded gardens around its streets, among them Athens' oldest resi-

3 days – Approximately 262 miles (419km)

OLD GEORGIA'S ANTEBELLUM TRAIL

Atlanta ● Georgia's Stone Mountain Park
Athens ● Madison ● Eatonton
Milledgeville ● Clinton ● Macon ● Atlanta

This journey through Georgia's historic heartland east of Atlanta takes you back more than a century to those romantic pre–Civil War days when rich white folk of the Old South lived in grand plantation homes and elegant townhouses. It is a dream that was shattered by the War Between the States, when General Sherman's Union forces cut a final, vengeful swath of destruction across lovely Georgia. Miraculously, the devastation passed by places like Athens, Madison, Eatonton, Macon and even Milledgeville, the state capital at that time, and today their historic beauty and charm remain to remind us of times that are now, as you might say, gone with the wind.

dence, the **Church-Waddel-Brumby House** of 1820. Here you can get information on self-guided tours of the university, neighborhoods with antebellum homes, and the downtown area, with its quaint shops and outdoor cafés. As you wander around, don't miss the city's two

FOR HISTORY BUFFS

7 On the east side of Macon, off **I-16**, is the **Ocmulgee National Monument**, a large archaeological site which has traced over 10,000 years of Indian settlement here. You can see huge platform mounds, a restored earth lodge and a museum with exhibits of artifacts. Worth a detour 16 miles (26km) north of Macon off **US 23** is the **Jarrett Plantation**, near Dames Ferry, where you can take a tour of a working 19th-century farm complex.

FOR CHILDREN

7 A special treat for kids at the end of the tour is the fascinating **Museum of Arts and Sciences** at Macon, where they can explore a simulated limestone cave, see a local whale fossil, collections of gems and minerals and exhibits of art, and enjoy the exciting space shows at the **Mark Smith Planetarium**.

BACK TO NATURE

5 If you are interested in wild plants, don't miss a tour (free, by appointment weekdays) of the 50-acre (20-hectare) **Lockerly Arboretum**, just south of Milledgeville on **US 441**. A tour guide will tell you about the plants as you walk the pleasant wooded trails.

6 For a glimpse of Georgia's wildlife, visit **Piedmont National Wildlife Refuge**, some 12 miles (19km) north of Clinton via **SR 11**. The mosaic of abandoned farmland and forest—hardwoods, loblolly and shortleaf pines—harbors bobwhite quails, wild turkeys, red-cocked woodpeckers, tufted titmouse and numerous species of warblers.

RECOMMENDED WALKS

Sightseeing walks around town streets are tiring, so for gentler strolls in more countrified surroundings make for the recreational areas along the tour. They include **Lake Oconee**, east of Madison (3), and **Lake Sinclair** and **Oconee National Forest**, west of Eatonton (4). There are also miles of pleasant walking trails at the **State Botanical Garden** at Athens (2).

special curiosities: the **Double-Barreled Canon**, a failed invention of 1862 that wreaked havoc when test-fired, and the **Tree That Owns Itself**, which stands in a small patch deeded to it by a professor who loved to sit in its shade. Garden lovers won't want to miss the 2½-acre (1-hectare) **Founders Memorial Garden**, at historic **Lumpkin House** on the university campus, or the beautiful 293-acre (118-hectare) **State Botanical Garden**, down by the Oconee River south of town. It is on the way to Watkinsville, where you can see the famous **Eagle Tavern**, built as Fort Edwards in 1789 and later used as a stagecoach stop and store.

ⓘ 280 E Dougherty Street

From Athens take **US 129/441** *south for 30 miles (48km) through Watkinsville to Madison.*

Madison, Georgia

3 As early as 1864, this small community of tree-lined streets and beautiful old homes fronted with columns or lacy Victorian fretwork was praised as 'the most picturesque town in Georgia'. Fortunately, pleas by local citizens saved it from destruction during the Civil War, and it became known as 'the town that Sherman refused to burn'. Today most of Madison is designated as a National Historic District. You can get walking-tour maps and cassettes from the Chamber of Commerce and watch a short slide show on the town's historic homes at Heritage Hall farther down the road. Among Madison's treasures are such beautiful mansions as **Bonar Hall** and the **Kelly House**, charming cottages, historic churches, Morgan **County Courthouse**, the **Old Stagecoach Inn** and the **Madison-Morgan Cultural Center**, a focus of performing and visual arts events.

ⓘ Main Street

From Madison continue south on

US 129/441 *for 21 miles (34km) to Eatonton.*

Eatonton, Georgia

4 Before entering Eatonton, make a stop at the **Rock Eagle Center** about 5 miles (8km) north of town to see one of the area's best-known attractions, the 6,000-year-old Indian **Rock Eagle Mound** built in the shape of a bird.

At Eatonton, neatly laid out around its public square, you will see fine examples of antebellum architecture, including the much-altered **Bronson House**, now occupied by the local historical society. The town is best known, however, as the home of Br'er Rabbit and the beloved 'critters' of the Uncle Remus tales written by Joel Chandler Harris, who lived in Eatonton until 1864. Kids enjoy discovering the statue of Br'er Rabbit on the courthouse lawn and visiting the slave cabin in nearby **Turner Park**, a replica of the one in which Uncle Remus lived. It serves as the **Uncle Remus Museum** and contains many mementos of Harris's work.

Follow **US 441** *south from Eatonton for 20 miles (32km) to Milledgeville.*

Milledgeville, Georgia

5 Milledgeville has a proud history as Georgia's capital during the prosperous years from 1803 to 1868 and boasts many imposing buildings in its Historic District. On Tuesdays and Fridays there are two-hour trolley bus tours of its treasures starting from the Chamber of Commerce on South Jefferson Street. Among the highlights are the impressive **Old State Capitol** of 1807, which now forms part of the **Georgia Military College**; the **Old Governor's Mansion** of 1838, now a National

Stone Mountain, its natural face bearing the marks of man's art

*Macon's Old Cannonball House
with antebellum furnishings*

Historic Landmark; **St Stephen's
Episcopal Church**; and the beautiful
1812 **Stetson-Sanford House**. If you
are here in mid-April you will also
enjoy a wide range of entertaining
events and activities in the city's
famed Old Capitol Celebration.

ⓘ 200 W Hancock Street

*From Milledgeville take **SR 22**
southwest for 21 miles (33km) to
Gray, then **US 129** for another
3 miles (5km) to Clinton.*

Clinton, Georgia

6 If you arrive here on a particular
weekend in mid-April, you might
think you have stumbled into a time
warp and gone back to the Civil War.
In their War Days festival each year at
this time, Georgians re-enact, with
terrifying realism, the fierce battles
fought here in 1864. In those clashes
the thriving little town was badly
damaged and later began to decline.
But about a dozen houses and the
Methodist Church, all dating from
1810 to 1830, survived and have
been preserved. Today Old Clinton is
a place where you can feel history all
around you. As Georgians say, it's
'the town that time forgot'.

*Continue south on **US 129/SR 22**
for 12 miles (19km) to Macon.*

Macon, Georgia

7 The city of Macon lies beside the
Ocmulgee River at the southern
end of Georgia's Antebellum Trail. Its
downtown Historic District was originally laid out in the 1820s in a neat
grid of broad streets and garden
squares, and is now a showcase of
carefully preserved and restored
buildings, many of them on the
National Register of Historic Places.
You can see them by following the
Heritage Tour Markers as you walk
or drive around. The most entertaining way to see the city, however, is to
take **Sidney's Old South Historic
Tour** from the Convention and
Visitors Bureau, during which you will
hear stories you won't find in the
guidebooks. Either way, be sure to
visit elegant **Hay House** (1850s); **Old
Cannonball House** (1853) and
Confederate Museum; **Woodruff
House** (1836); the pretty cottage
where the Georgia poet Sidney
Lanier was born in 1842; and the
elegant **Grand Opera House**. For an
evening's entertainment you might
catch a concert or play here, or a
show or sporting event at the **Macon
Coliseum** across the river.

ⓘ 200 Coliseum Drive

*From Macon take **I-75**
northbound for the fast 82-mile
(131km) drive back to Atlanta.*

Atlanta – Georgia's Stone Mountain
Park **24 (39)**
Georgia's Stone Mountain Park –
Athens **49 (78)**
Athens – Madison **30 (48)**
Madison – Eatonton **21 (34)**
Eatonton – Milledgeville **20 (32)**
Milledgeville – Clinton **24 (38)**
Clinton – Macon **12 (19)**
Macon – Atlanta **82 (131)**

SCENIC ROUTES

The entire **Antebellum Trail**
along **US 129** and **US 441**
between Athens and Macon
is a pleasant drive through
the pastoral scenery and
forests of central Georgia.
For a scenic alternative route
back to Atlanta from Macon,
during spring blossom time,
drive south to Perry on **I-75**
and follow the famed **Peach
Blossom Trail** north along
US 341.

SPECIAL TO ...

7 Lively annual festivals add
to the enjoyment of the
historic towns along this
itinerary. Among the best
known is **Macon's Cherry
Blossom Festival** in late
March. It is a celebration
with music, craft shows,
firework displays, tours of
historic homes and other
events devised to salute the
spectacular Yoshino cherry
trees, more than 50,000 of
them, that brighten the city's
streets with clouds of pale-
pink blossom at this time.

THE SUNSHINE STATE

Miami:

With an average year-round temperature of 76°F (24°C) and 15 miles (24km) of silvery beaches shelving into a warm, blue-green sea, Miami, not surprisingly, is a major international vacation center drawing about 7 million visitors each year. Clustered around the glittering skyscrapers of the downtown business district, the 26 municipalities known as Greater Miami are linked by causeways across Biscayne Bay to a necklace of offshore resort islands, from the Sunny Isles in the north to fabled Miami Beach and Key Biscayne in the south. And sheltered in the bay, sleek cruise ships line the wharves of the busy Port of Miami.

A rich potpourri of ethnic groups—South American, Cuban, Black, and white Anglos—has produced an exciting cultural mix, creating a lively performing and visual arts scene, colorful festivals, and a mouthwatering range of international cuisine. Following large influxes of Cubans in the early 1960s and '80s, Miami has acquired an especially strong Latin flavor, so you are just as likely to hear Spanish spoken as English.

Although the press and the TV series *Miami Vice* have spotlighted its high crime rate in recent years, Miami remains a fascinating and alluring place for the visitor, with a range of attractions too numerous to list. Apart from fine museums like the downtown **Historical Museum of Southern Florida**, sightseeing musts in Miami include the Latin enclave of **Little Havana**, centered on colorful Calle Ocho, or SW 8th Street; **Bayside Marketplace**, with its eye-catching boutiques and street performers down by the waterfront; the nostalgic 1920s and '30s architecture in the Art Deco district of South Miami Beach; and the performing dolphins and other marine animals at the **Miami Seaquarium** on Rickenbacker Causeway. There are also enjoyable one-day cruises with on-board entertainment from the Port of Miami, and yacht and sportfishing charters from the area's many marinas. But for sheer relaxation, you still can't beat soaking up the sun on one of the fabulous palm-dotted beaches.

Tampa:

The manufacturing port city of Tampa lies at the head of the immense natural harbor of Tampa Bay, midway along Florida's Gulf Coast. A well-known landmark among its downtown skyscrapers is the old Moorish-style **Tampa Bay Hotel** built by railroad tycoon Henry B Plant in 1891. The railroad Plant brought to this area some years earlier encouraged Cuban cigar-makers to set up business in the nearby neighborhood of Ybor City. This is now Tampa's Latin Quarter, and you can turn back the clock to those days by touring its cobblestoned streets.

Miami Beach caters almost exclusively for the tourist

The 'Sunshine State' of Florida, America's premier vacationland, has for many years been *the* place to go in winter to escape from snowbound northern states. More recently, it has also become an increasingly popular year-round destination for overseas visitors, who flock in by the plane-load to enjoy the warm, sunny climate, the superb beaches, the vast family entertainment complexes, the outdoor recreational opportunities and the exotic wildlife.

For centuries after its discovery in 1513 by the Spanish explorer Ponce de León, the 400-mile (640km) peninsula remained largely unexploited. Except for its idyllic coastline, it seemed an unlikely place for colonization—a gigantic, flat, waterlogged slab of limestone pockmarked with lakes, deep sinkholes and springs, and blanketed in moss-draped forests, mangroves and swamps. It was also inhabited by fearsome alligators and even more hostile Seminole Indians. But in the 1880s and '90s railroads were brought down its coasts to Tampa Bay and Miami, and Florida's destiny was sealed. Development boomed, tourism took off, and older folk moved in to retire. Today the economy is based not only on tourism, but also on agriculture and industry.

Florida's attractions are many and varied. The Atlantic coast is fringed with beaches, lagoons, islands and resort towns. Here you will find the charming old city of St Augustine; Daytona Beach and its International Speedway; the NASA Kennedy Space Center; busy Fort Lauderdale, the 'Venice of America'; the glitzy oceanfront hotels of Miami Beach; and the skyscrapers and cruise ships of Miami. At the state's southern tip lies the vast wilderness of the Everglades, whose life-giving waters are now threatened by Miami's relentless growth. The Florida Keys arc into the ocean to the bustling vacation center of Key West.

Known for tarpon fishing, seashells, sponges and pirates, Florida's Gulf Coast boasts delightful seaside communities and more superb beaches. The most popular stretch is the Pinellas Suncoast, near St Petersburg and Tampa and linked by fast highway to Orlando's entertainment parks.

Florida's 220-mile (350km) panhandle encompasses the state capital, Tallahassee, and historic Pensacola. It is a region of silent pine forests, salt marshes, springs and sun-splashed beaches, where the atmosphere of the Old South still survives in the quiet backwaters.

Tampa's other visitor attractions include several fine museums and the new, prestigious **Tampa Bay Performing Arts Center**, where you can enjoy anything from ballet to jazz. There are also boat cruises, water activities such as sailing, water skiing and sailboarding, and lots of fun at the water theme park of **Adventure Island**. But not to be

Bayside Marketplace, Miami's newest shopping center

missed is a visit to fabulous **Busch Gardens**, a 300-acre (121-hectare) amusement park on an African theme, with live entertainment, animal shows and exhibits, shops, exciting rides and a huge zoo.

4/5 days – Approximately 341 miles (545km)

FLORIDA'S EVERGLADES & CORAL KEYS

**Miami ● Coconut Grove and Coral Gables
Homestead ● Everglades National Park
Key Largo ● Islamorada ● Marathon and the
Lower Keys ● Key West ● Miami**

Head off south through the sprawling suburban communities of Miami—with a pause to explore the refreshing oases of Coconut Grove and Coral Gables and the tourist attractions along the way. Suddenly you are on the threshold of two of the Sunshine State's great outdoor experiences: first the sawgrass-and-alligator swampland of Everglades National Park, a unique wonderland of semitropical wildlife, then the vacationer's paradise, the Florida Keys, a necklace of sparkling coral islands forever associated with sportfishing, palm-fringed beaches, pirates' treasure and wrecked Spanish galleons, and the adventure-packed tales of Key West's favorite resident, Ernest Hemingway.

🛈 4770 Biscayne Boulevard, Penthouse G, Miami

*From downtown Miami take either **I-95** or Brickell Avenue and South Bayshore Drive for the short drive to Coconut Grove and Coral Gables.*

Coconut Grove and Coral Gables, Florida

1 Just minutes from downtown Miami, these two distinctly different communities have a special appeal. Lively, carefree, chic and

Key West captivates with its silver sands and azure sea and sky

artistic, Coconut Grove draws visitors with its smart boutiques, outdoor cafés, art galleries, night spots and frequent festivals. It also has sightseeing attractions, among which pride of place goes to magnificent **Villa Vizcaya** and its fine gardens.

Planned by the poet George Merrick as the ultimate 'city beautiful', Coral Gables is an architectural showcase, with Spanish-style buildings, tree-lined boulevards, shady plazas and fountains, and imposing entrance gates. Take a drive around to see the shops on the **Miracle Mile** (Coral Way), the **Venetian Pool**, the marvelous **Lowe Art Museum** with its exhibits of American, Asian, African, baroque, pre-Columbian and southwest American Indian art, and 83-acre (33-hectare) **Fairchild Tropical Garden's** rare plant house and rain forest.

🛈 2820 McFarlane Road, Coconut Grove; 50 Aragon Avenue, Coral Gables

*From Coral Gables pick up the South Dixie Highway **(US 1)** southbound for the 22-mile (35km) drive through the residential communities of Greater Miami South to Homestead.*

Homestead, Florida

2 The urban sprawl of Greater Miami South has little interest for passing visitors except for a few special attractions with names that are self-explanatory. Even if you are not into performing animals, you will probably enjoy **Parrot Jungle**, on SW 157th Avenue; the immense, state-of-the-art, cageless **MetroZoo**, on SW 52nd Street; and **Monkey Jungle**, on SW 216th Street, where, in an ironic reversal, you will be put in a cage to be watched by free-roaming animals. For plant lovers there is a colorful show of blooms at **Orchid Jungle**, just north of Homestead; and for the romantic at heart, Homestead itself boasts the amazing **Coral Castle**, built single-handedly by a jilted lover

The Everglades, 50 miles (80km) wide and only inches deep, fed by Lake Okeechobee

FOR HISTORY BUFFS

Scattered along the Florida Keys are historic sites that tell the colorful story of these lovely islands. You can visit the wreck of the Spanish galleon *Herrera* off Islamorada (5); Indian mounds and village sites on the Lower Keys (6); and romantic **Fort Jefferson**, a National Monument on the Dry Tortugas Islands, 70 miles (113km) off Key West (7) accessible by charter boat or seaplane.

over a period of 20 years. The center of Florida's nursery and fruit production, Homestead is also the gateway to Everglades National Park. Don't miss a visit to **Preston B Bird and Mary Heinlein Redland Fruit and Spice Park** which has over 500 species of spice trees, nuts and fruit from 50 tropical countries.

ℹ 160 US Highway 1

*From the Homestead–Florida City area follow **SR 9336** southwest for 10 miles (16km) to Everglades National Park.*

Everglades National Park, Florida

3 This immense natural wilderness and wildlife haven at Florida's southern tip was created by spillage flowing south to the sea from Lake Okeechobee. Stretching into the distance are great expanses of sawgrass—Florida's 'River of Grass'—which grows in the shallow water. Here and there, islands of semitropical vegetation, called hammocks, provide a home for black bears, white-

natural habitat by exploring some of the side roads leading to walking trails and points of interest. You can also take boat tours into the park from Flamingo.

ℹ Parachute Key Visitor Center, park entrance, SR 9336

*From Flamingo return by the same road **(SR 9336)** to Florida City. Then take **US 1** south for about 20 miles (32km) to Key Largo, the first of the islands on the 110-mile (177km) drive on the Overseas Highway along the Florida Keys to Key West.*

Key Largo, Florida

4 Key Largo is your first sight of the string of coral islands known as the Keys, which arch westward into the sea from Florida's southern tip. A popular year-round vacation spot, the Keys are a Mecca for boating, fishing, swimming, scuba diving, camping, biking, walking, or just lying in the sun. With their exotic cuisine, they are also a gourmet's paradise.

FOR CHILDREN

1 The amazing sights and exciting adventures on this tour are made for kids. But there are also experiences that appeal to the mind, such as the hands-on exhibits at the excellent **Miami Museum of Science and Space Transit Planetarium** at Coconut Grove. The museum's attractions include computer exhibits, minitheater shows on flora and fauna in Florida and the Everglades, and an aviary and wildlife center, while the Planetarium houses changing displays and offers multimedia laser and star shows daily.

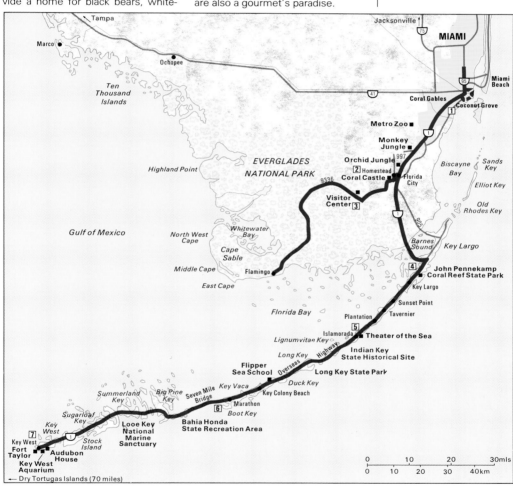

tailed deer, alligators, herons, egrets and many other wild creatures (especially mosquitoes!). And among the mangrove forests and mudflats along the coast, you can see white ibis, brown pelicans, roseate spoonbills and even flamingos.

Stop at the main Visitor Center near the park entrance and follow the paved road which meanders for 36 miles (58km) to the seaside community of Flamingo. Along the way take a closer look at this unique

Key Largo is known around the world for the Bogart-Bacall movie of the same name, and it still preserves Bogart's old boat from *The African Queen.* But its star visitor attraction is undoubtedly the underwater wonderland encompassed by the **John Pennekamp Coral Reef State Park.** By snorkeling, scuba diving or just sitting comfortably in a glass-bottom boat, you can see a dazzling array of colorful fish darting around the beautiful coral and the incongruous

BACK TO NATURE

3 The **Everglades National Park** is accessible via Homestead and visitors should not miss the Anhinga Trail at Royal Palm Hammock and Eco Pond at Flamingo. Look for alligators, terrapins, anhingas, egrets, herons, turkey vultures and black vultures. The Keys are generally rather built up and have lost much of their wildlife interest. However, shorebirds, herons and gulls are found almost anywhere, and magnificent frigatebirds are ever present in the skies as you approach Key West. A few sanctuary areas are set aside for the diminutive and endangered Key deer.

RECOMMENDED WALKS

In addition to the trails off the highway through Everglades National Park, there are enjoyable walks on the Keys in John Pennekamp State Park, Long Key State Park, Indian Key State Historic Site, Bahia Honda State Recreation Area and around the town of Key West.

SCENIC ROUTES

The highlight of the itinerary is the island-hopping drive along the Florida Keys on the Overseas Highway, with its bridges and constantly changing views of the ocean, beaches, craggy bays and forest wilderness. The Seven-Mile Bridge between Marathon and the Lower Keys is an especially exciting section, with expansive views of the ocean and of the old unused bridge which runs alongside, now frequented by anglers.

SPECIAL TO . . .

7 Key West's festive atmosphere is punctuated each year by three major celebrations that draw the crowds. During **Old Island Days**, from February 2 through April, houses are spruced up and opened to visitors, and various events take place, such as the **Conch-Blowing Contest**. The **Hemingway Days Festival**, in mid-July, features a Hemingway look-alike contest and a short-story contest among its events. And in the lively **Fantasy Fest**, in late October, the town is seized with a carnival atmosphere as people take part in colorful events that reach a climax in the Grand Parade.

spectacle of a submerged statue, 'Christ of the Deep'. Even more unusual are Key Largo's **Undersea Art Gallery** and ocean-floor hotel.

ⓘ 103400 Overseas Highway

Drive southwest for 20 miles (32km) to Islamorada.

Islamorada, Florida

5 West of Key Largo, the group of islands known collectively as Islamorada, or 'Purple Isles', is a major center for charter fishing but also has other visitor attractions. Not to be missed are the dolphin and sea-lion shows and other sea creatures at the **Theater of the Sea** on Windley Key; the tropical hardwood forest on Lignumvitae Key; the reefs and historic wrecks off the southern shores; and the beach and nature trails in **Long Key State Park**.

*Continue on **US 1**.*

Marathon and the Lower Keys, Florida

6 Midway along the Keys, the Marathon group of islands is best known for golf, sportfishing, and angling from 'the world's longest fishing pier'—still-standing segments of the former highway bridge. The spectacular new **Seven-Mile Bridge** that replaced it links Marathon to the Lower Keys.

The main attraction for visitors to the Lower Keys is the unspoiled forest wilderness and abundant wildlife in the specially protected areas. When you have sampled the pleasures of Bahia Honda's fine beach, be sure to see the beautiful undersea reefs at **Looe Key National Marine Sanctuary** and the rare miniature Key deer and great white herons at the special refuges on Big Pine Key.

*Continue on **US 1** to Key West.*

Key West, Florida

7 With its sophisticated, free-and-easy lifestyle, this lively island community has long been a favorite retreat for the rich and famous and a popular playground for vacationers. For a taste of Key West's unique atmosphere, walk the Pelican Path or ride an Old Town Trolley or the Conch Tour Train; explore the colorful shops, bars and outdoor cafés; sample the exotic local cuisine; and mingle with the evening crowds who gather in Mallory Square to watch free entertainment and the breathtaking sunsets. Rent a charter boat for some deep-sea fishing and tour the many sightseeing attractions. Not to be missed among these are the town's 'gingerbread' mansions (ornate Victorian style); **Hemingway House** and **Audubon House**, commemorating two of Key West's best-known celebrities; historic **Fort Taylor**; and the **Mel Fisher Maritime Heritage Society's Treasure Museum**, with its booty from wrecked Spanish galleons.

For underwater wildlife visit the **Key West Aquarium** and the popular **Turtle Kraals** and watch the dolphins under training at **Flipper's Sea School**. And if you have time, take a walk to the town's picturesque cemetery. You will find it hard not to chuckle when you read some of the epitaphs, like the one from a grieving widow which wrily observes: 'At least I know where he's sleeping tonight!'

ⓘ 402 Wall Street

*From Key West follow the Overseas Highway and **US 1** for 160 miles (256km) back to Miami.*

Miami – Coconut Grove **9 (14)**
Coconut Grove – Homestead **22 (35)**
Homestead – Everglades National Park **10 (16)**
Everglades National Park – Key Largo **35 (56)**
Key Largo – Islamorada **20 (32)**
Islamorada – Marathon **38 (61)**
Marathon – Key West **47 (75)**
Key West – Miami **160 (256)**

The extraordinary Seven-Mile Bridge, link-up to the Lower Keys, disappears near the horizon

4 days – Approximately 406 miles (650km)

FLORIDA'S FAMILY FUNLAND

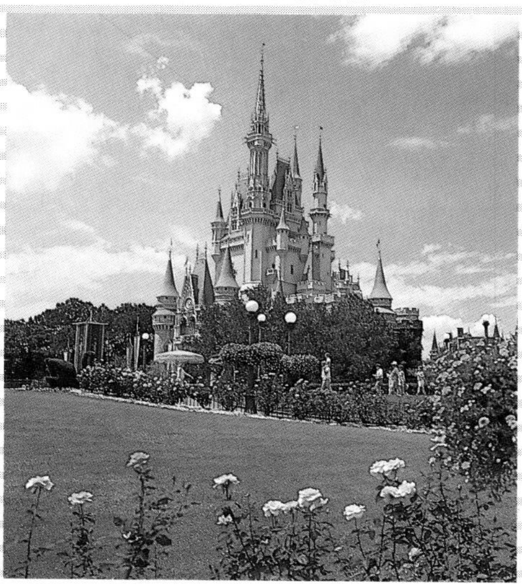

With the turreted outline of Cindarella's Castle in view, it could only be the Magic Kingdom

Tampa • The Pinellas Suncoast
St Petersburg • Bradenton • Sarasota
Walt Disney World • Merritt Island and Spaceport USA • Tampa

This four-day drive out of Tampa spans the whole width of Central Florida from the Gulf Coast to the Atlantic, from the superb beaches of the Pinellas Suncoast to the launchpads at Cape Canaveral. It is a tour of manmade entertainments rather than scenic attractions but with enough variety to satisfy most tastes and interests. Apart from beaches and space shuttles, there is the cluster of family entertainment parks in the central region around Orlando and the cultural attractions of Sarasota. And scattered among all this are those historic places and stretches of countryside that show what Florida was like before tourism took off.

[i] The Market on Harbour Island, Tampa

*From downtown Tampa follow **I-275** west for 5 miles (8km), turn onto **SR 60** and continue via the Courtney Campbell Causeway, Gulf Boulevard to Bay Boulevard and Clearwater Causeway to Clearwater Beach. Cross the Clearwater Pass toll bridge and follow Gulf Boulevard **(SR 699)** south for about 18 miles (29km) along the Pinellas Suncoast.*

The Pinellas Suncoast, Florida

1 With its unbroken sunshine and 28 miles (45km) of sparkling white beaches shelving gently into the Gulf of Mexico's warm blue waters, the coast of Pinellas County and its string of offshore sandbar islands are among America's top vacation destinations. Here you will find accommodations and dining establishments from the inexpensive to the luxurious. High on the list of popular outdoor activities—in addition to swimming and soaking up the sun—are windsurfing, waterskiing, parasailing, golf and tennis. Boat cruises are also available, and there are many opportunities for fishing.

On the drive south from Clearwater Beach visit the **Suncoast Seabird Sanctuary** at Indian Shores, where nearly 5,000 injured birds get hospital treatment every year; take a walk around the shops at **John's Pass Village**, a re-created turn-of-the-century fishing community at Madeira Beach; and take a sightseeing cruise on the bay to glimpse dolphins and feed seabirds at St Petersburg Beach, location

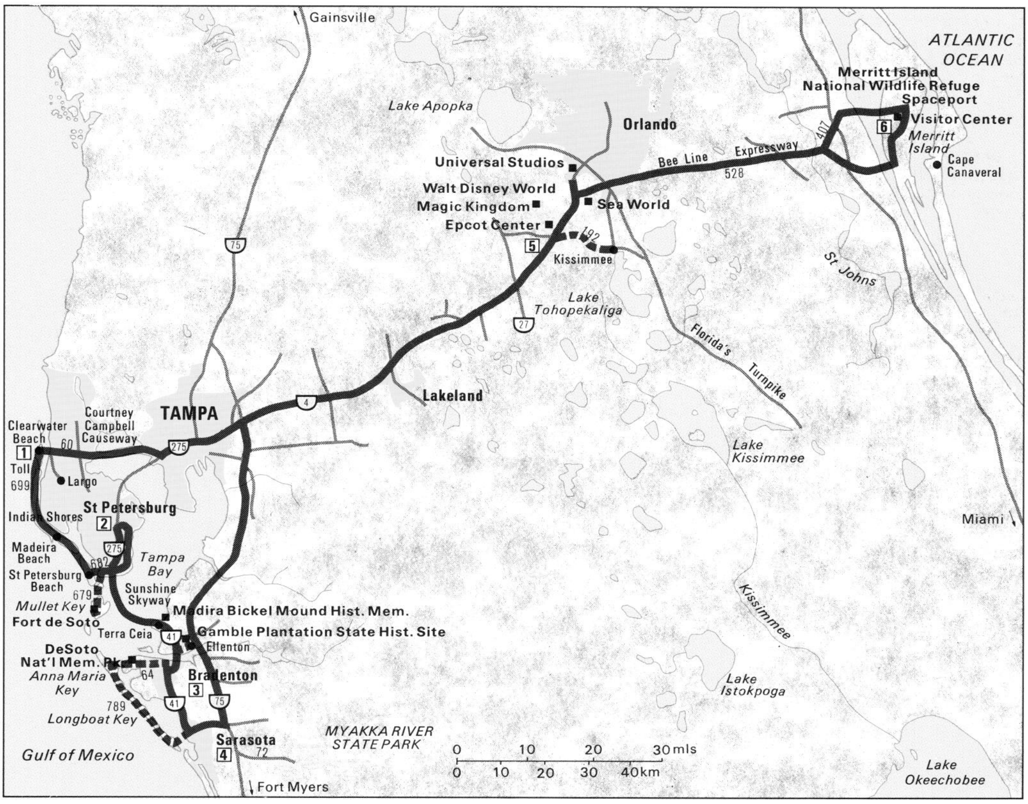

FOR HISTORY BUFFS

1 On exhibit at **Heritage Park and Museum**, in Largo, adjacent to Clearwater, is a replica of a Benoist airboat, the plane that began the age of scheduled commercial air services with a flight from St Petersburg across the bay to Tampa on January 1, 1915. The park also displays a collection of historic buildings of the area in the wooded grounds. The museum portrays aspects of pioneer life, with frequent displays of weaving, spinning and other crafts and an old-fashioned rural fair, 'Country Jubilee', in late October.

of the old Don CeSar hotel resort, a noted landmark along the seafront.

ⓘ Welcome Center, 40 Causeway Boulevard, Clearwater Beach

Follow the Pinellas Bayway (SR 682) from the southern end of St Petersburg Beach and after about 4 miles (6km) take I-275 north for another 4 miles (6km) to downtown St Petersburg.

St Petersburg, Florida

2 Once known as a retirement area for senior citizens, the city of St Petersburg, on Tampa Bay, is now blossoming at the hub of Florida's west coast tourism boom. New hotel resorts and sightseeing attractions have sprouted to cater for visitors' needs. On your way into town you will pass one of the newest facilities, the **Florida Suncoast Dome**, an impressive arena for baseball, concerts, shows and other events. Jutting into the bay on the waterfront is St Pete's most famous landmark, **the Pier**, with its unusual, inverted pyramid-shaped marketplace. Nearby you can take a short luncheon or dinner cruise around the bay on the *Belle of St Petersburg*. North of the Pier you will find lovely **Straub Park**;

ⓘ 100 Second Avenue North

From St Petersburg take I-275 and the Sunshine Skyway south across Tampa Bay, then US 41 (the Tamiami Trail) south to the town of Bradenton, a 26-mile (42km) drive.

Bradenton, Florida

3 Several places of cultural and historic interest are scattered around the Bradenton area on the south side of Tampa Bay You can see displays of ancient Indian relics at the **Madira Bickel Mound Historic Memorial**, on Terra Ceia Island, also and at Bradenton's **South Florida Museum**, and tour a 19th-century sugar planter's home at the **Gamble Plantation State Historic Site** at Ellenton, off **US 301**. Drive west out of Bradenton on **SR 64** and you will find the **De Soto National Memorial Park**, which commemorates the Spanish explorer's landing in this part of Florida in 1539, an event that is re-enacted every year in April.

ⓘ Third Avenue West

Continue south from Bradenton for 13 miles (21km) on US 41 to the resort of Sarasota.

St Pete's, Pier, with fishing, an aquarium, and speciality shops

FOR CHILDREN

4 The sun, sea and sand of the Pinellas beaches, the excitement of Walt Disney World and the marvels of Spaceport USA are probably enough for most kids on this tour. But for something different, take them to see the delightful miniature trains and seashells on display at the **Lionel Seashell and Train Museum** at Sarasota.

the **Museum of Fine Arts**, with its fine collections, including ancient and oriental art and pre-Columbian goldware and pottery; and the famed **Sunken Gardens**, home to exotic birds and animals in a beautiful jungle setting. Drive south from the Pier and you can perhaps take in a show or concert at the Bayfront Center and enjoy the fascinating hands-on science, nature and art exhibits at the **Great Explorations Museum**. Not to be missed is the unique collection of Surrealist art dating from 1914 at the excellent **Salvador Dali Museum**.

Sarasota, Florida

4 With its offshore islands and silvery beaches, Sarasota is another popular west coast vacation center offering a wide range of seaside activities. But it is especially known for its important cultural attractions, which owe much to the contributions made to the town by circus impresario John Ringling who used the town as winter quarters for his Ringling Brothers and Barnum and Bailey Circus. On **US 41** just north of town he built his lavish dream home, **Ca'd'Zan** (John's House, in Venetian dialect). It is now part of the complex that also includes the **John and Mabel Ringling Museum of Art** containing his priceless Rubens

The marina is just one of Sarasota's recreation facilities

collection and other treasures; the nostalgic **Circus Galleries**; and the reconstructed 18th-century **Asolo Theater** from Italy. Nearby is another very popular attraction, the three museums of **Bellm's Cars and Music of Yesterday**, one featuring antique automobiles, another displaying mechanical musical boxes, and a third featuring early forms of arcade pinball machines. And for a complete change of mood, go to see the tropical plants, Gardens of Christ, alligators and flamingoes on show at the **Sarasota Jungle Gardens** on Bayshore Road.

ℹ️ 655 North Tamiami Trail

*Pick up **I-75** northbound from Sarasota, then take **I-4** east for the 129-mile (206km) drive to Walt Disney World.*

Walt Disney World, Florida

5 Don't expect scenic beauty or natural wonders in this part of Florida. This is 'Vacationland USA' — a brash and breezy fantasy world created specifically, and successfully, to entertain you. The variety of theme parks, water parks, entertainment complexes and other attractions here are enough to make any adventurous soul, from seven to 70, wide-eyed with wonder. At the top of the list, without question, is **Walt Disney World**, off I-4 at **Exit 25**. This huge resort complex includes the Magic Kingdom, the EPCOT Center, the Disney/MGM Studios, Typhoon Lagoon, River Country and Shopping Village and much more. But be warned: a brief visit simply cannot do it justice, so plan your day carefully and get there early in the morning.

A few miles further along I-4 you can watch the antics of performing killer whales and dolphins at **Sea World of Florida** (Exit 28) and enjoy the fun in favorite movie settings at **Universal Studios Florida** (**Exit 30B**), two of the area's other outstanding attractions.

*Leave **I-4** at **Exit 28** and continue east for about 55 miles (89km) on the Beeline Expressway and **SR 407** to Merritt Island and Spaceport USA.*

Merritt Island and Spaceport USA, Florida

6 Merritt Island and the other offshore barrier islands and lagoons of Florida's eastern shoreline — the 'Florida Space Coast' — are home not only to seabirds but also to the rockets and spacecraft launched from famous Cape Canaveral. If you can't watch a launch, do the next best thing and tour the awesome complex and the technological marvels on display at **NASA Kennedy Space Center's Spaceport USA**, where every aspect of space flight — past, present and future — is explored. You can watch the birds in the peace and quiet of **Merritt Island National Wildlife Refuge**, which surrounds the space complex.

*Follow the Beeline Expressway **(SR 528)** and **I-4** westbound for the 117-mile (187km) return drive to Tampa.*

Tampa – Pinellas Suncoast 27 **(43)**
Pinellas Suncoast – St Petersburg 36 **(58)**
St Petersburg – Bradenton 26 **(42)**
Bradenton – Sarasota 13 **(21)**
Sarasota – Walt Disney World 129 **(206)**
Walt Disney World – Merritt Island 58 **(93)**
Merritt Island – Tampa 117 **(187)**

BACK TO NATURE

Unexpected encounters with Florida's wildlife can happen anywhere on the tour. However, it is more than likely you will see pelicans fishing and egrets stalking fish on a walk along the boardwalk at **John's Pass Village**, Madeira Beach (1). There are also special wildlife refuges that offer guided walks, such as **Moccasin Lake Nature Park**, at Clearwater (1); **Boyd Hill Nature Trail Park**, at St Petersburg (2); and **Myakka River State Park**, on SR 72 about 14 miles (23km) southeast of Sarasota (4).

SCENIC ROUTES

The most scenic routes on this tour are those sections of **SR 60** and the **Sunshine Skyway** that span Tampa Bay. For an additional treat, instead of taking **US 41** from Bradenton to Sarasota, follow the more pleasant shoreline route on **Routes 64** and **789** along Anna Maria Key and Longboat Key, with its broad views of rolling dunes, dazzling beaches and the ocean.

RECOMMENDED WALKS

Pleasant places for a stroll, apart from the sightseeing attractions, are the boardwalk at John's Pass Village and the waterfront and Pier at St Petersburg (2). There are also the half-mile (800m) nature trail by the Manatee River at De Soto National Memorial Park, at Bradenton, and quiet walks along the dunes and beaches of Anna Maria Key, Longboat Key and little Egmont Key, off the coast between Bradenton and Sarasota (3).

SPECIAL TO . . .

Among the myriad events and festivals that draw thousands of visitors to Florida's central west coast every year are the **Fun 'n' Sun Festival**, a 10-day extravaganza in late April at Clearwater (1), with music, sports events and a regatta; the big **Festival of States**, held at St Petersburg over a two-week period in March and April and featuring band competitions, concerts, three parades, various sports events and fireworks displays; and the exciting **St Petersburg Grand Prix** (2), held every fall, when racing cars roar around the waterfront circuit.

THE MIDWEST

America's Midwest region stretches for more than 1,000 miles (1,600km) across the center of the country from the Appalachians to the Rockies and from the northern forests and lakes of Minnesota and Wisconsin to the Ozark Mountains of Arkansas. Drained by the Mississippi, Missouri, Ohio and other great rivers, this huge territory is the nation's agricultural heartland. From Ohio to Nebraska an immense checkerboard of fields known as the Corn Belt yields abundant harvests of farm produce, while in the west, treeless expanses of wheat and vast cattle ranches extend across the Great Plains that border the Rockies from Montana to Kansas.

This region conjures up eternal images of sultry, hot summers and bleak, snowy winters; isolated farmsteads with tall shiny silos, red-painted barns and water tanks on towers; and quiet little towns with no more than a few clapboard houses, a church, wooden schoolhouse, diner and general store. Yet there are also big manufacturing cities, often hugging the great river arteries, like Cincinnati, Minneapolis and St Paul, or the shores of the Great Lakes, like Chicago, Milwaukee, Detroit and Cleveland.

The tranquillity of today's Midwest belies its often violent past. Chapters in its story tell of the early Indian inhabitants and great buffalo herds; the region's exploration by the French; westward expansion by settlers and the railroads; the lawless Wild West, featuring characters like Wild Bill Hickock and Jesse James; and bloody conflict with the Indians, culminating in the epic massacre of Colonel George Custer's Seventh Cavalry at Little Big Horn in 1876.

Cincinnati:

This livable city of some 385,000 people lies in an amphitheater of hills on the north bank of the Ohio River in southwest Ohio. Established in 1788, it developed as an important river port linked to the Mississippi and the newly opened-up lands in the west. The city's German heritage is reflected in its vibrant cultural life, fine restaurants, and events like its famous Oktoberfest.

A steamboat cruise on the river today takes you beneath photogenic old bridges and past the landmark **Riverfront Stadium** and the **Riverfront Coliseum** entertainment complex. Other fine views of the city are available from the top of the 49-story **Carew Tower**, which rises above busy Fountain Square, with its famous Tyler Davidson Fountain, in the heart of the downtown area.

Not to be missed is a tour of the charming old hilltop neighborhood of **Mt Adams**, with its fashionable boutiques and restaurants, and nearby **Eden Park**, location of the prestigious **Cincinnati Art Museum**, the **Museum of Natural History**, the **Playhouse in the Park** professional theater, and the **Krohn Conservatory** botanical showcase. For family fun there are also the superb **Cincinnati Zoo** and several amusement and water parks, including the popular **Kings Island theme park**.

Chicago:

Three of the world's five tallest buildings puncture the magnificent skyline of America's third largest city, a bustling metropolis of nearly 3 million people at the southern tip of Lake Michigan. Since its birth in 1830, infusions of immigrants, many of them Poles, have helped turn Chicago, the Windy City, into a major business, financial and manufacturing center, transportation hub and lake port. Tough and assertive, its character has also been molded by such factors as the Great Fire of 1871, the gang warfare of the 1920s Prohibition era, domination by political bosses, and ethnic tensions.

For the visitor, Chicago is a

sophisticated, cosmopolitan place with fine hotels, restaurants and shops, exciting entertainment, nightlife and spectator sports, and numerous cultural and sightseeing attractions. Outstanding among these are museums like the marvelous **Art Institute of Chicago** and the free **Museum of Science and Industry**.

On the lakefront are the **Navy Pier**, with its boat cruises; **Grant Park** and the famous **Buckingham Fountain**; and the **Adler Planetarium**, **John G Shedd Aquarium** and **Field Museum of Natural History**. Among the sky-scrapers of the downtown business and shopping district, known as the Loop, are small plazas embellished with modern sculptures, and old architectural landmarks like the Carson Pirie Scott and Marshall Field department stores. North of here are the shops of North Michigan Avenue, Chicago's 'Magnificent Mile', and the throbbing nightlife of Rush Street and Old Town.

Breathtaking bird's-eye views of this captivating city are available from the observation decks in the 110-story **Sears Tower** and the 100-story **John Hancock Center**, Chicago's two loftiest skyscrapers.

Minneapolis and St Paul:

Minneapolis and St Paul, the Twin Cities, face each other across the Mississippi River amid the rolling farmlands of southeast Minnesota. Minneapolis is the dynamic business and financial center of the Upper Midwest, while more con-servative St Paul serves as state capital. In addition to their fine downtown skyway systems, Minneapolis presents a bold skyline of sleek modern architecture, while St Paul still preserves many renovated old landmarks among its newer structures. Together the Twin Cities enjoy a thriving cultural life, a factor which adds to their already considerable appeal to resident and visitor alike.

Minneapolis is known for its world-famous **Guthrie Theater**; the IDS building's **Crystal Court**; the shops of Nicollet Mall, quaint St Anthony Main and the Riverplace mall; Vikings football and Twins baseball at the **Hubert H Humphrey Metrodome**; and fine museums like the **American Swedish Institute**. St Paul has the impressive **State Capitol complex**, **Cathedral of St Paul** and renovated **Landmark Center**; the magnificent **Ordway Music Theater**; the shops of Grand Avenue, St Paul Center and Bandana Square; the fine 19th-century homes along Summit Avenue; and the marvelous hands-on **Science Museum** with its superb Omnitheater and displays on anthropology biology, technology and natural sciences.

Other area attractions include historic **Fort Snelling**, **Minnehaha Falls** and the **Canterbury Downs** horse-racing track at Shakopee, the location also of the colorful Renaissance Festival held every August through September.

The modern face of Cincinnati, seen from Central Bridge

3/4 days – Approximately 437 miles (699km)

KENTUCKY BLUEGRASS & MAMMOTH CAVE

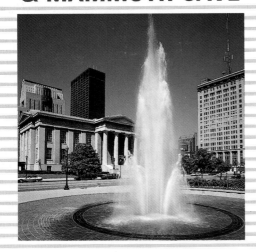

Cincinnati • Louisville • Mammoth Cave National Park • Hodgenville • Bardstown Lincoln Homestead State Park • Frankfort Lexington • Cincinnati

Mention Kentucky and many things spring to mind: Kentucky Fried Chicken and bluegrass music, the Kentucky Derby and thoroughbred horses, bourbon whiskey, tobacco and mint juleps—and, of course, Daniel Boone and young Abraham Lincoln. All of these appear at some point on this tour, which includes both the big-city attractions of Louisville and Lexington and the natural delights of Bluegrass Country and Mammoth Cave. Add in the historic places, from the elegant mansions of the rich to the modest cabins of Lincoln's childhood, and you have a tour of rich and rewarding experiences.

FOR HISTORY BUFFS

4 **Spalding Hall**, in Bardstown, is perhaps an odd choice for the location of the **Oscar Getz Museum of Whiskey History**, when you consider it was once a Catholic seminary and college, a hospital, an orphanage and a school. It chronicles the role of whiskey over 200 years, and collections exhibited include advertising posters, rare documents and memorabilia from pre-Colonial days to Prohibition years. Among the containers and bottles is an 1854 E C Booz bottle, the brand which gave its name to 'booze'.

FOR CHILDREN

1 Most stopping places along the itinerary have places of interest to children. They include the **Louisville Zoo and Metropolitan Children's Museum**. At the zoo the mammals and birds are exhibited zoogeographically in spacious surroundings. You can view smaller creatures through microscopes, see the world through the eyes of an insect and watch amphibians from underwater.

ℹ 300 West 6th Street, Cincinnati

*From downtown Cincinnati take **I-71/75** south across the Ohio River via the Brent Spence Bridge to Covington and northern Kentucky and continue south on **I-71** for about 103 miles (165km) to Louisville.*

Louisville, Kentucky

1 One of the world's great Meccas of horse racing, Louisville is the home of the prestigious Kentucky Derby, the climax to 10 days of varied events in the city's annual **Kentucky Derby Festival** in early May. Even if you are not there on the day, you can experience the thrills of the race by watching the multi-image show in the **Kentucky Derby Museum** at the Churchill Downs track south of downtown. But first explore this historic city's other attractions. At the entrance to the city, just off **I-71**, don't miss **Locust Grove**, the plantation home built around 1790 by Louisville's founder, General George Rogers Clark. Then drive to the Ohio riverfront to see the famous **Louisville Falls Fountain** and the sternwheeler *Belle of Louisville*. Wander through the downtown streets and you will see the **Museum of History and Science, Kentucky Center for the Arts**, the **Actors Theater** and the **Galleria** shopping center. Then make your way south

The Jefferson County Courthouse (1837) in historic Louisville

along Third Street to charming Old Louisville, location of the marvelous **J B Speed Art Museum** and the **Rauch Planetarium**, just minutes away from Churchill Downs track.

ℹ 400 S First Street

*Follow the Henry Watterson Expressway **(I-264)** east to pick up **I-65** southbound. Continue for 95 miles (153km) through Elizabethtown to Mammoth Cave National Park.*

Mammoth Cave National Park, Kentucky

2 About 45 miles (72km) out of Louisville take a break at Elizabethtown to visit the unique **Schmidt's Museum of Coca-Cola Memorabilia**, with displays, memorabilia and collectables connected with this popular drink over the last 100 years, before driving on to Kentucky's Cave Country. Here the three small towns of Horse Cave, Cave City and Park City lure visitors to the area with their varied attractions both above and below ground. The center of interest here, however, is **Mammoth Cave**, with more than 300 miles (480km) of known passageways and caverns below ground and 52,000 acres (21,044 hectares) of forested hill country teeming with wildlife on the surface. In the cave guided walking tours of varying lengths start at the Visitor Center and take you past amazing, colorfully named rock formations and caverns shaped by the underground Echo River. And if you get hungry, don't worry: there is even a restaurant down there. On the surface the park's beautiful scenery and wildlife can be enjoyed either by walking the many self-guiding nature trails or by taking the delightful one-hour boat trip along the Green River.

ℹ Mammoth Cave National Park

*From Mammoth Cave drive north on **I-65** for about 38 miles (61km) to **Exit 81** and turn east (right) onto **SR 84** for another 10 miles (16km) to Hodgenville.*

Hodgenville, Kentucky

3 Within a few miles of this old town, Abraham Lincoln was born and lived until he was seven. In historic Lincoln Square you will see a statue of Honest Abe as a man and a **museum** that traces his life. Drive south out of town for 3 miles (5km) on **US 31E** and **SR 61** and you will find the **Abraham Lincoln Birthplace National Historic Site**, with a shrine and log cabin in the 116-acre (47-hectare) park. In the opposite direction, on **US 31E** at Knob Creek, is the **Lincoln Boyhood Home**, a reconstructed cabin on or near the site where he lived from 1811 to 1816.

*Continue north on **US 31E** for another 27 miles (43km) to Bardstown.*

Bardstown, Kentucky

4 You can see many of this historic town's attractions if you take a walking tour or the free one-and-a-half-hour tourmobile ride from

Stephen Foster Avenue. Among them are several fine historic houses; the **Old Nelson County Jail**; the **Talbott Tavern** of 1779; the **Civil War Museum** and old frontier community re-created at **Old Bardstown Village**; and paintings donated by King Louis-Philippe of France in **St Joseph's Proto-Cathedral**. Not to be missed, either, is the Bardstown house that really did inspire Stephen Foster, the great 19th-century songwriter, to write his immortal ballad *My Old Kentucky Home*. It is **Federal Hill**, his cousin's 1818 plantation house, which is now the focal point of **My Old Kentucky Home State Park** just outside town on **US 150**. Here you can see an outdoor evening performance of the popular show *The Stephen Foster Story*, featuring the composer's music.

*Follow **US 150** southeast for 18 miles (29km) to Springfield, then go 5 miles (8km) north on **SR 528** and **SR 438** to Lincoln Homestead State Park.*

Lincoln Homestead State Park, Kentucky

5 This 150-acre (60-hectare) park occupies land originally settled by the Lincoln family in the 1780s. Among several historic buildings preserved here is the original house in which Abraham's mother, Nancy Hanks, lived when being courted by his father, Thomas Lincoln, and a replica of the cabin in which Thomas and his brothers were raised. In Springfield you can see Nancy and Thomas's marriage certificate among other documents preserved at the County Courthouse.

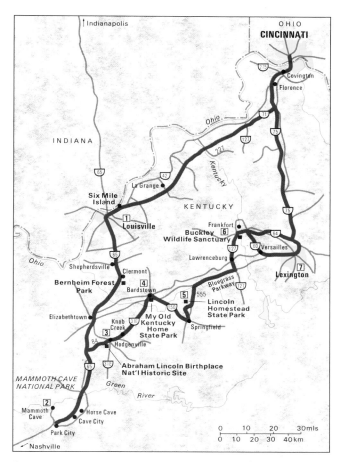

Stalactites at Mammoth Cave, here forming the Frozen Niagara. Tours last from 1¼ to 4½ hours; wear sturdy, nonslip shoes

BACK TO NATURE

The famed bluegrass of northern Kentucky is just one of the state's natural wonders. The lush countryside and forests abound with wild animals, birds and plants of all kinds, including the state symbols—the gray squirrel, the cardinal and goldenrod. Among the best places to observe wildlife are the three state Nature Preserves around Louisville (1), **(Beargrass Creek, Blackacre and Six Mile Island)**; **Bernheim Forest Park**, off **I-65** south of Louisville (1); **Mammoth Cave National Park** (2), which boasts 16 species of breeding warblers; and **Buckley Wildlife Sanctuary**, off **US 60** south of Frankfort. If you have no luck there, you will find black bears, bobcats, cougars, deer, raccoons, wolves and countless birds on display at **Game Farm** on **US 60** west of Frankfort (6).

SCENIC ROUTES

Away from the interstate highways, the smaller country roads you follow between Hodgenville and Frankfort, the **US 31E**, and **SR 528, SR 438,** and **SR 555,** offer scenic views of the beautiful Kentucky Bluegrass Country.

SPECIAL TO ...

1 No tour of Kentucky would be complete without touring enterprises that produce two of its major products: tobacco and bourbon. You can watch the cigarette-making process at **Philip Morris USA** in downtown Louisville, where the famous Kentucky barley tobacco is blended in the region's only cigarette-production facility, and learn some of the secrets of bourbon production at any of the distilleries open for tours along the route. Among the selection are **Heaven Hill Distilleries**, in Bardstown, and **Jim Beam's American Outpost**, at Clermont (4).

RECOMMENDED WALKS

2 At **Mammoth Cave** there is a choice of guided underground tours lasting from 1¼ to 4½ hours. Here you will see fantastic rock formations and huge caverns with names like Frozen Niagara, Onyx Colonnade and Bottomless Pit and historic relics recording mankind's long use of the cave. There are also special tours available for the disabled. Above ground, you can take a short walk on the **Cave Island Nature Trail** which starts and finishes near the Historic Entrance.

Continue north on **SR 438** and **SR 555** for about 8 miles (13km) and join the Bluegrass Parkway at eastbound **Entry 42**. After 11 miles (18km) take **Exit 59** north onto **US 127** and continue for about 17 miles (27km) through Lawrenceburg to Frankfort.

Frankfort, Kentucky

6 The Bluegrass State's capital city since 1792, Frankfort lies in the pleasant Kentucky River valley, overlooked by the grave of Daniel Boone, the intrepid pioneer who first opened up this territory. Get a brochure and map at the Visitor Center on Capital Avenue before starting a marked walking tour of the city's historic sights. Highlights include the majestic **State Capitol** and the **Governor's Mansion**; the **Old State Capitol** and the **Old Governor's Mansion**; and the posh 'Corner in Celebrities' district, where top people lived in such elegant homes as the **Vest-Lindsey House**, **Liberty Hall** and the **Orlando Brown House**. History buffs will also find much to see at the **Kentucky Historical Museum**, next to the Old Capitol, and at the **Kentucky Military History Museum**, with its fine collection of uniforms, flags, medals and weapons. But for something quite different, go and see bourbon whiskey candies being made at **Rebecca-Ruth Candies** or take a guided tour of the **Ancient Age Distillery**, where its well-known bourbon is produced.

ⓘ 100 Capital Avenue

*For the 23-mile (37km) drive from Frankfort to Lexington, take the fast route on **I-64**.*

Lexington, Kentucky

7 Lexington, Kentucky's second largest city, lies in the heart of the state's rolling Bluegrass Country, surrounded by horse farms with manicured paddocks, smart fences and colorful barns. Internationally recognized as the horse capital of the world, the city plays host to large numbers of visitors at **The Red Mile** and **Keeneland** race tracks, the **Kentucky Horse Center**, and the horse industry's major showcase, the **Kentucky Horse Park**, with its **American Saddle Horse Museum**, off I-75 (**Exit 120**) north of town.

Take a walking or driving tour from downtown Triangle Park, or a horse-drawn carriage ride, to see the city's other attractions. These include such places as Henry Clay's **Ashland Estate**, Federal-style **Hunt-Morgan House**, Mary Todd Lincoln's girlhood home, the Greek Revival mansion of **Waveland Estate**, Lexington's historic cemetery, and the **Headley-Whitney Museum**, with its varied

Lexington's horse farms are part of its graceful Southern tradition

changing exhibits and fine art collections, including jeweled ornaments designed by George Headley.

ⓘ 430 West Vine Street

*Pick up **I-75** north of downtown Lexington for the 82-mile (131km) drive back to Cincinnati.*

Cincinnati – Louisville **103 (165)**
Louisville – Mammoth Cave **95 (153)**
Mammoth Cave – Hodgenville **48 (77)**
Hodgenville – Bardstown **27 (43)**
Bardstown – Lincoln Homestead **23 (37)**
Lincoln Homestead – Frankfort **36 (58)**
Frankfort – Lexington **23 (37)**
Lexington – Cincinnati **82 (131)**

Robert Tinker's Swiss-inspired chalet, a wonder of woodwork

ℹ️ 310 S Michigan Avenue, Chicago

*From downtown Chicago follow the John F Kennedy Expressway and Northwest Tollway **(I-90)** westbound for 84 miles (134km) to Rockford.*

Rockford, Illinois

1 Illinois' second largest city was founded in 1834 at a crossing point on the Rock River used by travelers on the way to the booming town of Galena further west. It still has four well-preserved historic districts around the downtown area and many fine old buildings that you can visit, such as the **Tinker Swiss Cottage** (1865) and the **Erlander Home** (1871). But your first stopping point should be at the tollway exit on your way into town to see the fabulous collection of antique timepieces at the **Time Museum** in the Clock Tower Resort. For a change of pace in your tour of the city, board the *Forest City Queen* for a pleasant cruise on the Rock River, and ride an old trolley bus to the lovely Sunken Gardens in **Sinnissippi Park**. Leave enough time, though, to see the reconstructed turn-of-the-century village at **Midway Village** and **Rockford Museum Center** and to browse the shops at **Victorian Village**. Before driving on to Galena, head north out of town on **SR 173** for an enjoyable walk in beautiful **Rock Cut State Park**.

ℹ️ 220 East State Street

*From Rockport follow **US 20** west for 75 miles (120 km) past Freeport and Stockton to Galena.*

Galena, Illinois

2 Along the highway to Galena, amid the beautiful Black Hawk Hills just beyond Stockton, there is an enjoyable 7-mile (11km) side trip to the scenic splendors of **Apple River Canyon State Park**. There is also fine scenery along **US 20** further on as you drive into Galena, a charming old town clinging to the steep, wooded slopes above the river of the same name. Galena's name derives from the soft, heavy mineral galena, consisting of lead sulphide.

The town came into existence as a lead-mining community and pros-

THE BLACK HAWK HILLS & ROCK RIVER

Chicago ● Rockford ● Galena ● Fulton Dixon ● Oregon ● St Charles ● Chicago

Just a 90-minute drive from downtown Chicago, the nine-county region of northern Illinois known as the Black Hawk Hills lures many visitors with scenery of timeless beauty. It is a world of rolling hills and rich farmlands, woodlands and orchards, sparkling rivers and lakes, and historic towns where the past lives on in traditional festivals, gracious old homes and atmospheric museums—all bound on the west by the mighty Mississippi. And along the Rock River, vestiges of Abraham Lincoln and Indian chief Black Hawk recall the battles that were once fought over this beautiful land.

pered until the mid-1800s. Since then, it has remained much as it was, with its quaint streets studded with historic buildings. Many lovely old homes, like the **Belvedere Mansion, Dowling House** and **Turney House**, are open to visitors, as is the home of General Ulysses S Grant. As Galena is a compact town and its streets are narrow and difficult for driving, leave your car here and cross the foot-

FOR HISTORY BUFFS

3 To see what a small pioneer prairie town was like a century or so ago, take an 18-mile (29km) round-trip detour from Savanna along **US 52** to picturesque **Mount Carroll**, a treasure trove of Victorian architecture set on a hill amid the cornfields. Visit the **County Courthouse**, the historic **Miles House**, and the log cabins, schoolhouse and other old buildings at the Oakville complex nearby.

bridge into the center. Here you will find **Main Street**, a veritable gold mine of antique shops, art galleries, craft shops and restaurants. While in this area, be sure to see the **Old Stockade**, with its pioneer exhibits, the **Old Market House** and the **Old General Store**. Enjoy a tasting at **Galena Cellars Winery**, then drive out to the **Vinegar Hill Historic Lead Mine** for a nostalgic look back at Galena's early mining days.

ⓘ 101 Bouthillier Street

*From Galena follow the Great River Road by retracing **US 20** for 12 miles (19km) to the **SR 84** intersection, then continuing south through Hanover, Savanna and Thomson for another 38 miles (61km) to Fulton.*

and, some miles on, more engineering marvels to watch as Mississippi riverboats negotiate **Lock and Dam 13**. Before leaving the river at Fulton, take a walk through the woods to see the quaint old village created at **Heritage Canyon**.

*From Fulton drive east on **SR 136** for 2 miles (3km) and join **US 30** for about 24 miles (39km) to the twin cities of Sterling and Rock Falls. Follow the Rock River Valley on **SR 2** to Dixon.*

Dixon and the Rock River, Illinois

4 If you need a break on the drive from Fulton, turn onto **SR 78** just north of Morrison for a stroll by the lake in **Morrison Rockwood State Park**. If it is August you might then

The house presented to General Grant by Galena's citizens in 1865

FOR CHILDREN

1 Places with kids especially in mind are scattered along the tour. Rockford has the **Zitelman Scout Museum**, with uniforms, badges and other items going back to 1910; the **Burpee Museum of Natural History**, with dinosaurs and Illinois wildlife among the exhibits; the hands-on **Discovery Center Museum**, all about science; and water fun at the **Magic Waters theme park**.

2 There are also **Lolly's Doll and Toy Museum** in Galena and the toy trains at the **Thomson Depot Train Museum**.

Fulton, Illinois

3 Before turning onto SR 84 from US 20, stop at the **Long Hollow Scenic Overlook** rest stop to enjoy the views of the countryside from the observation tower. As you drive south beyond Hanover, with its huge **mallard duck hatchery**, the road approaches the Mississippi River, and you will get some spectacular views of it from the wooded bluffs and trails in **Mississippi Palisades State Park**. A few minutes away are the boat marinas of Savanna, a riverfront town lying amid prime fishing and duck-hunting country where you can visit the little **Hiawatha Train Museum**. Plagues of shadflies (mayflies) in this area each August have been turned to an advantage by local folk as an excuse to have a little fun in a celebration called Shadfly Days! South of Savanna there are another **train museum** at Thomson

catch the fun at the **Whiteside County Fair** in Morrison. When you reach Sterling call at the historic **Dillon Home** where, in addition to opulent furnishings, you will find yet another minirailroad museum. In Dixon itself, there is a statue of Abraham Lincoln, who served in the Black Hawk War that raged up this valley in 1832. He later confessed that he fought no Indians but had 'a good many bloody struggles with the mosquitoes'. On South Hennepin, in Dixon, is **Ronald Reagan's Boyhood Home**, which is open for tours. If you want to see his birthplace, you will have to drive out to Tampico, 16 miles (26km) south of Rock Falls on SR 88 and 172.

*Continue on **SR 2** through Grand Detour to Oregon.*

Oregon, Illinois

5 At the quaint little town of Grand Detour, on a great bend in the Rock River, you can tour the **John Deere Homestead**, complete with its own reconstructed blacksmith's shop, where, in 1837, he made the first steel plow that revolutionized prairie farming. A scenic drive along wooded bluffs then brings you to the river-front town of Oregon, nestled amid the beauty of three forested state parks: **Castle Rock, White Pines Forest** and **Lowden**. A landmark in Lowden State Park is a huge statue of an Indian popularly referred to as Chief Black Hawk.

*From Oregon follow **SR 64** east for 54 miles (86km) through Sycamore to the town of St Charles.*

St Charles, Illinois

6 If you are a browser, a collector of knick-knacks or a lover of good food, you will be happy in St Charles, one of the picturesque towns clustered along the Fox River west of Chicago. Three markets in Old St Charles, on the west bank of the

The riverside town of St Charles boasts of its antique flea market

river, are just bursting with antiques, while out at the fairgrounds on Randall Road they claim to have the 'largest antique flea market in the world'. In Old St Charles, at Fox Island Square and Piano Factory, and, on the other side of the river, in the Century Corners district, there are more than 50 restaurants and enough tempting shops to wear out your credit card. But don't miss a tour of the **St Charles History Museum** to see how the town was in the past or a pleasant riverboat cruise along the lovely Fox River valley aboard the *St Charles Belle* or *Fox River Queen*.

ℹ 201 North First Avenue

*Continue east on **SR 64** and **I-290** for the return to Chicago.*

Chicago – Rockford **84 (134)**
Rockford – Galena **75 (120)**
Galena – Fulton **50 (80)**
Fulton – Dixon **40 (64)**
Dixon – Oregon **16 (25)**
Oregon – St Charles **54 (86)**
St Charles – Chicago **36 (58)**

SCENIC ROUTES

Although the entire Black Hawk Hills region of northern Illinois is an area of remarkable natural beauty, there are especially attractive sections of highway along **US 20** (the Great River Road) between Freeport and Galena; along **SR 84** south from Galena to Fulton; and up the Rock River Valley on **SR 2**, especially between Dixon and Grand Detour and north to Oregon.

SPECIAL TO ...

1 The dairy country around Freeport in Stephenson County is said to produce some of the best cheeses and cream in America. The **Torkelson Cheese Company** on Louisa Road, off **Highway 73** north of Lena, is noted for its semisoft Muenster and brick cheeses.

BACK TO NATURE

Along the itinerary you are quite likely to come across Illinois' varied wildlife, such as white-tailed deer, squirrel, raccoon, opossum, fox, skunk and perhaps even coyote. Among the birds you might see various species of duck, Canada geese, wild turkey, quail and pheasant. Good places for sightings are the trails in state parks and special places along the Mississippi River, such as the Thomson Causeway, a favorite spot for great blue heron, and Lock and Dam 13, where you can watch for eagles from the observation deck.

RECOMMENDED WALKS

Beautiful walks abound on this tour. In addition to the walking tours around the historic streets of Rockford (1) and Galena (2), there are pleasant trails in **Mississippi Palisades State Park**, near Savanna (3), in the state parks along the Rock River near Oregon (5), and along the Fox River at the delightful old town of St Charles (6).

3/4 days – Approximately 492 miles (787km)

IN THE FOOTSTEPS OF ABE LINCOLN

Chicago • Starved Rock State Park Peoria • Lincoln • Petersburg and New Salem • Springfield • Decatur Champaign/Urbana • Kankakee • Chicago

This long trip across the wide prairie farmlands of Illinois follows much of the route of the historic Illinois-Michigan Canal and the Illinois River Valley. It is a land once frequented by Indians and explored by the French more than three centuries ago and where sightseeing attractions and historic sites draw thousands of visitors every year. The focal point of the tour is the cluster of towns and log cabins in the center of the state, where the memory of Abraham Lincoln still remains strong. You will come away from places like Springfield, Lincoln, New Salem and Decatur enriched by the spiritual legacy left behind by the 16th president.

FOR HISTORY BUFFS

1 An important factor in the development of Illinois' central region was the construction of the Illinois-Michigan Canal, which linked the Great Lakes and Mississippi River through the valleys of the Chicago, Des Plaines and Illinois rivers. You can trace the history of this waterway at the **Illinois-Michigan Canal Museum** at Lockport, which recalls 19th-century life along the canal, and at the **Illinois Waterway Visitor Center** at Utica.

ⓘ 310 S Michigan Avenue, Chicago

From downtown Chicago take the Adlai E Stevenson Expressway (I-55) southwest for 47 miles (75km) and at Exit 250 turn west onto I-80. Continue for 36 miles (58km) past Morris to Ottawa, then go another 11 miles (18km) on SR 71 to Starved Rock State Park.

Starved Rock State Park, Illinois

1 This spectacular state park beside the Illinois River is one of the most popular visitor attractions in Illinois. Together with **Matthiessen State Park**, which adjoins it on the west, Starved Rock is a jumble of sandstone bluffs, ravines, streams and waterfalls that vie for your attention as you walk along the network of trails. Once the site of a French trading post, the park got its name from an Indian legend of the 1760s, which relates how a band of braves, cornered on a high rock in a war with another tribe, refused to surrender and so starved to death.

ⓘ 1740 Bell School Road, Cherry Valley

Fine architecture old and new is a hallmark of Chicago, which claims the first skyscraper

Continue west on SR 71 past Hennepin for about 24 miles (39km) and join SR 29 southbound along the Illinois River for another 43 miles (69km) to Peoria.

Peoria, Illinois

2 The Peoria area was settled by the French more than 300 years ago and today contains many historic gems. As you enter the city from the north, drive up to **Tower Park** in Peoria Heights for a magnificent view of the Illinois Valley from the top of the water tower. Touring the city you will see the elegant mansions on Grand View Drive, the **Pettengill-Morron House** in the historic Moss District, and the mineral springs on Dr Martin Luther King Jr Drive, which years ago brought whiskey and beer manufacturing to Peoria and are still flowing. Down on the riverfront don't miss a tour of the fascinating **Maritime Museum** aboard the tugboat *Belle Reynolds* and a sightseeing cruise on the river. Other visitor attractions are the **Lakeview Museum of Arts and Science** and, west of town at Hanna City, the **Wildlife Prairie Park**, where you can see buffalo, bears, wolves, elk, bald eagles and other native Illinois animals. Not to be missed as you leave Peoria is **Fort Creve Coeur**, a reconstruction of the defensive fortress built by the French on the east bank of the Illinois River back in 1680, now the location for the **Fort Creve Coeur Rendezvous** festivities every September.

ⓘ 331 Fulton Plaza

From Creve Coeur drive east on I-474 and I-74 for about 13 miles (20km) and take Exit 101 onto SR 121 southbound for the 36-mile (58km) drive to Lincoln.

Lincoln, Illinois

3 Abraham Lincoln christened this town himself with the juice of a watermelon in 1853, and henceforth Postville was known as Lincoln. It was here, during his sessions at the Postville Courthouse as a traveling attorney and judge, that the future president earned his nickname, 'Honest Abe'. When you visit the reconstruction of this historic building today, you might meet huge Charlie Ott, a convincingly tall presidential look-alike, before going on to see the Lincoln memorabilia at the **Lincoln College Museum**. And if you are here during September, you can enter the annual National Railsplitter Contest, an art at which young Abe excelled. The restored **Lincoln Depot**, with its range of shops and a restaurant, offers a break from sightseeing before you leave town.

ⓘ 601 Pekin Street

From Lincoln follow I-55 for about 17 miles (27km) to Exit 109. Continue west through Athens on the marked Lincoln Heritage Trail for about 17 miles (27km) to Petersburg.

Petersburg and New Salem, Illinois

4 At Petersburg is an authentic reconstruction of the log cabin village of New Salem, where Abraham Lincoln worked as postmaster and store clerk and studied to be a lawyer in the 1830s. Today costumed interpreters re-enact village life of the time, and on summer evenings there is a thrilling outdoor performance by the Great American People Show company that retraces Lincoln's life. There are also pleasant short cruises along the Sangamon River on the sternwheeler *Talisman*.

Follow the Lincoln Heritage Trail (SR 97) for about 21 miles (34km) to Springfield.

Springfield, Illinois

5 The spirit of Abraham Lincoln pervades this city, the place where he lived for much of his life and now lies buried. As you approach across the prairie, the tall dome of the New State Capitol looms up in the distance, announcing that this is the seat of Illinois' government. Many places here are associated with Lincoln, and on a tour of the city you will visit the **Old State Capitol**, where he made his famous speech referring to slavery with the words 'a house divided against itself cannot stand'; **Lincoln's Home**, a National Historic Site in the pleasant restored district along 8th Street; the **Lincoln-Herndon Building**, where Lincoln practiced law with William Herndon; and **Lincoln's Tomb**, a moving

The only home Lincoln ever owned, built in 1839 in Springfield

monument dominated by a tall obelisk in Oak Ridge Cemetery, where visitors traditionally rub the nose on a bust of the president at the entrance for good luck. In a different vein, don't miss the **Dana-Thomas House** on East Lawrence, one of socialite Frank Lloyd Wright's famed 'prairie houses', furnished in his unique style.

🛈 109 North 7th Street

From Springfield follow I-72/US 36 east for 41 miles (66km) to Decatur.

Decatur, Illinois

6 This pleasant old city, set beside Lake Decatur, with numerous

FOR CHILDREN

If the children get bored with Mr Lincoln's varied activities, they can, for example, see life on the farm at the **McGlothlin Farm Park** in East Peoria (2); pet barnyard animals at the **Henson C Robinson Children's Zoo** in Springfield (5); or climb aboard a steam locomotive or caboose at the **Sangamon Valley Railway Museum** at Monticello on I-72 between Decatur and Champaign (6).

BACK TO NATURE

1 In addition to its scenic attractions, Starved Rock State Park is also an excellent spot for observing wildlife and wild flowers. Springtime is best for birdwatching when resident woodland species mingle with migrant warblers and thrushes passing through the region. Within the Chicago area there are also several good locations: **Lincoln Park, McGinnis Slough Wildlife Refuge** and **Palos Park Forest Preserve** are among them. They harbour a mixture of woodland birds and mammals as well as freshwater species.

RECOMMENDED WALKS

As well as 12 miles (19km) of walking trails in **Starved Rock State Park** (1), suitable and interesting places for a stroll include Decatur's community parks and **Rock Springs Center for Environmental Discovery** (6), with its nature trails (and wagon rides for the weary); the gardens at **Allerton Park** in Monticello (6); and charming **Lake of the Woods Park**, with its forest trails and delightful bridges, on I-74 west of Champaign (7).

Proportion and grace mark the State Capitol in Springfield, approached through verdant grounds

SCENIC ROUTES

Driving across flat prairielands on interstate highways is rarely ever scenic, but you will enjoy the ride along **SR 71** beside the Illinois River west of Ottawa and the marked routes on the **Lincoln Heritage Trail** around Petersburg.

SPECIAL TO . . .

The rural communities of Illinois' prairie country are in full swing throughout the year with all sorts of festivals and celebrations. Among the big-city events are the bubbling river festivities during **Steamboat Days** at Peoria in June (2); the July 4 weekend **Lincolnfest** and the huge **Illinois State Fair** over two weeks in August at Springfield (5); and **National Outboard Motorboat Race** at Decatur (6).

parks and golf courses, also has many associations with Abraham Lincoln. At Lincoln Square he delivered his first political speech, and at the **Lincoln Log Cabin Courthouse**, now in Fairview Park, he won his first court case. Other interesting places to visit are the **Historic District**; the **Oglesby Mansion** on West Williams Street; the imposing **James Milliken Homestead** on North Pine Street; and the **Macon County Museum**, with its delightful Prairie Village. But for something quite different, take a walk among the herb beds and gardens and along the deer trails at the **Mari-Mann Herb Farm and Gingerbread House**, where the products on sale are hard to resist.

🛈 Transfer House, 1 Central Park East

Continue northeast on I-72 for 47 miles (75km) past Monticello to Champaign/Urbana.

Champaign/Urbana, Illinois

7 One good reason for stopping at these twin cities in the heart of the Illinois cornbelt is to visit the cultural and architectural attractions on the prestigious University of Illinois campus. The highlights are the **Krannert Art Museum**, which has major collections of paintings, sculpture, textiles, pottery and glassware; the

Krannert Center for the Performing Arts, a showcase for music, drama and dance, which is open for tours in addition to performances; and the **World Heritage Museum**, with exhibits tracing the story of mankind.

🛈 40 East University Avenue, Champaign

Pick up I-57 west or north of Champaign and continue north for 77 miles (123km) to Kankakee.

Kankakee, Illinois

8 Just an hour's drive from Chicago, this industrial city and county seat has an Indian name meaning 'beautiful river', a reference to the relatively unspoiled river which runs through the area. If you feel like a break before driving on to Chicago, make for the **Kankakee River State Park**, a recreation area along the river northwest of town, where you will find opportunities for walking, picnicking and doing other outdoor activities in pleasant surroundings.

Continue north for about 62 miles (99km) on I-57 and the Dan Ryan Expressway to downtown Chicago.

Chicago – Starved Rock **94 (150)**
Starved Rock – Peoria **67 (108)**
Peoria – Lincoln **49 (78)**
Lincoln – Petersburg **34 (54)**
Petersburg – Springfield **21 (34)**
Springfield – Decatur **41 (66)**
Decatur – Champaign **46 (75)**
Champaign – Kankakee **77 (123)**
Kankakee – Chicago **62 (99)**

Renaissance Festival celebrations at Shakopee, near Minneapolis

ⓘ 81 South 9th Street, Minneapolis

THE GREAT RIVER ROAD RAMBLE

Minneapolis/St Paul ● Northfield Rochester ● Winona ● Wabasha ● Pepin and Maiden Rock ● Red Wing ● Hastings Stillwater ● Taylors Falls ● Minneapolis/ St Paul

*To leave the Twin Cities area, take **I-35W** from Minneapolis or **I-35E** from St Paul south for about 35 miles (56km) to **Exit 69**. Take **SR 19** east for 7 miles (11km) to Northfield.*

Northfield, Minnesota

1 If you are enjoying your ride through the pleasant farmlands of southeast Minnesota and suddenly see a busload of visitors being hijacked by bandits, don't be alarmed. It is just a dramatic promotion stunt to highlight the little town of Northfield's main claim to fame: the attempted robbery of the local bank by Jesse James and his gang in 1876. If you are here in early September, you will also witness a shoot-out on the town's streets as the event is re-enacted in the annual Defeat of Jesse James Days celebration. For an account of the raid call in at the **museum** housed in the still-surviving bank building during your walking tour of Northfield's Historic Preservation District.

ⓘ 105 East Fourth Street

*Continue east on **SR 19** for 14 miles (23km) to Cannon Falls, then head south on **US 52** and **SR 57** for 34 miles (54km) through Hader to Mantorville. Three miles (5km) south of here take **US 14** east for 13 miles (21km) to Rochester.*

Rochester, Minnesota

2 On the drive to Rochester pause for a walk around old Mantorville, a former stagecoach stop with a board-walk and restored historic buildings, including an opera house where you can enjoy a lively melodrama during

the summer months.

Rochester, the largest city in this part of Minnesota, is a manufacturing

T his tour from the Twin Cities of Minneapolis and St Paul begins with a drive through the rolling farmlands and woods of southeast Minnesota. Here you will see a bank that was raided by Jesse James, an opera house where they still stage old melodramas, and one of the finest medical institutions in the world. A wide variety of other sights and experiences then accompanies you as you drive up the Mississippi and St Croix river valleys through landscapes of exceptional beauty, where you will be tempted to linger in charming old river towns that recall the great days of the steamboat.

FOR HISTORY BUFFS

9 The story of human settlement in this part of America is well documented in the museums along the itinerary. But at the **Ice Age Center** in Interstate Park at St Croix Falls, Wisconsin, you can see how the land itself was dramatically shaped by glaciation much further back in time.

FOR CHILDREN

9 Two special treats for kids on the tour are within a short distance of Taylors Falls. Seven miles (11km) north of town they can ride the chair lift and water slide at **Wild Mountain Ski Area**, while 4 miles (6km) east, beyond St Croix Falls in Wisconsin, they can pet and feed the animals during the summer at the **Fawn Doe Rosa Park**.

BACK TO NATURE

With their abundant wildlife, the Mississippi and St Croix valleys are a paradise for nature lovers, hunters and anglers alike. In remote spots you may glimpse a black bear, coyote, beaver, otter, mink or raccoon, and down by the water, great blue herons, woodcocks and all sorts of ducks. Among the special places are **Reads Landing**, near Wabasha (4), for bald eagles, and **Whitewater State Park** on **SR 74** north of St Charles (2), for a wide variety of bird life.

RECOMMENDED WALKS

6 Stop the car at any rivertown or state park along the Mississippi or St Croix and you will have an opportunity for a pleasant stroll. A particularly rewarding walk follows the trail to the top of Barn Bluff from East 5th Street in Red Wing, where you will enjoy a fine view of the Mississippi River.

center with a vibrant music and theater scene. But it is best known as the home of the world-famous **Mayo Clinic**, a medical research and treatment complex in the heart of the town. Take the guided tour of its facilities and visit the **Mayo Medical Museum**. Then drive out to see the local history exhibits at the **Olmsted County Historical Museum** southwest of town and take the special tour bus from here to visit impressive **Mayowood**, the 1911 home and estate of one of the Mayo Clinic's founders. Other sightseeing musts in Rochester include the restored 1875 **Heritage House** in downtown Central Park and the lovely Old English-style **Plummer House** completed in 1917.

ℹ 150 South Broadway, Suite A

From Rochester continue east on US 14 for 45 miles (72km) through St Charles to Winona.

Winona, Minnesota

3 From the 554-foot (169m) bluffs in Garvin Heights Park there is a spectacular view of the old river port of Winona lying along the sand plain beside the Mississippi River. Now the largest city on this stretch of the river, Winona has a fine **County Courthouse** and many 19th-century buildings. Its river town heritage is brought vividly to life at the **Julius C Wilkie Steamboat Center**, a replica old steamboat housing a museum. If you would like to sail on one of these old-timers down the Mississippi, you can take a short cruise aboard the *Jollie Ollie*.

ℹ 67 Main Street

Follow the Great River Road (US 61) north along the Mississippi River for 28 miles (45km) to Wabasha.

Wabasha, Minnesota

4 North of Winona as far as Hastings, the Great River Road, on both the Minnesota and the Wisconsin sides of the Mississippi, passes through a scenic patchwork of farmlands, wooded hillsides and historic river towns nestled beneath towering rock bluffs. For an authentic old river town atmosphere, explore historic Wabasha. Here you will find the renowned **Anderson House**, a gracious old inn dating from 1856, where you can get, if you wish, tasty Pennsylvania Dutch food, a house cat for overnight company and hot bricks to warm your bed. The **Arrowhead Bluffs Exhibits** has a large collection of pioneer and native American artifacts, with mounted displays of wildlife and a fine collection of firearms, including every Winchester model made from 1866 up to 1982.

From Wabasha take SR 25 for 4 miles (6km) across the Mississippi River to Nelson, Wisconsin. Then follow the Great River Road (SR 35) north for 20 miles (32km) through Pepin to Maiden Rock.

Pepin and Maiden Rock, Wisconsin

5 North of Nelson, where the Mississippi broadens to form Lake Pepin, stop at the little town of Pepin to visit the **Laura Ingalls Wilder Wayside Park**, which commemorates the author of the *Little House* books. Seven miles (11km) out of town on SR 183 you will also find a replica of the log cabin in which she was born. North along the lake, Maiden Rock is named for the 400-foot (122m) bluff from which, according to legend, a young Indian woman jumped to her death rather than marry a man she did not love.

Continue north from Maiden Rock for 12 miles (19km) on SR 35 before taking US 63 south across the Mississippi River for 3 miles (5km) to Red Wing.

Red Wing, Minnesota

6 The old community of Red Wing lies below Barn Bluff on a lovely stretch of the Mississippi known as the Hiawatha Valley. There is a fine view of its beautiful setting from the

Minnehaha Falls, in Minnehaha Park, made famous by Longfellow's epic poem The Song Of Hiawatha

summit of nearby Sorin's Bluff. In the compact downtown area you will find many architectural treasures, including the **St James Hotel** and historic **Mall District**. If you don't want to walk, you can take a delightful 45-minute narrated tour of the streets on a San Francisco-style cable car. Leave enough time, though, to visit the fine **Goodhue County Historical Museum** and to browse through the shops at **Pottery Place**, a restored former pottery factory at the west end of town. And to round off your visit, board the riverboat *Red Wing Princess* for a relaxing two-and-a-half-hour cruise on the Mississippi.

⊡ 416 Bush Street

Take US 61 northwest for 24 miles (39km) to Hastings.

Hastings, Minnesota

7 You can savor the 19th-century atmosphere of Hastings, a quiet rivertown with streets lined with historic buildings. The impressive **Dakota County Courthouse**, the **Gardner House** and the **LeDuc-Simmons Mansion** are just some of its notable landmarks.

⊡ 1304 Vermilion Street

From Hastings follow SR 95 north up the St Croix River valley for 24 miles (39km) to Stillwater.

Stillwater, Minnesota

8 The old logging community of Stillwater, on the lower St Croix River, is a bustling town with fine shops and restaurants housed in beautifully restored 19th-century buildings. Historic landmarks include the gracious **Lowell Inn**, **County Courthouse**, **Staples Mill**, and the

'Ye Olde City Hall' typifies Hastings' unchanged character

old prison warden's house presently used by the **Washington County Historical Museum**. Every July townsfolk recall their heritage and celebrate Lumberjack Days.

Head north out of town on SR 95 and you will find opportunities to walk by the lovely St Croix River at picturesque Marine on St Croix and nearby **William O'Brien State Park**.

⊡ 423 South Main Street

Continue on SR 95, then take US 8 east to Taylors Falls.

Taylors Falls, Minnesota

9 As you near Taylors Falls you will see the mood of the river change from the placid meanderings of the broad lower reaches to the turbulent surge through the rugged gorge of the Dalles, at **Interstate Park**, a favorite spot for both canoeists and rock climbers. At Taylors Falls don't miss the view of the river from the bridge, the old jail now used as a guest house (complete with barred windows) and, up the hill, the **W H C Folsom House** of 1855, which is open to visitors.

From Taylors Falls go west on US 8 for 13 miles (21km) before turning southeast on to SR 98 for 6 miles (10km) to Wyoming. Pick up I-35 southbound and continue for about 30 miles (48km) to downtown Minneapolis (I-35W) or St Paul (I-35E).

Minneapolis – Northfield	42 (67)
Northfield – Rochester	64 (103)
Rochester – Winona	45 (72)
Winona – Wabasha	28 (45)
Wabasha – Pepin	9 (14)
Pepin – Red Wing	30 (48)
Red Wing – Hastings	24 (39)
Hastings – Stillwater	24 (39)
Stillwater – Taylors Falls	30 (48)
Taylors Falls – Minneapolis	49 (79)

SCENIC ROUTES

Although the drive through southeast Minnesota passes through beautiful farm country and woodlands, the most scenically spectacular sections of the itinerary are along the Great River Road between Winona and Red Wing and along **SR 95** up the St Croix valley between Stillwater and Taylors Falls.

SPECIAL TO . . .

Among the many memorable experiences you can savor on this tour are a concert recital played on the 56-bell Mayo Carillon at Rochester's **Plummer Building** (2); a taste of delicious Wisconsin cheeses as you tour the **Nelson Cheese Factory** north of Wabasha (4) or the cider and apples at **Hay Creek Apple Farm** just outside Red Wing (6); and a look at the piano that was twice dumped in the Mississippi River while on its way to the **Octagon House** at Hudson on the St Croix River.

THE MISSISSIPPI HEARTLAND

On the last lap of its long journey south to the Gulf of Mexico, the Mississippi River flows through a region of low plains that stretch for miles across the states of Arkansas, Tennessee, Alabama, Mississippi and Louisiana. Much of the land is patterned with rich farmland, forests and man-made reservoirs, while the coast is edged with white sandy beaches, lagoons, barrier islands, the swamps and bayous of the Mississippi's waterlogged delta, and the offshore oil rigs of Louisiana.

After brief, relatively mild winters these southern states swelter through long, sultry summers, which culminate dramatically in spectacular thunderstorms and the occasional hurricane that lashes the coast.

But rather than the land and its climate, it is the unique history, culture and lifestyle of its people that fascinate visitors in this part of America. For this is the heart of the traditional Deep South. Nothing evokes its spirit so powerfully as a cruise on an old-time sternwheeler down the Mississippi from St Louis to New Orleans. In your mind you can recapture the world of *Huckleberry Finn*, with its imposing old plantation houses, fields white with cotton, and soul-baring spirituals and gospel songs.

Many memories of the past linger on in this region. Old communities like Sainte Genevieve, Cape Girouard, even New Orleans itself, recall the time when it was part of the enormous French territory of Louisiana before it was finally bought by the United States in 1803. Battle sites, like the one at Vicksburg, Mississippi, commemorate the War Between the States, while beautiful antebellum homes and gardens survive as melancholy reminders of the now-vanished way of life over which it was fought.

The cultural identity of America's Mississippi heartland is especially colored by its music, a complex tapestry of rhythm and sound woven by blues, jazz, bluegrass, country, gospel and rock 'n' roll, not forgetting the fiddle and accordion music of Louisiana's Cajun folk. Cajun, too, is some of the region's finest cuisine, with dishes like *andouille*, *boudin*, *jambalaya* and *gumbo* offering more exotic flavors than the traditional fried chicken and grits. Everywhere there are year-round festivals and gatherings to celebrate, in particular, the region's colorful arts and crafts, though few can match the exuberance of New Orleans' renowned Mardi Gras.

Narrated riverboat cruises glide past St Louis' Gateway Arch

St Louis:

St Louis, Missouri, an important Mississippi river port and manufacturing city of around 430,000 people, lures visitors with sightseeing attractions, live entertainment, riverboat rides, fine shopping malls, and museums ranging from art and history to transport, magic and dogs.

Founded by the French in 1764, St Louis became the gateway for settlers moving into the newly opened-up western territories after the Louisiana Purchase of 1803. Many buildings and homes of the 1800s still stand in the city, and colorful riverboats, now packed with sightseers, still throng the busy waterfront. Here the city's most famous landmark, the spectacular 630-foot (192m) **Gateway Arch**, offers marvelous views for miles around from the observation room at the top. At its foot is the **Museum of Western Expansion** and, nearby, the **Old Cathedral**, **Old Courthouse**, impressive **Busch Stadium**, and the shops, restaurants and night spots of the

revitalized riverfront district of Laclede's Landing.

Other major visitor attractions include the redeveloped old **Union Station**; the imposing **New Cathedral**, with its magnificent mosaics; the **Missouri Botanical Garden** and its famous Climatron greenhouse; and the varied attractions of immense **Forest Park**, which include the **St Louis Art Museum** and **Science Center** with its hands-on Discovery Room, the **Zoo** and the popular outdoor entertainment amphitheater known as **The Muny**.

New Orleans:

Mention Bourbon Street, Mardi Gras and Creole cooking and you can only be talking about New Orleans, one of America's most fascinating cities. Founded by the French in 1718 on a bend in the Mississippi River, Louisiana's 'Crescent City', now a major international port of some 560,000 people, exhibits a unique cultural blend derived from its French, Spanish and Creole heritage.

The historic heart of the city is the Vieux Carré, or French Quarter, a potpourri of little shops, house museums, restaurants, cafés, bars and night spots, where snatches of music and spicy aromas constantly waft on the air. A walking tour or carriage ride along the narrow streets takes you past colorful old buildings, many with lacy ironwork balconies, and small hidden courtyards filled with exotic greenery. At night, Bourbon Street bubbles with jazz clubs, burlesque revues and lively bars, while **Preservation Hall**, the mecca of jazz, is around the corner on St Peter Street. Focal point of the French Quarter is lovely **Jackson Square**, flanked by the 1794 **St Louis Cathedral** and other historic buildings. Nearby is the bustling French Market, where the **Café du Monde** serves its famous *café au lait* and *beignets*.

From Canal Street, with its hotels and department stores, you can take a St Charles Avenue streetcar ride past the elegant 19th-century homes of the Garden District on the way to **Audubon Park and Zoo**. Another ride north takes you to immense **City Park** and the excellent **Museum of Art**, while back on the riverfront there are wonderful old-style steamboats offering nostalgic narrated cruises.

3/4 days – Approximately 510 miles (816km)

THE LAND BETWEEN THE RIVERS

St Louis • Sainte Geneviève • Kaskaskia Island • Ellis Grove • Carbondale and the Western Shawnee Hills • Vienna • Cave in Rock • Delwood • Cape Girardeau St Louis

This long but delightful drive from St Louis, Missouri, takes you through the historic towns of the Mississippi River region once trod by French explorers and traders three centuries ago and into the forested hill country lying between the Mississippi and Ohio rivers at the southern tip of Illinois. This beautiful region, known as the Shawnee Hills or the Illinois Ozarks, is a land of great scenic beauty and abundant wildlife, where you can get close to nature along pleasant wooded trails and enjoy a wide range of outdoor activities that cater for almost every interest and age.

FOR HISTORY BUFFS

8 According to legend, the monument in **Trail of Tears State Park**, near Cape Girardeau, marks the grave of Princess Otahki, just one of the 4,000 who died during the forced removal of 15,000 Cherokee Indians from their homeland in the southern Appalachians to Oklahoma in the winter of 1838. Their march into exile, the cruel 'Trail of Tears', took them through southern Illinois and across the Mississippi at Cape Girardeau.

FOR CHILDREN

8 If there is too much to see and not enough to do for the children on the tour, give them a ride, complete with clanging bells and hissing steam, on the **St Louis Iron Mountain and Southern Railroad**. It starts at weekends from Jackson, just north of Cape Girardeau. (By the way, it is just possible there will be a train hold-up by 'Jesse James and his gang'—an exciting re-enactment by the local sheriff's men of a real raid in 1873.)

ℹ️ 10 South Broadway, St Louis

Follow I-55 south from downtown St Louis for about 55 miles (88km), then turn east on SR 32 for another 4 miles (6km) to Sainte Geneviève.

Sainte Geneviève, Missouri

1 This charming small town, Missouri's oldest permanent community, was established beside the Mississippi River by French settlers in about 1735. Despite a devastating flood in 1785, many fine buildings dating from those early years have survived, including the **Amoureaux House** of 1770 and the **Green Tree Tavern** of 1790. French tradition remains very much alive, as you will see if you are here during the Jour de Fete celebrations in August. On your walk around the town don't miss the **Felix Valle Historic Site**, a store and home built in 1818 in the American Federal style of the time; the local history exhibits at the **Sainte Geneviève Museum**, which has Indian relics, Civil War items and birds mounted by John James Audubon when he lived here; and the charming **Sainte Gemme Beauvais Inn**. Take a look, too, inside the **Catholic Cathedral** and visit the town's **winery** on Merchant Street.

ℹ️ South Third Street

Follow US 61 south for about 10 miles (16km) to Kaskaskia Island.

Kaskaskia Island, Illinois

2 Kaskaskia Island is an enclave of Illinois on the Missouri side of the

---

The St Louis Iron Mountain and Southern Railroad gives passengers a taste of the Old West – watch out for outlaws!

Mississippi River. From 1818 to 1820 it was the site of Illinois' first state capital, washed away long ago by the river. All that remains is the **Liberty Bell of the West**, a gift from King Louis XV of France.

Continue for another 7 miles (11km) on Highway H and SR 51 across the Missouri River to Chester and north on SR 3 to Ellis Grove.

Ellis Grove, Illinois

3 Across the Mississippi at Ellis Grove, north of Chester, you can visit the elegant period-furnished home of Illinois' first lieutenant governor at the **Pierre Menard Home State Historic Site**, with its small museum, herb garden and smokehouse, and enjoy panoramic views of the river from the remains of historic **Fort Kaskaskia**. As you drive back through Chester, look out for the **statue of Popeye** and, just south of town, stop at the **Turkey Bluffs Scenic Overlook** for more fine views of the river.

Continue southeast on SR 3, SR 149 and SR 13 for 47 miles (75km) through Grimsby and Murphysboro to Carbondale. From SR 13, just east of Carbondale, meander south on SR 26 back roads past Crab Orchard Lake and through Makanda to Alto Pass.

Carbondale and the Western Shawnee Hills, Illinois

4 Beyond Grimsby, in the recreational area centered on Kinkaid Lake and Big Muddy River, you pass through the orchard country around Murphysboro, where there is a lively Apple Festival every September. You then come to Carbondale, site of Southern Illinois University and gateway to the western end of the Shawnee Hills, a spectacularly beautiful region of rugged, forested hills and valleys and quaint little towns. Drive on through **Crab Orchard National Wildlife Refuge**, with its three recreational lakes, where you might see beavers, coyotes, bald eagles or migrating Canada geese. But stop for a walk in **Giant City State Park**, near Makanda, where spectacular sandstone bluffs soar above the thick forest, before driving on to Alto Pass, a little town known for its quilts. Nearby, offering superb views of the surrounding hills from the top of Bald Knob Mountain, is a well-known Illinois landmark, the impressive **Bald Knob Cross**, a Christian monument 111 feet (34m) high, which is illuminated at night.

ℹ️ 714 East Walnut Street

From Alto Pass take SR 127 and SR 146 to Jonesboro, then follow SR 146 east for 19 miles (30km) to West Vienna. Make a 28-mile (45km) detour south on SR 37 through Cypress, east on SR 169 through Karnak and north on US 45 to Vienna.

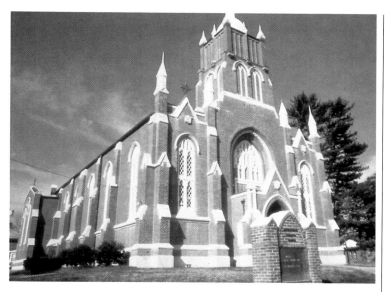

Vienna, Illinois

5 It is hard to believe you are in Illinois when you explore the remote unspoiled swamp country along the lower Cache River south of Vienna. Here you can see stands of majestic white oaks, cypresses standing in the water, and all sorts of wildlife, perhaps even beavers, otters and bobcats, and colonies of great blue herons nesting amid the peace of **Heron Pond Nature Preserve**.

Continue east on **SR 146** *for about 50 miles (80km) through Dixon Springs, Golconda and Elizabethtown to Cave in Rock.*

Gothic-style Old St Vincent's Church, in Cape Girardeau

Cave in Rock, Illinois

6 After stretching your legs in **Dixon Springs State Park**, drive on to the historic little town of Golconda, tucked away amid deer-hunting country beside the mighty Ohio River. There is a lively little Deer Festival here every November. Further east, don't miss the historic **Illinois Iron Furnace** on Hog Thief Creek, before turning south on a side road to visit the **Fluorspar Museum** at the small riverfront town of

BACK TO NATURE

Botanists and wildlife lovers will find much of interest on this tour, which lies on the Mississippi Flyway used by migrating birds. If you are in luck you will spot not only the more common wild creatures but perhaps also beavers, otters, bobcats and bald eagles—even timber rattlers and water moccasins in out-of-the-way places in the Shawnee Forest.

RECOMMENDED WALKS

Although many of the best-known state park trails in this region are quite long and strenuous, there are stretches which you can follow for a gentle stroll. Among them are the Pirates Bluff and Hickory Ridge trails at **Cave in Rock State Park** (6) and the famed Red Cedar Trail and shorter trails in **Giant City State Park** (4). You will also find pleasant walking trails in **Trail of Tears State Park**, near Cape Girardeau (8).

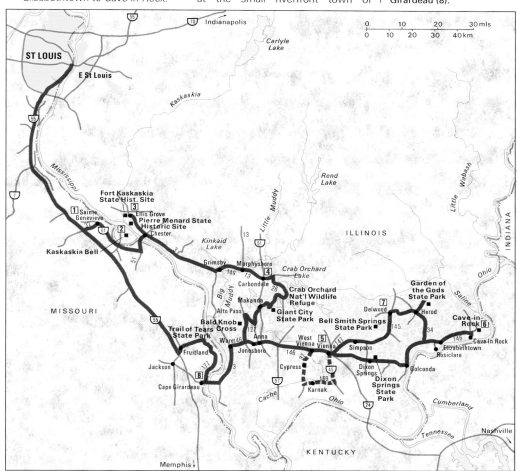

SCENIC ROUTES

In addition to magnificent panoramas of the Mississippi and Ohio rivers from the viewpoints and riverfront towns mentioned along the itinerary, there are many wonderful mountain vistas to be enjoyed along the roads through the Shawnee Hills, especially the back roads around Makanda, Alto Pass, Herod and Delwood.

SPECIAL TO ...

8 Cape Girardeau's unusual method of recording local history will probably catch your eye on this tour. Look out for the big colored murals. The **Water Street Riverfront Mural** is a brightly colored celebration of life on the Mississippi River at Cape Girardeau, and the **Missourian Murals** on Lorimer Street are made of tiles and depict the local role in the story of printing, while the **Jake Wells Mural** at Kent Library on the campus of the University of Southeast Missouri portrays the history and natural resource of southeast Missouri.

Rosiclare. At Cave in Rock you must see the colossal cavern that gave the town its name. Two centuries ago it was a famous landmark for pioneers sailing down the Ohio River on their way west. It was also a notorious hideout for the river pirates who preyed on them.

Retrace SR 146 for about 17 miles (27km) through Elizabethtown and turn north on SR 34 for about 15 miles (24km) to the Garden of the Gods, near Herod, and west on the local road for about 13 miles (21km) to Delwood.

Delwood, Illinois

7 Weave your way along the trails in Garden of the Gods State Park and you will understand how this scenic wonderland got its name. Set against the dark forest are spectacular rock formations, with such colorful names as Camel Rock, Buzzard's Roost, Tower of Babel and Fat Man's Squeeze. To the west, hidden in the breathtaking scenery around Delwood, there are more beautiful trails in **Bell Smith Springs State Park**, along which you will see a winding canyon, Indian caves, a lovely waterfall and, nearby, a natural stone bridge.

From Delwood take SR 145 and SR 147 south to Vienna, then continue west on SR 146 for 30 miles (48km) through Anna and Jonesboro to Ware. Turn south on SR 3 for 16 miles (26km) across the Mississippi River to Cape Girardeau.

Cape Girardeau, Missouri

8 Despite the French name it acquired during French Colonial times, Cape Girardeau was not laid out as a planned riverfront town until 1806, just after it became part of the United States. So the historic buildings you see on a downtown walking tour are not French but 19th-century American. Among them are the imposing **Common Pleas Courthouse** of 1854; the Gothic-style **Old St Vincent's Church** dedicated in 1853; the lovely **Hoche House** of 1838; and the elegant **Glenn House** of 1883. As you walk around, see if you can also spot the old **Opera House** and General Grant's headquarters, now disguised behind other uses. **Arena Park** is the site of the Southeast Missouri District Fair in September. Don't miss a stroll along Riverfront Park and a tour of the **Cape River Heritage Museum** before driving out to see the famed **Rose Display Garden** at Capaha Park. Then make your way northeast of town to enjoy Mississippi River views from **Cape Rock Park** and **Trail of Tears State Park**.

🚩 601 N Kingshighway

From Trail of Tears State Park continue on SR 177 to Fruitland and pick up I-55 northbound for the 100-mile (160km) drive to St Louis.

St Louis – Sainte Genevieve **59 (94)**
Sainte Genevieve – Kaskaskia I **10 (16)**
Kaskaskia I – Ellis Grove **21 (34)**
Ellis Grove – Carbondale **47 (75)**
Carbondale – Vienna **84 (134)**
Vienna – Cave In Rock **50 (80)**
Cave In Rock – Delwood **45 (72)**
Delwood – Cape Girardeau **72 (116)**
Cape Girardeau – St Louis **122 (195)**

The Garden of the Gods in Shawnee National Forest, southern Illinois

Avery Island, home of Tabasco

ⓘ 529 St Ann Street, New Orleans

*Cross the Mississippi River from New Orleans on either Greater New Orleans Bridge or Huey P Long Bridge and follow **US 90** west for the 55-mile (89km) drive to Houma.*

Houma, Louisiana

1 Nicknamed the 'Venice of America' on account of its many waterways and bridges, the city of Houma is a shrimp-fishing and seafood-processing center. From here you can take boat excursions into the surrounding cypress swamps to see alligators and other wild creatures. Walk around the Historic District and see the porcelain birds and other fine exhibits at **Southdown Plantation's Terrebonne Museum**. From Houma, you can take boat trips into the deep swamp and bayou country of southern Louisiana where you can spot alligators, raccoons, herons and other wildlife if you are sharp-eyed.

*Follow **SR 24** north to Thibodaux.*

Thibodaux, Louisiana

2 The university city of Thibodaux is another community with fine 19th-century architecture. Here you should visit the **Laurel Valley Village and Rural Life Museum**, southeast of town on SR 308, where you will learn about life on a sugar plantation. Still in operation, the complex includes a schoolhouse, general store, boarding house and the remains of an old sugar mill.

ⓘ 100 Green Street

*Go south on **SR 24** and pick up **SR 20** going southwest for 16 miles (26km) to Gibson, then **US 90** west for about 62 miles (99km) through Morgan City, Patterson and Franklin to New Iberia.*

New Iberia, Louisiana

3 The old city of New Iberia, on Bayou Teche, is the center of

THE BAYOUS OF ACADIANA

New Orleans ● Houma ● Thibodaux ● New Iberia ● St Martinville ● Lafayette ● Baton Rouge ● Burnside and the Mississippi River plantations ● New Orleans

This tour takes you through the steamy swamps and along the sleepy bayous of the Mississippi delta to experience the unique atmosphere of Louisiana's Cajun Country. You will visit the historic communities of the French-speaking Cajun people, taste spicy home cooking, hear foot-tapping music and perhaps dance a *fais-do-do*. You will gather memories of live oaks and cypresses festooned with Spanish moss, alligators, swamp tours, a cruise on the bayou, a Tabasco sauce factory and gracious old sugar plantations filled with nostalgia. Capture, as you go, the spirit of Cajun *joie de vivre* and, as they say, 'Laissez les bons temps rouler!' 'Let the good times roll!'

Louisiana's sugarcane industry. A tour of its downtown Historic District reveals many architectural treasures and, surprisingly, a genuine 2nd-century Roman statue of the Emperor Hadrian. Not to be missed is the beautiful and romantic **Shadows-on-the-Teche Plantation**, standing by the bayou amid moss-draped live oaks. East of town there are other sightseeing musts: the **Armand Broussard House** of about 1790 and the adjacent **Mintmere Plantation**. On the way back call at **Trappey's**

FOR HISTORY BUFFS

2 Historic houses, plantations and museums are plentiful along this itinerary, but for a break from the long Thibodaux to New Iberia drive, stop to explore the historic districts and houses at Morgan City and Franklin and to see exhibits depicting life along Bayou Teche at the small **Jeanerette Museum** further west.

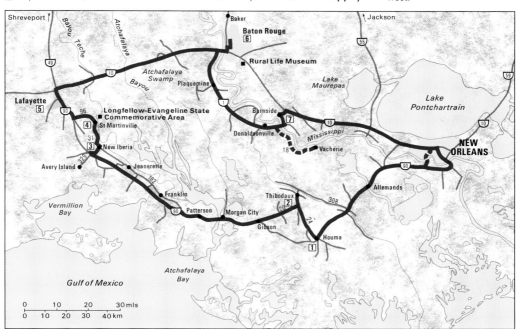

FOR CHILDREN

2 If the kids on the tour prefer familiar, homey animals to wild alligators and swamp creatures, they can see and feed farm animals at the **Barnyard Zoo** in Morgan City, northwest of Thibodaux.

6 Another favorite with kids is the **Greater Baton Rouge Zoo**, at Baker with animals from around the world in naturalistic outdoor habitats. There is a small zoo for children, with goats and rabbits and a variety of rides.

BACK TO NATURE

Alligators, nutria (coypu), crawfish, herons, egrets and a long list of other wild creatures inhabit the moss-draped cypress swamps, marshes, bayous and creeks of southern Louisiana. An easy way to see this rich variety of flora and fauna is to visit such special places as the **Wildlife Gardens** at Gibson, **Brownell Memorial Park** at Morgan City (2), and **Cypress Lake/Swamp** on the University of Southwestern Louisiana campus at Lafayette (5).

RECOMMENDED WALKS

Walks in Louisiana's hot and humid summer climate are best kept to a short stroll at the many places of interest along the itinerary. You will find easily walkable trails at Lafayette's **Acadiana Park** (5) and a pleasant walk along **Front Street** overlooking the Atchafalaya River at Morgan City (2).

famous Cajun shop for a tour of the adjoining Tabasco pepper sauce factory or visit the **Konriko Company Store** to see the rice mill and watch the slide show on Cajun culture. If you then feel like relaxing, there is a pleasant cruise on the bayou aboard the *Teche Queen*.

⊡ 2690 Center Street

*Follow West Main Street and **SR 31** from New Iberia for about 10 miles (16km) to St Martinville.*

St Martinville, Louisiana

4 It helps if you have already read Henry Wadsworth Longfellow's poem *Evangeline* when you visit this quiet little town with its strong French atmosphere beside Bayou Teche. It was here that Longfellow's heroine (in real life, Emmeline Labiche), like many other Acadian settlers, ended her journey into exile from Nova Scotia in the 1760s. On a tour of the town you will see Evangeline's statue and grave; the **Evangeline Oak**, beneath which she disembarked; and the **Longfellow-Evangeline State Commemorative Area**, a 157-acre (63-hectare) park dedicated to the early settlers north of town. Be sure, too, to visit **St Martin de Tours Church** and to see the historic exhibits in the adjacent **Petit Paris Museum**. And, for a leisurely one-hour cruise on the bayou, board the *Cajun Queen* at Evangeline Oak.

*Leave St Martinville on **SR 96** and after 7 miles (11km) pick up **US 90** northbound for about 10 miles (16km) to Lafayette.*

'The Shadows' (1834), restored by the builder's great-grandson

Lafayette, Louisiana

5 This city of more than 94,000 people is the cultural capital of Acadiana, with busy restaurants that serve traditional Cajun and Creole cuisine and foot-stomping music. The best times to be here are spring, when there is a big Mardi Gras celebration and the city is ablaze with azalea blossom, and September, for the Festivals Acadiens. Downtown landmarks include the **Old City Hall**, the **Cathedral of St John the Evangelist**, the **Lafayette Museum** and the **Lafayette Natural History Museum and Planetarium**. But the highlight for visitors is a tour of the reconstructed **Acadian Village** southwest of town, which captures the atmosphere of a small 19th-century Cajun community. There is also a two-hour sightseeing cruise along Bayou Vermilion aboard the steamboat *Vermilion Queen*, docked at Pinhook Bridge.

⊡ 310 16th Street

*Take **I-10** eastbound from just north of downtown Lafayette for 53 miles (85km) across the Atchafalaya Swamp and Mississippi River to the state capital, Baton Rouge.*

Baton Rouge, Louisiana

6 This vibrant Mississippi river port, with its lovely old homes and tree-lined streets, has been the capital of Louisiana since 1850, and today it is home to a quarter of a million people. For a panoramic view of it, go to the top of the 34-story **State Capitol**. The **Old Governor's Mansion**, which Mark Twain once dismissed as a 'sham little castle', is another of the government buildings you can tour

New Orleans' Mardi Gras figures burst with personality

(by appointment) in this city. Along the riverfront you can explore the Catfish Town old warehouse area, tour the World War II destroyer *USS Kidd*, and take a one-hour narrated cruise aboard the steamboat *Samuel Clemens*. But not to be missed is the representation of a working 19th-century plantation at the **Rural Life Museum**, one of Louisiana State University's four excellent museums in the south part of town. For the real thing, you can visit **Magnolia Mound** and **Mount Hope** plantations, two early 19th-century houses not far away.

Cross the Mississippi River bridge from downtown Baton Rouge and follow the Great River Road (SR 1) south for 35 miles (56km) through Plaquemine to Donaldsonville. Cross the Mississippi on SR 70, then turn north onto SR 44 to Burnside.

Burnside and the Mississippi River plantations, Louisiana

7 As you drive through the sugarcane fields along this stretch of the Mississippi, you will be reminded of the vanished way of life of the old plantations. A few miles beyond historic Plaquemine, with its old locks and fine views of the river, be sure to visit the imposing **Nottoway Plantation**, the biggest of them all. Then, if you have time, drive on down **SR 18** to see the impressive avenue of live oaks at **Oak Alley Plantation**, near Vacherie. Across the river, at Burnside, you will see other fine mansions, none more beautiful than the Greek Revival **Houmas House Plantation**. Rebuilt in 1840, it is furnished with early 19th-century antiques, and especially interesting are a graceful, three-story spiral staircase and a collection of armories.

Leave Burnside on SR 44, then take SR 22 to join I-10 eastbound for the 49-mile (78km) drive back to New Orleans.

New Orleans – Houma **61 (98)**
Houma – Thibodaux **14 (22)**
Thibodaux – New Iberia **78 (125)**
New Iberia – St Martinville **10 (16)**
St Martinville – Lafayette **17 (27)**
Lafayette – Baton Rouge **53 (85)**
Baton Rouge – Burnside **45 (72)**
Burnside – New Orleans **54 (86)**

THE LONE STAR STATE

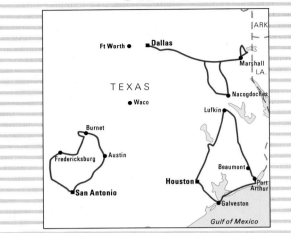

Decades of Hollywood movies and TV series have helped to perpetuate the image of Texas as one vast dusty plain swarming with cattle and slow-talking John Wayne-style cowboys, and dotted with cities of glittering mirror-glass skyscrapers where tough business entrepreneurs like J R Ewing play for high stakes.

This, of course, is the larger-than-life version of Texas, but it is one which even Texans themselves enjoy acting out. They walk around downtown Dallas or Houston, for example, wearing cowboy boots, jeans and wide-brimmed Stetsons; they play the cowboy at the state's many dude ranches and rodeos; and they will dance the Cotton-Eyed Joe or Two Step at a country music honkytonk one night and be seated at the opera or a symphony concert the next.

Self-reliance, getting things done, taking risks, and winning are qualities Texans admire, and these people of action are justifiably proud of their state. Until Alaska joined the Union in 1959, Texas was America's largest state, with 267,339 square miles (692,408 sq km) of territory between the Oklahoma state line on the Red River and the Mexican border on the Rio Grande. Larger than France, Italy or Britain, it was a country in its own right for nine years after Texans won their independence from Mexico in 1836. Texas then became the 28th state of the US, and from the 1840s to the '80s, the Golden Age of the cowboy, vast herds of cattle were driven from its ranches along the legendary Chisholm Trail and others to markets elsewhere in the country. Oil transformed the economy after 1901, building the fortunes of Houston and Dallas — and the rest is history.

Geographically, Texas encompasses terrain of considerable diversity. Behind the long, sandy beaches and islands of the Gulf shoreline, the flat coastal plain extends in an arc from the fertile farmlands, lakes and forests of the Piney Woods region of East Texas to the semitropical croplands near the Mexican border south of San Antonio. Inland, the irrigated wheat prairies and ranches of the Great Plains region stretch north from the Hill Country near Austin to the Oklahoma line. West Texas has the rugged canyon country of the Panhandle around Amarillo and, west of the Pecos River, the dramatic desert and mountain scenery that includes the Guadalupe Mountains and Big Bend National Parks.

Dallas:

Dallas is part of the vast urban 'metroplex' of some 3 million people which has grown along the Trinity River on the plains of north-east Texas. As a business center engrossed in banking, oil and the high-technology industry, Big 'D' has an atmosphere of wealth and sophistication and boasts beautiful residential districts, well-manicured parks, fine shops and restaurants and a flourishing cultural life. Glistening skyscrapers rise above the clean downtown streets, where many of the buildings are linked by underground and elevated walk-ways. Of special interest here is the permanent exhibit called '**The Sixth Floor**' in the former **Texas School Book Depository**, which commemorates the assassination of President John F Kennedy in Dallas in 1963. Nearby are the revitalized West End Historic District, with its shops, restaurants and night spots, and the Arts District, which contains the **Dallas Museum of Art** with its fine pre-Columbian works, and the stunning **Morton H Meyerson Symphony Center**.

Other premier attractions around Dallas include **Southfork Ranch**, the setting of the famous *Dallas* TV series; the cluster of family amuse-

The skyline in Dallas is a study in 20th-century architecture

ment parks west of the city; and the **Stockyards** and outstanding **art museums** of Fort Worth.

Houston:

A cluster of historic pioneer buildings stands today in Houston's downtown **Sam Houston Park**, dwarfed by the surrounding futuristic skyscrapers—an eloquent symbol of this vibrant port city's remarkable development since its modest beginnings by a hot, swampy bayou back in 1836. Now America's fourth largest city, with a metropolitan area population of more than 3 million, Houston has many sightseeing, cultural and entertainment attractions for visitors, and shopping opportunities such as the popular **Galleria** west of downtown. The city has an especially lively performing arts scene, with permanent companies offering ballet, opera, symphony concerts and theater. There are also fine museums, such as the **Museum of Fine Arts**, **Menil Collection** and **Museum of Natural Science**. South of downtown are the **AstroWorld** amusement park and the famous huge **Astrodome** arena, which hosts year-round spectator sports, including Oilers football games, and many other events, such as the exciting Houston Rodeo and Livestock Show every February.

San Antonio:

The downtown **Tower of the Americas** offers marvelous bird's-eye views of this captivating southwest Texas city, founded by the Spaniards on the San Antonio River in 1718. But the city's best-known landmark is the **Alamo**, the old mission where Davy Crockett

Dallas's glass skyscrapers are transformed by night

explore the quaint adobe craft shops and galleries of **La Villita**, where the city began. Other city attractions include the old **San Fernando Cathedral**, **Spanish Governor's Palace** and the colorful **Mexican Market**, or El Mercado.

South of town are the 19th-century homes of the **King William Historic District** and a chain of old

and a band of Texas volunteers were massacred by Mexican forces in the struggle for Texas independence in 1836. Nearby, you can enjoy the festive atmosphere of the **Paseo del Rio**, or River Walk, with its mariachi bands, outdoor cafés, restaurants and shops, and

Spanish missions; north, several impressive art museums and lovely **Brackenridge Park**, where you can see koalas in the fine **San Antonio Zoo**; and west, the showcase of marine animal entertainment at **Sea World of Texas**.

3 days – Approximately 470 miles (751km)

THE PINEY WOODS OF EAST TEXAS

Dallas ● Tyler ● Rusk ● Alto
Nacogdoches ● Kilgore
Marshall ● Karnack and Caddo Lake
Jefferson ● Dallas

With its wide range of attractions, this relatively unknown corner of Texas east of Dallas may come as a pleasant surprise. Much of its appeal derives from the natural beauty of its dense forests, lakes and streams and its rich wildlife. There are also charming towns with lovely old homes and historic sites that tell of the Indians and early Spanish colonists. At each point on the tour something new awaits you—a rose garden, a doll museum, a replica oil-boom town and a delightful steam train—all tucked away amid the timeless scenery.

FOR HISTORY BUFFS

3 For an interesting 30-mile (48km) side trip, follow the old *Camino Real* (**SR 21**) southwest from Alto to Weches. Just outside town, at **Mission Tejas State Park**, you will see a replica of the first Spanish mission in East Texas, built in 1690. Also in the park is the historic **Rice Stagecoach Inn**, of 1828.

ℹ️ Union Station, 400 S Houston Street, Dallas

*For the 98-mile (157km) drive to Tyler, take **US 80** east from downtown Dallas and pick up **I-20** eastbound. At **Exit 556** turn south onto **US 69** to Tyler.*

Tyler, Texas

1 Every September large crowds descend on this manufacturing center and college town to attend the

---

In Rusk, travel as folk did at the turn of the century, choo-chooing on a special excursion

six-day East Texas State Fair, a major livestock event linked to the local agricultural business. Roses, however, are Tyler's best-known product, and they feature in magnificent displays at the 22-acre (9-hectare) **Municipal Rose Garden** on West Front Street. Another popular visitor attraction is **Caldwell Zoo**, designed with children especially in mind. Among the animals on show is a cow, which youngsters can watch being milked. A well-known city landmark is the **Goodman-LeGrand Home**, a stately mansion of 1859 that now houses a museum displaying historic artifacts.

*Drive south on Broadway and **US 69** for 42 miles (67km) through Jacksonville to Rusk.*

Rusk, Texas

2 Highway 69 passes through beautiful rolling forest country. Between the towering pines of **Jim Hogg State Historic Park** and **Rusk State Railroad** is the historic community of Rusk, birthplace of two Texas governors. Here you can walk across the nation's longest footbridge at 546 feet (166m), and enjoy a ride on the antique steam train operated by the **Texas State Railroad** between Rusk State Park and Palestine, 25 miles (40km) away.

*Continue on **US 69** for another 12 miles (19km) to Alto.*

Alto, Texas

3 Where **US 69** crosses the old Spanish *Camino Real*, or Royal Highway (**SR 21**), is the little town of Alto, famous for tomatoes. It is also the gateway to the **Caddoan Mounds State Historic Site**, an ancient Indian site 6 miles (10km) southwest of town on **SR 21**. Here you can see a reconstructed Caddoan Indian dwelling which resembles a beehive, two ceremonial mounds

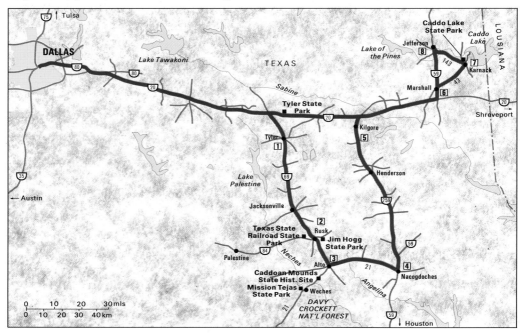

and various exhibits at the Visitor Center. The whole site is thought to date back some 15 centuries.

*From Alto take **SR 21** east for 27 miles (43km) to Nacogdoches.*

Nacogdoches, Texas

4 This charming old city, a paradise for history buffs, was the site of an Indian settlement long before the arrival of the Spaniards. The main gateway to Texas from the east, the city grew at the crossroads of an old

around the realistic dioramas, the boomtown street scene and other fascinating exhibits explaining the oil industry. Downtown, in the block at Main and Commerce Streets nicknamed 'The World's Richest Acre', you can still see one of the 24 derricks that once stood on this site, one of them actually piercing the terrazzo floor of the Kilgore National Bank.

107 South Martin Street

*Continue north on **US 259** for 5 miles (8km) and pick up **I-20***

FOR CHILDREN

Attractions along the itinerary include the **Hudnall Planetarium** and the space vehicle exhibits at **Tyler Junior College** (1); the hands-on learning center in the warehouse at the **Depot Museum and Children's Discovery Center**, at Henderson (4); and the fine doll collection at **Jefferson's Carnegie Library** (8).

Drink in the haunting beauty of nature at Caddo Lake State Park

Indian highway (named the *Calle del Norte* by the Spanish, now North Street) and the Camino Real, which was blazed through the area by the Spaniards in 1691. You can see ancient Indian artifacts excavated from the Washington Square archaeological site on display at the nearby **Old Stone Fort**, a reconstruction of the Spanish trading post built here in 1779. Other historic city landmarks worth seeing date from the 1800s; they include the fine group of buildings at Millard's Crossing; the **Sterne-Hoya Home** (1828), which houses a library; **Oak Grove Cemetery**, with several historic monuments; **Old Nacogdoches University** (1845), now used as a museum of antique furniture and silver; and **Old North Church** (1852), just outside town off **US 59**.

*Follow **US 259** north from Nacogdoches for 59 miles (94km) through Henderson to Kilgore.*

Kilgore, Texas

5 One good reason to visit this oil-producing town is to tour the excellent **East Texas Oil Museum** on Kilgore College campus. You can relive the exciting boom days that followed the discovery of the East Texas oilfield in 1930 as you wander

eastbound for 32 miles (51km) to Marshall.

Marshall, Texas

6 As a wealthy manufacturing center back in the 19th century, Marshall played an important part in keeping the Confederacy supplied with ammunition and other equipment during the Civil War—hence the **Confederate Monument** on the lawn of the courthouse. You will learn more about such aspects of the city's past if you stop by the **Harrison County Historical Society Museum**. Also worth visiting are the 1896 **Ginocchio Hotel** and 1877 **Allen House Museum** in the three-block Ginocchio National Historic District downtown. Another prominent city landmark open for tours is **Maplecroft**, an impressive Italianate mansion built by a leading Texas family in 1870 and now officially designated the **Starr Family State Historic Site**. But don't leave Marshall without seeing the fine collection of 1,200 dolls and other toys at the **Franks Doll Museum** on Grand Avenue or visiting the famous **Marshall Pottery** southeast of town. Here you can watch the potters at work and see their creations in the showrooms.

*From Marshall take **SR 43** northeast for 15 miles (24km) to Karnack and Caddo Lake.*

BACK TO NATURE

If you thought Texas was just one great expanse of grass, the **Piney Woods** of East Texas will be a pleasant surprise with its junglelike forests of loblolly pines and all sorts of hardwood trees, often festooned with Spanish moss, vines and creepers and shading a dense undergrowth of dogwood, sumac, sassafras, ferns and countless wildflowers. This 'Garden of Eden' is home to white-tailed deer, squirrels, wild turkeys, barred owls, Acadian flycatchers and pine warblers.

RECOMMENDED WALKS

Numerous hiking and nature trails crisscross the Piney Woods region of East Texas: for example in **Tyler State Park** (1), in **Jim Hogg State Park**, near Rusk (2), and beside **Caddo Lake** (7). You can also stroll through the pleasant gardens at the **Goodman-LeGrand House** and the **Rose Garden and Park** at Tyler (1).

Jefferson's House of the Seasons, with frescos and stained glass

SCENIC ROUTES

Lovely forest scenery awaits you around every corner along this tour of the Piney Woods region. The drive along **US 69** through Cherokee County between Tyler and Alto is exceptionally enjoyable, with vistas of hills, woodlands and lakes bordering the highway. For especially fine views of the countryside, stop at Love's Lookout Park just north of Jacksonville.

SPECIAL TO ...

8 Jefferson hasn't totally spurned the railroad, for on display is the luxurious private railroad car used by tycoon Jay Gould. It is across the street from the Excelsior House hotel, in whose register Gould left his prediction of 'the end of Jefferson' when townsfolk rejected his railroad proposals. It is a nice touch of irony.

Karnack and Caddo Lake, Texas

7 Along the highway just south of Karnack you will pass the birthplace of Mrs Lyndon B Johnson, a fine, two-story brick house dating from before the Civil War (it is not, however, open for tours). North of Karnack you will come to **Caddo Lake**, shrouded in parts by lush, moss-draped forest and an atmosphere of mystery. Mississippi steamboats once plied its waters on their way up Big Cypress Bayou. Access to the lake is by **Caddo Lake State Park**, where you will find facilities for camping, boating and fishing, and hiking and nature trails.

*From Caddo Lake follow **SR 143** west for about 11 miles (18km) to Jefferson.*

Jefferson, Texas

8 In the historic little community of Jefferson, time almost seems to have stood still since its citizens refused to let businessman Jay Gould bring a railroad through the town more than a century ago. Before then it was a flourishing river port on Big Cypress Bayou, with an ironworks, a lumber industry, an ice plant and gas street lighting. With no railroad, however, Jefferson failed to develop, so today you can see it more or less as it was. The town is packed with historic homes and bed-and-breakfast inns, most of them listed on the National Register of Historic Places. Many are regularly open for tours, others only during the annual Historical Pilgrimage in early May. One of the most famous is **Excelsior House**, a beautifully furnished old hotel, where many prominent people have stayed, including Ulysses S Grant and Irish writer Oscar Wilde. When you have seen the exhibits depicting Jefferson's colorful past at the **Historical Society Museum** on Lafayette Street, take a 45-minute narrated tour around the streets in a horse-drawn surrey. Then cast your mind back to the days of the steamboats while enjoying a cruise along **Big Cypress Bayou** departing from Polk Street Bridge landing.

ⓘ 223 West Austin Street

*Follow **US 59** south from Jefferson for 19 miles (30km) through Marshall and pick up **I-20** westbound for another 150 miles (240km) to Dallas.*

Dallas – Tyler	**98 (157)**
Tyler – Rusk	**42 (67)**
Rusk – Alto	**12 (19)**
Alto – Nacogdoches	**27 (43)**
Nacogdoches – Kilgore	**59 (94)**
Kilgore – Marshall	**37 (59)**
Marshall – Karnack	**15 (24)**
Karnack – Jefferson	**11 (18)**
Jefferson – Dallas	**169 (270)**

Take a narrated tour of Galveston Bay aboard the triple-deck 'Colonel'

ⓘ 3300 Main Street, Houston

Follow the Gulf Freeway (I-45) south from downtown Houston for about 61 miles (98km) to Galveston.

Galveston, Texas

1 This historic port city, at the eastern end of Galveston Island, boasts excellent beaches and a growing number of visitor attractions. The most enjoyable way to see them is to ride the Galveston Flyer trolley or the Treasure Island Tour Train. A major city attraction is the revitalized **Strand National Historic District**, the 19th-century commercial area once known as the 'Wall Street of the West', which now bustles with shops, restaurants, pubs, galleries and even a candy factory. Other historic landmarks are the **Bishop's Palace** of 1886, the opulent **Ashton Villa**, built in 1859, and the fascinating **Railroad Museum**, which incorporates the former Santa Fe Depot. Along Seawall Boulevard performing dolphins and other marine animals top the bill at **Sea-Arama Marine World**, while on the waterfront you can tour the restored 1877 sailing ship *Elissa*, now a museum of seafaring technology, and board the paddlewheeler *Colonel* for a two-hour cruise around Galveston Bay.

ⓘ 2106 Seawall Boulevard

Take the free ferry across the ship channel between Galveston and Port Bolivar and follow SR 87 along the Bolivar Peninsula for 77 miles (123km) to Port Arthur.

Port Arthur, Texas

2 This important oil-refining center lies inland on Sabine Lake and is linked to the Gulf by a broad ship channel. You will see the tankers pass by from **Sabine Pass Battleground State Historical Park**, south of Port Arthur, which commemorates a Confederate Civil War victory. You can discover more about the battle and local history at the **Port Arthur Historical Museum** downtown. Also of interest is the **Pompeian Villa**, a mansion built in grand style in 1900 by a local industrialist and now open to visitors.

Follow US 69/287 from downtown Port Arthur for 20 miles (32km) to Beaumont.

Beaumont, Texas

3 Now a major industrial city and port on the Neches River, Beaumont was suddenly transformed from a small logging community when an oil rig at Spindletop struck black gold in 1901. Exhibits recording those times are displayed at **Spindletop Museum** on the Lamar University campus, while nearby, at the **Gladys City-Lucas Gusher Monument**, there is an excellent re-creation of the old town in the early days of the oil boom. Also worth visiting are the **John Jay French Trading Post** of 1845; the richly furnished **McFaddin-Ward House** of 1906, with its silver, china, porcelain and oriental rug

THE UPPER GULF COAST & BIG THICKET

Houston ● Galveston ● Port Arthur ● Beaumont ● Woodville Lufkin ● Houston

This break from the bustle of Houston takes you on a relaxing tour of the East Texas Gulf Coast and the Big Thicket forest region. Along the shoreline you will see fine sandy beaches, fishing piers, the historic seaside city of Galveston and modern oil refineries that form a bizarre backdrop to teeming wildlife refuges. Inland you will drive through old logging towns nestled in dense forests, where you can look for wild animals or rare plants as you walk the quiet trails. And, for something completely different, you can enjoy the colorful activities at an Indian reservation.

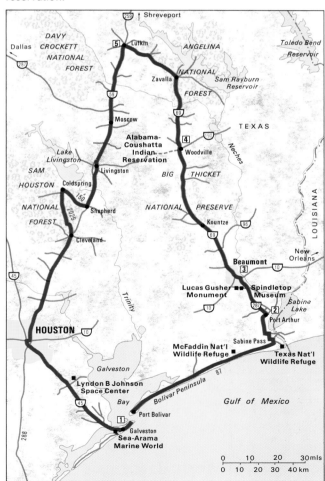

FOR HISTORY BUFFS

5 In the quaint Old Town area of Coldspring is the **San Jacinto County Museum**, on Slade Street, housed in a restored jail of about 1887 and complete with hangman's drop, jailer's quarters and cell block. Exhibits such as household objects, old photographs and farming implements depict the settlers' life.

FOR CHILDREN

In addition to the Lyndon B Johnson Space Center (NASA) and Galveston's beaches, places of interest to kids include the **Edison Plaza Museum** at Beaumont (3), with its exhibits of scientific inventions from Edison's time to the present and into the future, and **Lufkin City Zoo**, which has, a miniature railroad (5).

BACK TO NATURE

2 Some of Texas' rich wildlife can be viewed at the **McFaddin National Wildlife Refuge** near Port Arthur, which has a large population of American alligators. The refuge at nearby Texas Point contains great numbers of shorebirds and waterfowl. In the lush forests inland look out for the pileated woodpecker and such exotic plants as wild orchids and insectivorous pitcher plants.

RECOMMENDED WALKS

5 Opportunities for walking include the short **Moscow Trail**, just south of Moscow on **US 59**; nature trails beside **Lake Livingston**, just west of Livingston; and hiking trails in **Sam Houston National Forest**, south of Coldspring and northwest of Cleveland.

SCENIC ROUTES

Take any highway out of **Woodville** and you will enjoy a scenic drive through rolling forest country punctuated by streams, bubbling springs and colorful wildflowers. Another scenic route follows **SR 150** and **Route 2025** from Coldspring to the Double Lake Recreation Area.

SPECIAL TO ...

The NASA space complex, southeast of Houston off **I-45**, offers the new Disney-planned **Space Center Houston**. Here you can experience flying in space, watch real flights on giant screens and see spacecraft and other exciting exhibits.

collections; and the **Babe Didrikson Zaharias Memorial Museum**, containing golfing trophies and other memorabilia of the famous American sportswoman who was one of the world's greatest athletes.

*Continue north on **US 69/287** for 62 miles (99km) through Kountze to Woodville in the Big Thicket.*

Woodville, Texas

4 The Big Thicket National Preserve is a vast area of dense woodlands, marshes, bayous and streams containing a rich variety of wildlife and exotic plants. It extends north from Beaumont in 12 units penetrated by nature and canoe trails. For details stop at the Information Station on **Route 420** just north of Kountze. In the midst of the area is the small logging town of Woodville,

Big Thicket: a unique diversity of habitat and life forms

where you can visit the **Shivers Library and Museum** at the restored Victorian home of a former Texas governor. West of town on **US 190** is the fascinating **Heritage Garden**, with its outdoor historic exhibits depicting Texas life. The **Alabama-Coushatta Indian Reservation**, further on, is the oldest in the state; its excellent visitor program includes craft-making displays, swamp tours, miniature railroad rides, and Indian

dances on weekends in fall and spring.

*Continue north from Woodville on **US 69** for 51 miles (82km) through Zavalla to Lufkin.*

Lufkin, Texas

5 This important manufacturing and logging center city lies in the heart of the East Texas Piney Woods region, where the **Davy Crockett** and **Angelina National Forests** and **Sam Rayburn Reservoir** provide facilities for camping, hiking, swimming, hunting and fishing. Worth a visit in Lufkin is the **Forestry Museum**, which has botanical exhibits, an old railroad and depot and sawmill steam engines, and the **Museum of East Texas**, with changing art exhibits, a general store and the Angelina Room containing porcelain, china and other artifacts belonging to early Lufkin residents.

*From Lufkin follow **US 59** south for 62 miles (99km) to Shepherd. Make a 28-mile (45km) detour west on **SR 150** through Coldspring, then south on **Route 2025**, and rejoin **US 59** near Cleveland. Continue south for 43 miles (69km) to Houston.*

Houston – Galveston **61 (98)**
Galveston – Port Arthur **83 (133)**
Port Arthur – Beaumont **20 (32)**
Beaumont – Woodville **62 (99)**
Woodville – Lufkin **51 (82)**
Lufkin – Houston **133 (213)**

Cool viewing from a boat taxi on San Antonio's downtown River Walk

ℹ 317 Alamo Plaza, San Antonio

Pick up the Pan Am Expressway (I-35/US 81) northbound from downtown San Antonio and continue for 36 miles (58km) to New Braunfels.

New Braunfels, Texas

1 There is a strong German flavor to New Braunfels, established by German settlers on the Guadalupe River back in 1845. It is especially evident during the colorful 10-day Wurstfest celebration held every November to honor the German sausage. You will notice it, too, in the architecture of historic buildings like the **Baetge House** and the **Lindheimer Home**, built in the 1850s. Take a drive around the historic Gruene district, with its old homes, shops, galleries and 1880 **beer hall**; visit the **Museum of Texas Handmade Furniture**, and tour the exhibits on pioneer life at the **Sophienburg Museum**. For outdoor recreation, you will find good facilities for golf, boating and swimming in beautiful **Landa Park**, while on the river you can enjoy canoeing, rafting and float trips. Not to be missed, however, before leaving New Braunfels, are the wonders of **Natural Bridge Caverns**, some 17 miles (27km) southwest of town.

Continue north on I-35/US 81 for 17 miles (27km) to San Marcos.

San Marcos, Texas

2 This city was laid out for Anglo-American settlers in 1851 in an idyllic setting beside a crystal-clear river fed by natural springs. The site is now occupied by the **Aquarena Springs** family entertainment complex, complete with glass-bottom boats,

THE TEXAS HILL COUNTRY

San Antonio • New Braunfels • San Marcos • Austin • Burnet and Lake Buchanan • Johnson City and Lyndon B Johnson National Historical Park • Fredericksburg Kerrville • Bandera • San Antonio

If you have ever dreamed of riding the range, cowboy-style, with a herd of Texas Longhorns, this tour may just have the answer. Close to San Antonio and Austin, the state capital, is the scenic Hill Country. It is a land of limestone hills dotted with gnarled trees and wildflowers, of canyons and caverns, sparkling streams and green valleys and historic communities where folk still speak German, enjoy western music and dance the Cotton-eyed Joe. This is where President Lyndon B Johnson had his own spread and where you, too, can sample the outdoor life at the ranches of Kerrville and Bandera.

FOR HISTORY BUFFS

3 Austin has many special places of interest to history buffs, including the 50-year-old **Treaty Oak** on Baylor Street, beneath which agreements with local Indians were made; the home of the writer O Henry on E 5th Street; and the **Elisabet Ney Museum**, which houses sculptures of the famous German immigrant artist at her studio on E 44th Street.

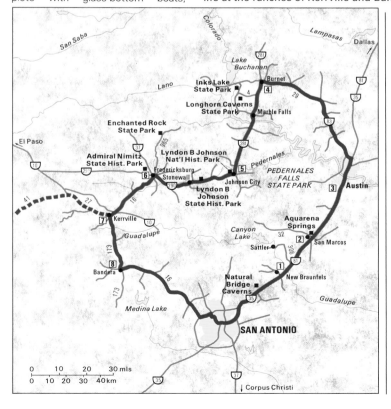

FOR CHILDREN

Of special interest to children on the tour are the **Schlitterbahn Water Park** at New Braunfels (1) and the animals at the **Wildlife Wilderness** and the **Natural Bridge Wildlife Ranch** west of town; exciting rides and petting animals at **Wonder World**, San Marcos (2); and the old autos and wax figures of Hollywood stars featured at the **Classic Car Showcase and Wax Museum** at Kerrville (7).

BACK TO NATURE

3 Among the prolific wildflowers that color the Texas Hill Country through the seasons are the bluebonnet (the state flower), Indian blanket and Mexican hat. Giant cypress trees hug the streams, while live oaks and cedars shade the hillsides. Wild animals that frequent this natural paradise include white-tailed deer, wild goats, coyotes, wild boars and armadillos. You may also see bald eagles, golden eagles, wild turkeys, great blue herons and perhaps even roadrunners or a rare golden-cheeked warbler.

RECOMMENDED WALKS

Special places for a stroll include the picturesque **San Marcos River Walkway** at San Marcos (2); lovely **Zilker Park**, location of the popular Barton Springs swimming hole, at Austin (3); the trails in **Inks Lake State Park**, near Burnet (4); and **Pedernales Falls State Park**, near Johnson City (5).

submarine theater shows, sky rides, alligator pits, historic buildings, Old West village and many other visitor attractions. As a contrast, take a stroll or drive around the Belvin Street Historic District, with its beautiful 19th-century homes and shady live oaks, and you will see the other side of San Marcos's appeal.

Continue north on I-35/US 81 for 30 miles (48km) to Austin (Exit 233 for the free parking lot on West Riverside Drive).

Austin, Texas

3 The Lone Star State's capital, a city of fine shops and a thriving cultural and entertainment center, stands on the Guadalupe River, its skyline pierced by the unmistakable shapes of the pink-granite Capitol and the Tower of the University of Texas. Leave your car at the free parking lot on West Riverside Drive and take a green 'Dillo (Armadillo) trolley to see the main downtown sights. In addition to the **Capitol**, you should see the **Governor's Mansion**; the **Old Bakery** and **Emporium** and **Old Paramount Theater** on Congress Avenue; and the revitalized center of city life, historic **Sixth Street** (Old Pecan Street), with its shops, drugstores, restaurants, bars, night spots and street entertainers. Best reached by car are the historic **French Legation**, the only building erected by a foreign government in Texas, established in 1841 when Texas was an independent republic; and on the University of Texas campus town, the **Lyndon B Johnson Presidential Library and Museum** and the **Harry Ransom Center**, whose art treasures include a copy of the historic Gutenberg Bible.

i 901 West Riverside Drive

Follow US 183 north for about 29 miles (49km), then take SR 29 west for 23 miles (37km) to Burnet and the Lake Buchanan area.

Burnet and Lake Buchanan, Texas

4 Make a stop at Burnet to see the historic exhibits at old **Fort**

Originally called Waterloo, the capital was renamed Austin in 1839

Croghan. The museum here preserves a variety of artifacts, including antique saddles and pianos, while in the grounds are eight restored 19th-century buildings. Then drive on to explore the area around Lake Buchanan. The lake lies amid the rugged scenery of the Texas Hill Country, the highest of the seven manmade Highland Lakes along the Colorado River northwest of Austin. Visitor attractions in the area include facilities for swimming, boating and fishing at **Black Rock Park** and **Inks Lake State Park**; the awesome **Longhorn Cavern** on Park Road 4; and the 2½-hour **Vanishing Texas River Cruise**, during which you will see towering cliffs, water-falls and Texas wildlife.

From Burnet, take US 281 south for 37 miles (59km) to Johnson City and on to Lyndon B Johnson National Historical Park.

Johnson City and Lyndon B Johnson National Historical Park, Texas

5 Dedicated to the memory of the 36th president, this popular visitor attraction has two separate units: one in Johnson City, the other at Stonewall, 16 miles (26km) west along the Pedernales River valley on US 290. Stop first at the Visitor Center in Johnson City for a guided tour of the president's boyhood home and his grand-parents' homestead (the **Johnson Settlement**).

Near Stonewall make another stop at the **LBJ National Historical Park**, where you can see native Texas animals, historic frontier buildings, and costumed interpreters re-enacting German pioneer life at the **Sauer Beckmann Farmstead**. From the Visitor Center a free National Parks Service bus will take you on a tour of President Johnson's birthplace, boyhood school, Texas White House and ranch and his grave in the family cemetery.

Continue west on US 290 for 30 miles (48km) to Fredericksburg.

Fredericksburg, Texas

6 Established by German settlers in 1846, this picturesque old town, has a distinct German atmosphere

LBJ's boyhood home, restored to its 1920s appearance

and many German-style buildings in its National Historic District. Be sure to see the old **Vereins Kirche**, a rebuilt eight-sided church, **the Pioneer Museum**, and the tiny stone 'Sunday Houses' used as weekend town homes by pioneer farmers. The town's best-known visitor attraction, however, is the **Admiral Nimitz State Historic Park**, dedicated to the people who served with the admiral in World War II. The complex consists of the Museum of the Pacific War, Garden of Peace, Art Gallery and displays of guns, tanks and aircraft.

ⓘ 112 W Main Street

From Fredericksburg follow SR 16 south for 22 miles (35km) to Kerrville.

Kerrville, Texas

7 Nestled beside the Guadalupe River in the heart of the Hill Country, Kerrville attracts large numbers of visitors, both young and old, to its annual summer camps and to guest ranches offering a taste of traditional cowboy life, with horseback riding, hayrides and cookouts. A popular destination is the Y O Ranch—30 miles (48km) west via **Routes 27** and **41**—with its Longhorn cattle and its collection of native Texas animals, zebras, ostriches and giraffes. Among Kerrville's other attractions are its music festivals and its museums, including the fine **Cowboy Artists of America Museum** just south of town. This is a showcase for contemporary cowboy artists and exhibits permanent and changing displays of paintings and sculpture on Western subjects.

ⓘ 1200 Sidney Baker Street

Follow SR 173 south for 26 miles (42km) to Bandera.

Bandera, Texas

8 At Bandera, a small Hill Country town that claims to be the 'Cowboy Capital of the World', you can sample the outdoor life of the Old West at the area's many working and guest ranches, watch thrilling rodeos and join in country-and-western dancing on sawdust floors at honky-tonks like **Arkey Blue's Silver Dollar**. You can also look back at pioneer life as you tour the exhibits at the **Frontier Times Museum** with its Old West relics and the **Old Jail Museum and Art Gallery's** exhibits of local history.

From Bandera take SR 16 for 50 miles (80km) to San Antonio.

San Antonio – New Braunfels	**36**	**(58)**
New Braunfels – San Marcos	**17**	**(27)**
San Marcos – Austin	**30**	**(48)**
Austin – Burnet	**52**	**(83)**
Burnet – Johnson City	**55**	**(88)**
Johnson City – Fredericksburg	**30**	**(48)**
Fredericksburg – Kerrville	**22**	**(35)**
Kerrville – Bandera	**26**	**(42)**
Bandera – San Antonio	**50**	**(80)**

SCENIC ROUTES

There are many beautiful stretches of highway in the Texas Hill Country. Highlights on this tour include short drives along **Route 306** north of New Braunfels and the 'Devil's Backbone', **Route 32** west of San Marcos; **Route 2341** to the Vanishing Texas River Cruise, east of Lake Buchanan; roads off **US 281** in the Marble Falls area; the roads to the Y O Ranch and to Enchanted Rock north of Fredericksburg; and **SR 173** between Kerrville and Bandera.

SPECIAL TO . . .

To make your visit to the Texas Hill Country complete, add the following things to do and see to your plans: footprints of prehistoric monsters at Dinosaur Flats, near Sattler, north of New Braunfels (1); nine days of parades, water fun, races and other events at Austin's tremendous Aqua Festival in July and August (3); the Easter Fires and pageant at Fredericksburg; and atmospheric and spectacular Enchanted Rock, off scenic Route 965 north of Fredericksburg. (6)

THE MOUNTAIN WEST

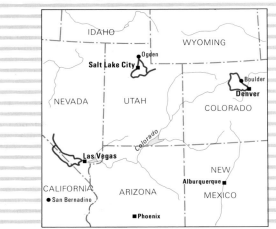

The World Trade Center in Denver

Whether you call it the Old West or even the Wild West, this is that ruggedly romantic part of America which decades of Hollywood Western movies have taught us to associate with stagecoaches, wagon trains, leather-faced cowboys and dusty cattle drives, saloon brawls and shoot-outs, Indian ambushes and US Cavalry rescues.

Geographically, the Mountain West covers an immense tract of territory stretching from Canada to Arizona and New Mexico and from the Rocky Mountains to the Sierra Nevada of California. Along the eastern edge, the Rockies rise from the Great Plains just west of the gateway city of Denver in a series of spectacular forested ranges that run from Montana to New Mexico, the highest peaks soaring above 14,000 feet (4,267m) in Colorado. Scenery of indescribable beauty is encompassed in Glacier, Grand Teton and Rocky Mountain National Parks, while in other places, like Yellowstone National Park, hot-water springs, geysers and mud pools provide dramatic evidence of continuing volcanic activity.

West of the Rockies, in western Colorado and in Utah and Nevada, a vast arid wilderness extends across rugged plateaus, parallel mountain ridges, blazing desert basins and shimmering salt flats, where nature has carved immense flat-topped mesas and buttes, towering rock pinnacles and precipitous canyons. Utah's magnificent national parks and Monuments are a showcase of the region's amazing natural wonders.

The only major centers of population in this sparsely inhabited part of the Mountain West are Salt Lake City, Utah, and Las Vegas, Nevada, although cliff dwellings in places like Mesa Verde National Park, Colorado, show that Indian peoples lived in the area long before the arrival of the white man. The first Americans to see the wonders of the Mountain West were the explorers, mountain men, fur trappers and traders who wandered through the area in the early 1800s. They paved the way for the exodus of pioneer wagon trains along the Oregon and California Trails to the west coast in the 1840s and '50s. Gold and silver strikes across the region brought floods of prospectors, miners and all sorts to the booming new camps, which soon became ghost towns as the precious ores ran out. Law and order was primitive, and the Wild West was born.

Denver:
A cluster of futuristic skyscrapers towers above the 'Mile High City' of Denver, an attractive, clean city lying at the foot of the Rocky Mountains on Colorado's Great Plains. Born in the 'Pikes Peak or Bust' gold rush of 1859, Denver prospered as the gateway to the booming mining communities in the west. Today it is the main business and cultural center of the entire Mountain West region, with a metropolitan area population approaching 2 million.

Among the city's many attractions are the shops of 16th Street Mall and Larimer Square; outstanding museums, such as the **Denver Art Museum**, with its fine collection of American Indian art, and the excellent **Museum of Natural History** in City Park; and the busy nightlife and entertainment, including the theatrical productions and concerts at the **Denver Arts Center**. Major sightseeing highlights include the gold-domed **State Capitol**, the fascinating **US Mint**, the **Denver Botanic Gardens**, and such historic buildings as the **Molly Brown House**, the Victorian home of the unsinkable survivor of the *Titanic* disaster.

Salt Lake City:

Salt Lake City was founded by Mormon pioneers led by Brigham Young at the end of their great trek west to Utah in 1847. It lies 4,300 feet (1,312m) above sea level between the Great Salt Lake and the towering Wasatch Mountains to the east. The heart of the city is Temple Square, a walled precinct containing the main buildings of the Mormon faith, including the Gothic-style **Temple** and the **Tabernacle** where the famed Mormon choir sings in rehearsal Thursday evenings.

Nearby are other Mormon buildings, including the historic **Beehive House**, Young's official home; the **Utah State Capitol**; the **Pioneer Memorial Museum**; and the ultramodern **Salt Palace Center** which is used for a wide variety of cultural and sports events. Other visitor attractions include the **Trolley Square shopping center** and, east of town, **Pioneer State Park**, which contains a reconstructed Mormon settlement and the imposing monument commemorating the Mormons' arrival in Utah.

Las Vegas:

Surrounded by the awesome desert scenery of southwest Nevada, the gaudy, neon-lit resort city of Las Vegas, home to half of Nevada's population, has been a mecca for gamblers since the 1930s. Fronted by glittering billboards, fantasy-style hotel-casinos like **Caesar's Palace, Circus-Circus** and the **Aladdin** line the famous 3½-mile (5.6km) boulevard known as 'The Strip' and the busy streets of the downtown Casino Center, often labeled 'Glitter Gulch'. To tempt you inside, there is non-stop gambling at slots, roulette, blackjack, craps, poker, baccarat and keno; gargantuan drinks bars and subsidized food buffets; and spectacular entertainment featuring top-name show-business stars, unusual specialty acts, and lavishly costumed (and topless) dancing girls.

The 'Entertainment Capital of the World' also has excellent golf courses, cultural attractions that include theaters, concerts and museums, spectator sports at **Cashman Field**, the spectacular Helldorado festival every May—and lots of little wedding chapels offering instant wedding ceremonies for a fee. Further afield are the recreational facilities of **Lake Mead**, above the impressive **Hoover Dam**. One of the largest artificial lakes in the world by volume, Lake Mead is 115 miles (185km) long and averages 200 feet (60m) in depth.

THE ROCKY MOUNTAIN WONDERLAND

Denver ● Boulder ● Estes Park ● Rocky Mountain National Park ● Granby ● Winter Park and Empire ● Georgetown ● Idaho Springs ● Central City Golden ● Denver

One of America's great scenic experiences is the drive along the magnificent Trail Ridge Road around the 12,000-foot (3,600m) peaks of Colorado's Rocky Mountain National Park, northwest of Denver. Amid the breathtaking mountain scenery you will also see the university town of Boulder, the attractions of lovely Estes Park and the ski resort town of Winter Park. And in the 'Gold Circle' of old mining towns up Clear Creek—Empire, Central City, Idaho Springs and Georgetown—you will step back in time to the riproaring boom days that followed the discovery of gold.

Estes Park, where bagpipes resound during the annual Scottish Highland Festival in September

ℹ 225 W Colfax Street, Denver

*From downtown Denver pick up **I-25** northbound, and at **Exit 217** take **US 36** northwest for 25 miles (40km) to Boulder.*

Boulder, Colorado

1 The pretty town of Boulder lies at the edge of the Rockies overlooked by the red-rock cliffs of the Flatirons. Four blocks of its old Victorian downtown district now form **Pearl Street Mall**, a lively pedestrian area of boutiques, art galleries and outdoor cafés. Most of the year Boulder is home to the 20,000 students of the University of Colorado, who periodically enliven the town with events like the zany Kinetic Conveyance Sculpture Race in May or the more dignified Shakespeare Festival, in July and August. If you are interested in the Old West, drop in at the **Leanin' Tree Museum of Western Art** on Longbow Drive, where you can see some fine paintings and sculptures by contemporary artists. If you are more scientifically minded, you might learn something about the weather and solar astronomy at the **National Center for Atmospheric Research** on Table Mesa Drive.

ℹ 2440 Pearl Street

*Continue north on **US 36** for about 38 miles (61km) through Lyons to Estes Park.*

Dividing the continent, the majestic Rockies are the source of several major rivers of the West

FOR HISTORY BUFFS

8 Among the fascinating buildings you can visit on a tour of Central City's historic streets is the **Thomas-Billings Home** at 209 Eureka Street. It stood fixed in a silent time warp for some 70 years after being closed up around 1916, and now you can see it just as it was, furnishings and all, when it was lived in all those years ago.

FOR CHILDREN

9 By the time you reach Golden the kids may be tired with all the sights and adventures on the tour. But for a final fling of fun you should visit **Heritage Square**, off **US 40** south of town, a family entertainment and shopping park designed as a Victorian village. There are lots of rides, a Ferris wheel and the exciting Alpine Slide.

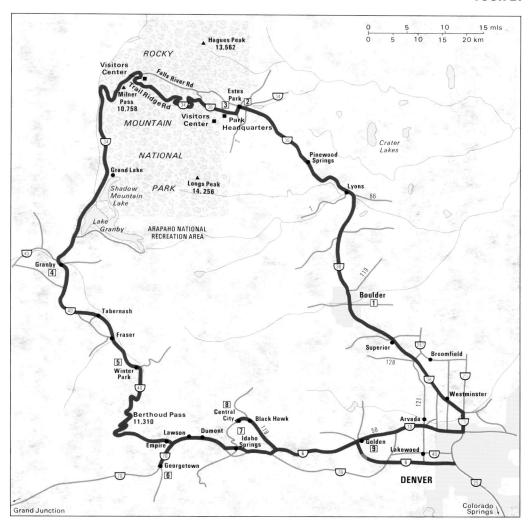

Estes Park, Colorado

2 This popular resort village, the location of the old **Stanley Hotel**, a noted landmark, lies amid beautiful forest-clad mountain scenery at the eastern gateway to **Rocky Mountain National Park**. Visitors flock here in the summer to enjoy the shops and fine restaurants along quaint Main Street and the area's varied attractions. You can tour the **Estes Park Area Historical Museum**, go horseback riding at one of the local guest ranches and take the exciting **Aerial Tramway** to the top of 8,700-foot (2,652m) Prospect Mountain for magnificent views of the surrounding peaks and valleys.

*Follow **US 36** west for about 2 miles (3km) to Rocky Mountain National Park.*

Rocky Mountain National Park, Colorado

3 This scenic mountain wonderland is one of America's most impressive spectacles. Clustered within its 414-square-mile (1,071sq km) area are more than 18 rugged peaks towering way above 13,000 feet (3,962m). To appreciate its grandeur, see the orientation slide program at Park Headquarters before starting the 50-mile (80km) drive along Trail Ridge Road. Open only in summer, this famed—and sometimes busy—highway winds above the timberline across the Continental Divide at

12,183 feet (3,713m), offering breathtaking mountain vistas, with glaciers and snowfields, cold alpine lakes, streams and waterfalls, wildflower meadows, stands of aspen and pine and perhaps a glimpse of the elusive wildlife. After a break at the Fall River Pass restaurant, turn south down the Kawuneeche (Colorado River) Valley and leave the park at the yachting and boating center of Grand Lake.

*From Grand Lake follow **US 34** south for 16 miles (26km) to Granby.*

Granby, Colorado

4 Guest ranches, rodeos, hunting and fishing are the main visitor attractions of the area around Granby, at the start of the scenic drive up the Fraser River valley to Winter Park. This former railroad center is now the western gateway to the **Arapaho National Recreation Area**. Lake Granby, 3 miles (5km) north on **US 34**, provides irrigation water for northeastern Colorado, and tours of Granby Pumping Plant are available Memorial Day to Labor Day.

*Take **US 40** south for 46 miles (74km) through Winter Park and over Berthoud Pass to Empire.*

Winter Park and Empire, Colorado

5 The winter ski resort of Winter Park draws visitors in summer with its fine restaurants, weekend rodeos and art and jazz festivals. Beyond

RECOMMENDED WALKS

Many hiking trails cross the spectacular landscapes of Rocky Mountain National Park. Two of the shorter trails are the **Tundra World Nature Trail**, where you will get magnificent panoramic views of the Continental Divide; and the half-mile (1km) walk along **East Inlet**, east of Grand Lake, to impressive Adams Falls. You can get details of routes at the park's visitor center.

SCENIC ROUTES

Extraspecial sections of this outstanding scenic tour include the mountain-top **Trail Ridge Road** in Rocky Mountain National Park (3); **US 40** over Berthoud Pass (4); and the rugged **US 6** route through Clear Creek Canyon west of Golden (9). For a special adventure, however, take the unpaved, twisting, wild scenic route from Central City (8) to Idaho Springs on the appropriately named 'Oh My God Road' (Virginia Canyon). It is not for the faint-hearted!

SPECIAL TO . . .

8 Central City's glorious past included a colorful establishment run by Madam Lou Bunch that was very well patronized in its heyday. In June every year grateful citizens honor her memory with a day-long celebration that features a costume parade, bed races down Main Street and a culminating grand Madam and Miners Ball.

Berthoud Pass, where the highway climbs over the Continental Divide at 11,310 feet (3,447m), is Empire, where you can see the restored 19th-century **Peck House**, Colorado's oldest hotel still in operation.

*From Empire pick up **I-70** southbound for 4 miles (6km) to Georgetown.*

Georgetown, Colorado

6 In the 1860s Georgetown, on Clear Creek, blossomed as a silver-mining town and soon became Colorado's third largest city. Justifying its tag as 'Silver Queen of the Rockies', it quickly acquired the usual lavish Victorian houses, hotels, gambling saloons, restaurants and the obligatory opera house. It also had a first-rate fire brigade, so, unlike other wood-built mining towns of the time, it suffered no major conflagrations. What you will see today is a quaint little town with more than 200 restored Victorian buildings lining its atmospheric streets. Don't miss the **Hamill House** (with its delightful six-seater privy), and the famous **Hotel de Paris**, built by the eccentric French restaurateur Louis du Puy, in 1875. An irresistible attraction is the exciting ride on the narrow-gauge **Georgetown Loop Railroad** to the nearby old mining town of Silver Plume, an excursion which also includes a fascinating mine tour.

*Backtrack on **I-70** and continue east to Idaho Springs.*

Idaho Springs, Colorado

7 Named for its hot mineral springs, the Victorian resort town of Idaho Springs, on Clear Creek, was the site of Colorado's first big gold strike in 1859. A monument southwest of Chicago Creek Road marks the spot. More than 200 mines in the area still produce gold, lead, silver, zinc, tungsten and molybdenum. In summer you can follow the old-timers and pan for gold yourself on a tour of the **Argo Mine and Mill**.

*From Idaho Springs follow **US 6** northeast for about 3 miles (5km), then take **SR 119***

northwest for 6 miles (10km) through Black Hawk to Central City.

Central City, Colorado

8 In the same year as the 1859 gold strike at Idaho Springs, the discovery of a rich gold-bearing lode in the mountains created the new boom town of Central City, 'the richest square mile on earth'. Despite a big fire in 1874, the town survived more or less intact and is now a National Historic Landmark. Its colorful Victorian streets are lined with old saloons with swing doors, boisterous music halls, elegant hotels, little museums, fine restaurants and shops. Well-known landmarks are the splendid old **Opera House**, built in 1878 and still offering a summer season of opera, and, next door, the 1872 **Teller House** hotel, where you will see the famous 'Face on the Barroom Floor', painted in 1936. There is also a narrow-gauge railroad. Despite the Victorian atmosphere, however, Central City is no dull museum. Colorful festivals and events draw the crowds throughout the year, such as the internationally known Jazz Festival in August.

*Backtrack through Black Hawk on **SR 119** and continue on **US 6** for another 12 miles (19km) through Clear Creek Canyon to Golden.*

Golden, Colorado

9 At the edge of the Rocky Mountain foothills lies the city of Golden, Colorado's first territorial capital of the 1860s and gateway to the gold-fields, and now perhaps best known as the home of Coors beers. You can visit the famous brewery—one of the largest in the world—and sample the products while touring the nearby Historic District along 12th Street. Other places of interest are the **Pioneer Museum**, the **Foothills Art Center** and the **Geology Museum and National Earthquake Center** at the prestigious Colorado School of Mines. Two of the most popular attractions, however, are just outside town. To the west, atop Lookout Mountain via the Lariat Loop Trail, is the **Buffalo Bill Memorial Museum**, with a large observation deck, and the famous old frontiersman's grave. To the north, on W 44th Avenue, there is the excellent **Colorado Railroad Museum**, with its impressive collection of historic locomotives and passenger cars.

*From Golden follow **US 6** (W 6th Avenue) or **US 40** (W Colfax Avenue) eastbound for about 12 miles (19km) to downtown Denver.*

From early days Central City, relatively staid for a mining town, has had an interest in the arts

Temple Square has Salt Lake City's most important religious buildings

ⓘ Council Hall, Capitol Hill, Salt Lake City

*The tour, begins on **I-80** west from Salt Lake City near the south shore of the Great Salt Lake. After about 20 miles (32km) turn south onto **SR 36** for 23 miles (37km) to Tooele.*

Tooele, Utah

1 About 15 miles (24km) west of Salt Lake City the highway reaches the Great Salt Lake, where you can experience the strange sensation of bobbing like a cork in water so salty it is almost impossible to sink. Inland, just off **Route 138** at Mills Junction, the renovated **Benson Grist Mill**, built by the Mormons in 1854, makes an interesting stop before driving on to Tooele. Pronounced 'Too-will-a', this is the region's biggest town, and it lies between two rugged mountain ranges. Of interest are its **golf course** and several **historical museums**. A 9-mile (14km) drive east up Middle Canyon into the Oquirrh Mountains brings you to one of America's most awesome sights: the vast open pit nearly two-and-a-half miles (4km) wide and half a mile (0.8km) deep excavated at the famous **Kennicott (or Bingham) Copper Mine**. From the mountaintop overlook there are magnificent views of the mine, the populated Salt Lake Valley in the east, and the forested mountains topped by Deseret Peak in the west.

*Continue south from Tooele on **SR 36** for 12 miles (19km) to St John Station. Then follow **SR 73** to Fairfield.*

GREAT SALT LAKE COUNTRY

Salt Lake City ● Tooele ● Fairfield Lehi ● Timpanogos Cave National Monument ● Provo Canyon ● Heber City ● Midway ● Mirror Lake Park City ● Echo ● Farmington Salt Lake City

Few short driving tours cross such varied terrain as this loop tour of north-central Utah out of Salt Lake City. The route takes you from the shores of the Great Salt Lake to the edge of the desert, then up lush green valleys into the cool, forested wildernesses of Utah's highest mountains. Along the way you will see breathtaking natural scenery, historic mining towns, old stagecoach inns, dazzling rock caverns, quiet mountain villages and glossy ski resorts buzzing with year-round activity. It is a great outdoor adventure with plenty of opportunities for fun and recreational enjoyment.

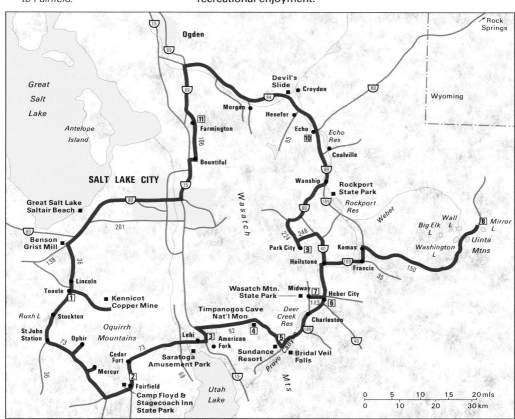

FOR HISTORY BUFFS

Route 65 south of Henefer will take you along part of the historic trail which the Mormon pioneers followed to cross the Wasatch Mountains during their emigration to the Great Salt Lake in 1847. The little town was established as a supply and repair base for later travelers using the trail and is a good base from which to tour the surrounding area.

FOR CHILDREN

3 There are lots of outdoor adventures suitable for youngsters along this itinerary. But for kids who love the thrilling rides and boisterous fun of a family entertainment park, you can make an extra stop at the **Saratoga Amusement Park** off Route 68 on the northwest shore of Utah Lake near Lehi.

Fairfield, Utah

2 Along the Rush Valley south of Tooele you will find once-booming gold- and silver-mining communities such as Stockton, now better known for sailboating and windsurfing on nearby Rush Lake; Ophir, now a quiet village, which once had a big silver nugget exhibited at the 1904 St Louis World's Fair; and Mercur, a ghost town whose history you can trace at the **Barrick Mercur Gold Mine Visitor Center** off **Route 73**,

A few miles south you will come to the ghost town of Fairfield, once an overnight stop on the old Pony Express and overland stagecoach routes across the Great Salt Desert to the west. The two-story adobe hotel has been renovated and refurnished and is now open for tours at **Stagecoach Inn State Park**. Nearby is the site of **Camp Floyd**, where US troops were billeted in the late 1850s during a minor spat with the Mormons.

Continue on SR 73 to complete the Oquirrh Loop drive at Lehi.

Lehi, Utah

3 Lehi was named after a character in the Book of Mormon. Don't miss the **John Hutching's Museum of Natural History**, which has displays of western Americana among its exhibits of pioneer and Indian artifacts and an extensive mineral collection. Highlights include Butch Cassidy's sawn-off shotgun.

Just north of Lehi pick up SR 92 eastbound for the 20-mile (32km) Alpine Loop drive round Mt Timpanogos and Timpanogos Cave National Monument.

Timpanogos Cave National Monument, Utah

4 Although closed in winter to everyone except cross-country skiers and snowmobilers, the Alpine Loop is probably Utah's most popular scenic drive. It is noted for its spectacular fall foliage and magnificent mountain views as it winds around the slopes of impressive Mt Timpanogos. There is a 6-mile (10km) hiking trail up the mountain to the 11,788-foot (3,593m) summit via lovely Emerald Lake, but most visitors are content just to explore the underground wonderland of **Timpanogos Cave National Monument**. Even so, it is a fairly strenuous one-and-a-half-mile (2.5km) walk from the Visitor Center up to the cave entrance, 1,065 feet (325m) above the canyon floor. Inside, there are three caves connected by man-made tunnels and filled with amazing, beautifully colored limestone formations and sparkling rock crystals. The guided tour takes you past such poetically named wonders as the Cavern of Sleep and Father Time's Jewel Box.

Continue southeast on SR92 to Provo Canyon.

Mount Timpanagos in winter

Provo Canyon, Utah

5 In Provo Canyon is movie actor Robert Redford's year-round **Sundance Resort**, where you can stay in elegant cottage or mountain home accommodations and enjoy excellent winter skiing facilities, fine dining in the Tree Room restaurant and musical shows during the Sundance Summer Theater season.

One of the most popular visitor attractions is the aerial tramway that soars to 1,753 feet (534m) above Provo Canyon just south of Wildwood and provides magnificent views of lovely **Bridal Veil Falls** and the surrounding green countryside.

ℹ 2545 N Canyon Road, Provo

*From Bridal Veil Falls follow **US 189** north up the Heber Valley for 15 miles (24km) to Heber City.*

Heber City, Utah

6 The most pleasant way to see the lush green countryside and forested mountain slopes along the Heber Valley is from the famous Heber Creeper steam train that chugs up Provo Canyon and along the valley between Bridal Veil Falls and Heber City. But if you drive, you will at least have the opportunity to stop at **Deer Creek Reservoir**, a 7-mile (11km) lake at the north end of Provo Canyon used for boating, sailing and fishing. Either way, don't miss the **Railroad Museum** in Heber City, where you will see an impressive collection of historic locomotives and other railroad memorabilia and a re-created turn-of-the-century village.

*Follow **SR 113** west to Midway.*

Midway, Utah

7 Midway lies at an altitude of 5,500 feet (1,676m) amid beautiful alpine scenery that reminded early Swiss settlers of home, so they stayed. Townsfolk remember their heritage during the colorful Swiss Days festival held here in late August. Midway is also known for the hot springs that supply the pools at the **Homestead** and **Mountain Spaa** resorts. It is also close to **Wasatch Mountain State Park**, just outside town on **Route 224**, a vast recreational area used for camping, hiking,

A land of contrast: farmlands abutting Utah's wilderness

picnicking, horseback riding and golf in summer, and for cross-country skiing and snowmobiling in winter.

*Return to Heber City and follow **US 189** north for 17 miles (27km) through Hailstone to Kamas, then take **SR 150** east for 35 miles (56km) to Mirror Lake.*

Mirror Lake, Utah

8 One of the most popular summer drives in Utah is to beautiful Mirror Lake, nestled amid the pine-clad 13,000-foot (3,962m) peaks of the Uinta Mountains, Utah's highest range. The lake offers excellent fishing, camping and boating and hiking and horsepacking trails into the surrounding mountains. No roads penetrate this remote unspoiled wilderness, designated the High Uintas Primitive Area, where you can unwind in breathtaking scenery encompassing spectacular peaks, dense forests, icy lakes, sparkling streams teeming with fish, lush wildflower meadows and an abundance of wildlife.

*Retrace **SR 150** and **US 189** to Hailstone, then turn north on **US 40** for 5 miles (8km) and west on **SR 248** for another 5 miles (8km) to Park City.*

Park City, Utah

9 Utah boasts 'The Greatest Snow on Earth' on the 10,000-foot (3,000m) peaks of the Wasatch Mountains, and the canyons carved into the slopes east of Salt Lake City provide rapid access to premier ski resorts at Alta, Snowbird, Brighton, Solitude and Park City. Park City was once a booming mining town following a silver strike in 1868 but is now Utah's largest winter sports area, with more facilities at the nearby Park West and Deer Valley resorts.

Despite the accent on skiing, Park City doesn't close when the snow melts. During the rest of the year you can play tennis and golf, ride down the exciting 3,000-foot (914m) Alpine Slide and walk along pleasant woodland trails. You can also browse along historic Main Street, with its

BACK TO NATURE

In addition to magnificent scenery, Nature has endowed this part of Utah with a rich variety of wildlife and plants. Among the waterfowl that frequent the Great Salt Lake shores are white pelicans, swans, ducks, geese and diving birds, while up in the mountains you might glimpse moose, elk, deer and mule deer and perhaps Rocky Mountain goats on Mt Timpanogos. In July and August wildflowers blanket the Uinta and Wasatch mountains with color, followed in the fall by the brilliant foliage of maples, oaks and aspen. The best locations to see it are Middle Canyon east of Tooele (1); the Alpine Loop (4); the Kamas-Mirror Lake drive (8); and the Park City (9) area.

RECOMMENDED WALKS

4 With so many places of interest, state parks and recreational areas to enjoy, you will find many opportunities for walking. Well worth the 12-mile (19km) round trip off the Alpine Loop is **Cascade Springs**, where a tree-lined walkway offers a pleasant stroll to the crystal-clear springs.

SCENIC ROUTES

It is difficult to pick out for special mention sections of a tour that has so much scenic splendor along the entire route. However, most people would agree that the highlights must include the **Middle Canyon Road** east of Tooele; the **Alpine Loop**; **Route 189** from Bridal Veil Falls to Heber City; **Route 150** between Kamas and Mirror Lake; **I-84N** through Weber Canyon; and the **Bountiful Peak Scenic Drive** between Farmington and Bountiful.

restaurants and galleries, boutiques and antique stores, saloons and taverns and lively nightspots like the popular **Claimjumper**. There are also changing art shows at the **Kimball Art Center** and mining and skiing exhibits at the **Park City Museum**.

A succession of festivals, summer concerts, dramatic productions and other cultural events also draw visitors throughout the year. Top annual events you might catch include the US Film Festival in January, and, during the summer months, the outdoor Shakespeare Festival and Park City Arts Festival.

ℹ️528 Main Street

*Leave Park City via **SR 224** north. Pick up **I-80** eastbound for 11 miles (18km) to Wanship, then go*

Weber River through the Wasatch Range, you will travel between high mountain slopes blanketed in pine and aspen in the area around the county town of Morgan.

*Continue northwest on **I-84** towards Ogden, turning south on **US 89** to Farmington.*

Farmington, Utah

11 Farmington is one of the historic Mormon communities clustered along the Great Salt Lake between Ogden and Salt Lake City and the location of the old **Farmington Rock Chapel** and the 7-acre (3-hectare) **Utah State University Botanical Gardens**. The town's best-known visitor attraction, though, is the **Lagoon Amusement Park**, which is

SPECIAL TO . . .

This part of Utah has two special adventures to offer bold outdoor types longing to escape to the wild. From trailheads at Mirror Lake you can take off into the Uinta wilderness on a guided horsepacking trip (8). Or, if you prefer a rugged four-wheel jeep adventure, you can follow the old Pony Express riders along the sagebrush trail they blazed years ago across the fearsome Great Salt Lake Desert.

*northbound for 12 miles (19km) to Echo and on **I-84** northwest to Morgan.*

Echo, Utah

10 From Kimball Junction **Route 80** descends the eastern slopes of the Wasatch Range and follows the north-flowing Weber River through Wanship down to the old stagecoach community of Echo. Good places to stop for a break along this stretch are **Rockport State Park** (at the reservoir) and **Echo Reservoir**, both popular for picnicking, swimming, boating and fishing. A few miles north of Henefer, a small community that developed on the old Mormon Pioneer and Pony Express trails, you will arrive at the curious geological feature in Weber Canyon known as the Devil's Slide—a good name, you will agree when you see it. It consists of two 40-foot high (12m) limestone reefs, 20 feet (6m) apart, which plunge hundreds of feet down the steep mountainside to the Weber River like two schoolyard slides. Further west, as you follow the

Scrub-covered Echo Canyon, home to the hardiest wildlife

the place to go in Utah for thrilling rides and an assortment of other entertainments.

From Farmington take the 21-mile (34km) **Bountiful Peak Scenic Drive**, which winds south along the Wasatch Front to Bountiful, providing breathtaking views of the Great Salt Lake and Antelope Island and of the stunning sunsets for which this area is famous.

*From Bountiful pick up **I-15** southbound for about 7 miles (11km) to Salt Lake City.*

Salt Lake City – Tooele	**37 (59)**
Tooele – Fairfield	**33 (53)**
Fairfield – Lehi	**21 (34)**
Lehi – Timpanogos Caves	**15 (24)**
Timpanogos Caves – Provo	**10 (16)**
Provo – Heber City	**15 (24)**
Heber City – Midway	**4 (6)**
Midway – Mirror Lake	**52 (83)**
Mirror Lake – Park City	**54 (86)**
Park City – Echo	**28 (45)**
Echo – Farmington	**55 (88)**
Farmington – Salt Lake City	**17 (27)**

Las Vegas has a love affair with lights: Fremont Avenue aglow by night

ⓘ 2301 East Sahara Av, Las Vegas

*Take Charleston Boulevard west out of Las Vegas and continue on **SR 159** for about 11 miles (18km) to the Visitor Center at Red Rock Canyon Recreation Lands.*

Red Rock Canyon, Nevada

1 Red Rock Canyon is a natural wonderland encompassing rugged scenery and unique desert vegetation. From the Visitor Center you can follow a self-guided 13-mile (21km) scenic drive along the multicolored rock escarpment, with its towering rock chimneys and boulder-strewn ravines. There is a pleasant spot for a break at Willow Springs picnic area, where, after rain, you may see temporary cascades of water tumbling from the high crags. Along the drive you may also catch a glimpse of the canyon's wild burros and bighorn sheep, Nevada's state animal.

Just south of Red Rock Canyon is **Bonnie Springs Old Nevada**, a re-created Old West town with various attractions, including a petting zoo. Not to be missed is a tour of the lovely old ranch home at nearby **Spring Mountain Ranch State Park**, which counted among its owners the millionaire recluse Howard Hughes.

*Continue south on **SR 159**, then go **SR 160** west for another 42 miles (68km) to Pahrump.*

Pahrump, Nevada

2 The first stretch of **Route 160** follows the Old Spanish Trail to California blazed through the deserts of the Great Basin in the 1820s. Further north, what used to be the

AN ENCOUNTER WITH DEATH VALLEY

Las Vegas ● Red Rock Canyon
Pahrump ● Death Valley and
Furnace Creek ● Scotty's Castle
Goldfield ● Beatty and Amargosa
Valley ● Mt Charleston ● Las Vegas

Leave the glitter and air-conditioned comfort of Las Vegas and you at once come face to face with Nature at her harshest and also at her most stunningly beautiful. Crossing the burning deserts of Nevada's Great Basin and California's Death Valley is an awesome experience that requires some precautions, especially in summer. But the rewards are unforgettable, with images of arid desert and mountain scenery, weird geological formations, amazingly tough desert plants, adaptable wild animals and, here and there, resilient little communities, comfortable resorts and ghost towns and ruins recalling the exciting, rough-and-ready mining days of old.

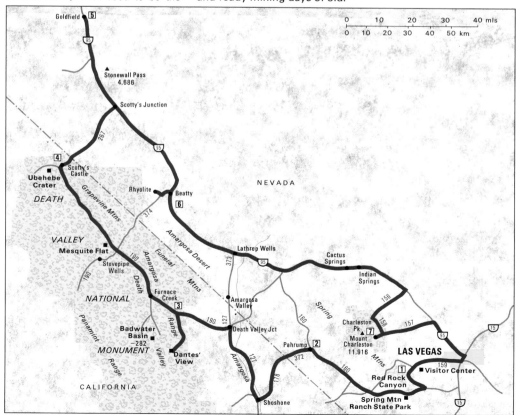

FOR HISTORY BUFFS

3 Many of the roads in Death Valley today follow the routes to the old borax mines that sprang up in the 1880s. They were carved out by the famed 20-mule wagon teams that shipped the mineral out in 20-ton loads. One of these roads traverses **Twenty Mule Team Canyon**, west of Death Valley Junction, from the old borax-mining town of Ryan. You can learn more about Death Valley's mining history at the **Monument Headquarters** near Furnace Creek.

FOR CHILDREN

Except for Bonnie Springs Old Nevada, places with attractions especially devised for kids are rare on this tour. Hopefully young companions will be fascinated by the scenic splendor and geological curiosities and the relics of Nevada's old mining towns. They will also have opportunities to see strange desert plants, walk among ancient sand dunes, picnic in the mountains, and perhaps even swim and ride horses at the **Furnace Creek Inn and Ranch**.

BACK TO NATURE

3 As far as living things are concerned, Death Valley does not really live up to its name, as many animals and plants have adapted to the harsh conditions. Animals tend to be nocturnal and often wear camouflage to hide their presence, so you will be lucky to see the resident antelopes, kangaroo rats, kit foxes, bobcats, desert coyotes and lizards, except perhaps at dawn or dusk. Among the plants, saltbush, creosote bush, sage and various kinds of cacti are common, but if you are here in spring you will see spectacular displays of wildflowers like the lovely desert primrose and fivepoint, especially if there have been winter rains earlier in the year.

quiet old farming community of Pahrump has developed rapidly in recent years into a desirable residential and retirement area, with championship golf courses and gaming opportunities. If you are here in September you may catch the town's Harvest Festival, Fair and Rodeo. Before leaving for Death Valley, check your car for fuel and water and, in summer, take extra water for your own consumption.

*From Pahrump follow **SR 372/178** southwest for 26 miles (42km) to Shoshone, California, then take **SR 127** north up the Amargosa River valley for 26 miles (42km) to Death Valley Junction (Amargosa). Take **SR 190** northwest and after 18 miles (29km) enter Death Valley National Monument.*

Death Valley and Furnace Creek, California

3 Walled in on three sides by high mountain ranges, the 140-mile (225km) desert cauldron of Death Valley National Monument contains the hottest, driest and lowest places in America. Temperatures are usually up to 126°F (52°C) in summer, but have reached 134°F (57°C); precipitation is normally less than 3 inches (76mm) a year; and the lowest point, at Bad Water, plunges to 282 feet (86m) below sea level.

The terrain encompasses rugged mountainsides and canyons of multi-colored rocks, expanses of sand dunes left by prehistoric seas, and

Death Valley's Zabriskie Point overlooks ancient eroded hills

parched salt flats that shimmer in the searing heat. But there are also a few permanent streams, freshwater springs and even a small salty pool, and various wild creatures and plants that have adapted to these inhospitable conditions. Here and there, abandoned gold, silver and borax mines indicate the puny incursions of humans into this inhospitable land.

About 19 miles (31km) west of Death Valley Junction, follow the winding 12-mile (19km) side road off Route 190 to **Dante's View**, where you will get breathtaking panoramic views of the valley and the Panamint Mountains in the west. There is another famous viewpoint at Zabriskie Point, off **Route 190** on the way to Furnace Creek Inn and Ranch, a luxurious palm-fringed hotel resort with excellent facilities for golf, swimming, tennis and horseback riding. Drop by the Visitor Center nearby for information on Death Valley's history and natural wonders, before driving down to see **Bad Water** and the expanse of crusty salt formations known as the **Devil's Golf Course**.

*Retrace the route back to Furnace Creek and continue north on **SR 190** to Scotty's Castle.*

Scotty's Castle, California

4 Just north of the intersection where **Route 190** turns west to Stovepipe Wells is **Mesquite Flat**, another curious geological phenomenon, a sea of great wind-blown sand dunes reminiscent of the Sahara Desert. Continuing north, with the red-and-black slopes of the Grapevine Mountains coloring the

Built by a wealthy Chicagoan, Scotty's Castle is filled with art

horizon on the right, you will eventually arrive at the amazing desert mansion known as **Scotty's Castle**, a well-known Death Valley landmark since the 1920s that is open for tours. Another interesting sight a few miles west is the **Ubehebe Crater**, an 800-foot (244m) deep volcanic cone with brightly colored walls.

From Scotty's Castle continue northeast into Nevada and follow SR 267 for another 21 miles (33km) to Scotty's Junction. Take I-95 northbound for 31 miles (50km) to Goldfield.

Goldfield, Nevada

5 Goldfield was one of those western Nevada mining towns that sprang to life around the turn of the century following the discovery of gold and silver. The strike promised to be, as the old rallying cry went, 'greater than the Comstock', Nevada's greatest-ever gold and silver bonanza. By 1907 Goldfield grew to 20,000 hardy souls, making it Nevada's largest city, but the ores soon ran out and people drifted away, leaving only memories among the crumbling ruins. Today, however, there are signs of new life, and the old **Goldfield Hotel**, once the finest hostelry between Salt Lake City and San Francisco, has undergone restoration. You can visit the old **Esmeralda County Courthouse**, with its original Tiffany lamps, and look for treasures of your own in the town's quaint antique stores.

From Goldfield retrace I-95 to Scotty's Junction and continue south for another 36 miles (58km) to Beatty, then 29 miles (47km) to Amargosa Valley.

Beatty and Amargosa Valley, Nevada

6 Unlike many other old Nevada mining towns, Beatty has survived,

and today offers hotel accommodations, restaurants, gaming facilities and other services. The town is a popular gateway to Death Valley, and about 4 miles (6km) west via **Route 374** you can visit the atmospheric ghost town of Rhyolite, a flourishing silver-mining community from 1905 to 1910 and now one of the most photographed ruins in the state.

Although Rhyolite's old opera house is now a silent memory, the one at Amargosa Valley, further south, still mounts theatrical and musical shows every year. While in the area you can also see the famous **Amargosa Sand Dunes**, relics of a long-vanished inland sea.

From Amargosa Valley continue south on I-95 for 57 miles (92km), then turn right and follow SR 156 and SR 158 for 27 miles (48km) to Mt Charleston in the Spring Mountains.

Mt Charleston, Nevada

7 One way to escape Nevada's blistering summer heat is to drive up the forested slopes into the cool air of Mt Charleston, at 11,918 feet (3,633m) the highest peak in the Spring Mountains, just northwest of Las Vegas. The scenic road climbs to 8,000 feet (2,438m) through stands of pinyon juniper and pine, providing access to numerous campgrounds, picnic sites and walking trails. In winter the area is popular with cross-country skiers, while the Lee Canyon resort has good facilities for downhill enthusiasts.

From Mt Charleston follow SR 157 east for 22 miles (35km) and pick up I-95 southbound for 16 miles (26km) to Las Vegas.

Las Vegas – Red Rock Canyon **11 (18)**
Red Rock Canyon – Pahrump **56 (90)**
Pahrump – Death Valley **70 (113)**
Death Valley – Scotty's Castle **89 (142)**
Scotty's Castle – Goldfield **52 (83)**
Goldfield – Beatty **67 (107)**
Beatty – Mt Charleston **113 (181)**
Mt Charleston – Las Vegas **38 (61)**

RECOMMENDED WALKS

1 Among Red Rock Canyon's many trails is the pleasant walk into the damp, cool recesses of Pine Creek Canyon, with its exotic vegetation at the foot of 3,000-foot (914m) cliffs.

7 On Mt Charleston there are short, easy trails off the Deer Creek Cutoff (**SR 158**) to Robber's Roost and to Desert View, with its spectacular panoramas of the surrounding desert and distant mountain ranges.

SCENIC ROUTES

Spectacular stretches of highway abound on this scenic desert tour, but the highlights are perhaps the 13-mile (21km) drive at Red Rock Canyon; **Route 190** and the side road to Dante's View in Death Valley; and the loop drive to Mt Charleston via **Routes 156, 158** and **157**.

SPECIAL TO ...

4 The flamboyant Walter Scott, a cowboy-prospector who had once performed in Buffalo Bill's Wild West Show, claimed that Scotty's Castle, Death Valley's most famous landmark, was financed in the 1920s from the proceeds of a secret gold mine. In fact, it was built and owned by a Chicago businessman, Arthur M Johnson, who came to Death Valley for health reasons and befriended the old desert rat. The ornate, turreted castle is filled with luxurious furnishings and art treasures, which you will see on a fascinating guided tour.

THE DESERT SOUTHWEST

In 1912 New Mexico and Arizona became, respectively, the 47th and 48th states of the Union, the last of the contiguous territories to reach statehood. Won in the Mexican-American War of 1846–48, these two southwestern territories had been part of Spain's, and later Mexico's, vast North American empire since the 16th century, when Spanish conquistadores passed through the area in a vain search for gold. As American settlers moved in, trouble with the indigenous Indians flared up, first with the Navajo, who were defeated by Kit Carson in 1864, and then, more devastatingly, with the Apache. Charismatic Apache leaders like Cochise and Geronimo waged a ferocious 25-year war.

Eventually the Apache, like the Navajo and others, were rounded up and packed off to the region's immense reservations. During these eventful frontier days, the silver-mining town of Tombstone wrote itself into the history books with the famed gunfight at the OK Corral.

The Spanish, Mexican, Indian and Old West heritage of Arizona and New Mexico is still much in evidence and contributes to the region's vitality and fascination. Everywhere you will encounter Spanish place names and hear Spanish spoken. You will also see ancient Indian archaeological sites, thriving adobe pueblos, Spanish missions, frontier ghost towns, old military forts and traces of the old Santa Fe Trail.

Above all else, however, the Southwest is a region of sunny skies and scenic splendor which draws large numbers of visitors each year. Dramatic canyons, rugged mesas, forested mountain ranges, and expanses of desert cactus form landscapes of breathtaking grandeur. Arizona is the land of the awesome Grand Canyon carved by the Colorado River, of the Painted Desert, Petrified Forest, Sunset and Meteor Craters, Monument Valley (often seen in old movie Westerns), the Canyon de Chelly and the magnificent Sonoran Desert. New Mexico, the 'Land of Enchantment', has the southernmost ranges of the Rocky Mountains and their ski slopes, jagged Shiprock Butte, Carlsbad Caverns with their great swarms of bats, the gleaming dunes of White Sands National Monument and many other natural wonders.

The fast-growing cities of Phoenix, Tucson and Albuquerque are not just gateways to the Southwest, but are themselves rewarding destinations.

Phoenix:

More than 2 million people live in metropolitan Phoenix, a cluster of 23 communities, including Phoenix itself, which sprawls across a great mountain basin in south-central Arizona. Often referred to as the 'Valley of the Sun', Phoenix has a dry, sunny climate—hot in summer, mild in winter—which helped make it one of the Sunbelt's fastest-growing cities in recent years.

Around 9 million visitors flock in every year to enjoy the area's excellent hotel resorts, shops and malls, performing arts, nightlife, and varied outdoor activities and events. In addition to spectator sports, there are golf, tennis, horseback riding, hot-air ballooning, desert four-wheeling, sailing, river rafting and tubing, fishing—and even covered-wagon trips that recapture the area's Old West atmosphere.

Phoenix began life here as a small frontier settlement back in 1860, but by 1889 it had grown enough to become Arizona's territorial and, in 1912, state capital. Today, it is a blend of the Old and New West, with a touch of Mexican and Indian flavor. The cultural mix is reflected in the city's main visitor attractions, which include the impressive **State Capitol** and **museum**; the excellent **Phoenix Art Museum** and **Heard Museum of Anthropology and Primitive Art**; the **Herberger Theater Center** performing arts complex; the excavated **Hohokam Indian ruins** at Pueblo Grande; and beautiful **Papago Park**, location of the large **Phoenix Zoo** and the cacti collections of the **Desert Botanical Garden**.

Albuquerque:

Albuquerque, New Mexico's largest city, spreads across the broad Rio Grande valley, overlooked by the rugged 10,000-foot (3,048m) wall of the Sandia Mountains. A major center of high technology industry and research, transportation and tourism, the city has a growing population that today stands at more than 460,000. Founded by Spanish colonists in 1706, Albuquerque has, over the years, acquired a distinct Spanish, Mexican and Indian flavor, which adds spice to the local architecture, art, music and cuisine.

The Old Town, near the Rio Grande, marks the site of the original Spanish settlement. The focal point is the **Plaza**, flanked by colorful shops, galleries and restaurants and the old church of San Felipe de Neri. Not far away are the delightful **Rio Grande Nature Center** and the **Zoo**, while scattered around the city there are many outstanding and unusual museums, such as the **Indian Pueblo Cultural Center**, the Maxwell Museum of Anthropology and the **National Atomic Museum**.

Central Avenue divides Phoenix east–west; all streets run east of Central; all avenues west

Twilight view over Phoenix, with its backdrop of mountains

Not to be missed while in Albuquerque are an exciting cable car ride up the Sandia Mountains on the **Sandia Peak Tramway** and a trip to **Coronado State Park and Monument**, where the first Spaniards in the area overwintered in 1540. Special events worth catching in Albuquerque include the colossal New Mexico State Fair in September and the city's famous nine-day International Balloon Fiesta in October.

3 days – Approximately 403 miles (646km)

APACHE & SAGUARO TRAILS

Phoenix ● Apache Junction and the Apache Trail ● Globe and Miami Superior ● Florence and the Casa Grande Ruins National Monument Tucson ● Tucson Mountain Park Phoenix

Southeast of Phoenix is a natural wonderland of dry, rugged mountains and unique cactus desert where Indian peoples long ago learned to scratch a living from irrigated agriculture and hunting. Here Spanish conquistadores searched in vain for the fabled Seven Cities of Cíbola while their missionaries hunted for souls, and rough mining prospectors, mean gunfighters and determined settlers gathered in frontier towns constantly harried by the Apaches. You can follow in their footsteps on this fascinating tour of Arizona's beautiful Sonoran Desert.

FOR HISTORY BUFFS

1 The appropriately named Superstition Mountains, which overlook the Apache Trail, are the source of many old tales about hoards of gold hidden in the wilderness. The best known is the legend of the Lost Dutchman Mine, the supposed secret cache of a German prospector (the so-called 'Dutchman') named Jacob Waltz, which no one has ever been able to find since his death in 1891. You could take a look yourself if you stop by **Lost Dutchman State Park** just north of Apache Junction.

ℹ 1100 West Washington, Phoenix

*Drive east from downtown Phoenix on East Van Buren Street and **US 60/89** through Tempe and Mesa for about 31 miles (50km) to Apache Junction.*

Apache Junction and the Apache Trail, Arizona

1 Named for an old Indian trail, this famous scenic road, unpaved in part, winds along the north side of the Superstition Mountains past towering rock buttes, rugged canyons, mountainsides dotted with saguaro cactus and blue manmade lakes. North of Apache Junction and beyond the old ghost town of Goldfield, you arrive at **Canyon Lake**, one of the four great reservoirs created by dams along the Salt River at the beginning of the century to provide water for Phoenix. They all have campgrounds, picnic areas and facilities for boating, fishing and water-skiing. A few miles past the quaint old stagecoach town of Tortilla Flat there is a 20-mile (32km) stretch of unpaved road and a scary descent into Fish Creek Canyon.

The hot Arizona sun dries strings of even hotter chilies for sale in Tubac, a magnet for artists and writers

Beyond tranquil Apache Lake you will see the 275-foot (84m) Theodore Roosevelt Dam, completed in 1911, and its 25-mile (40km) lake, a popular spot for anglers. At this point paved again, the road turns southeast through Roosevelt to **Tonto National Monument**, the site of prehistoric cliff dwellings. A foot trail leads to a well-preserved complex inhabited by Salado Indians in the 14th century. From mid-October through April there are three-hour ranger-led tours to a 40-room dwelling in the upper ruin. There is also a museum with various dioramas and exhibits of Salado crafts.

*Turn northeast and follow the scenic Apache Trail **(SR 88)** for about 76 miles (122km) to Globe and Miami.*

Globe and Miami, Arizona

2 Globe is an old mining town said to have been named after a large round nugget of almost pure silver found in these parts. Among its visitor attractions are the restored 1906 **Courthouse**, which houses the community's art gallery, and the **Gila County Historical Museum** (pronounced *hee-la*), which displays pioneer memorabilia and items relating to the area's early mining history. South of town, on Jesse Hays Road, is the site of excavated Indian ruins at **Besh-Ba-Gowah (Metal Camp) Archaeological Park**, where craftspeople have re-created what is probably the most realistic Indian dwellings in the state.

A few miles west you can tour the copper-mining operations and open pit at Miami. On the edge of town you will also see a marker indicating the site of the Bloody Tanks Massacre perpetrated by local settlers against the Indians in 1864.

ℹ 1360 North Broad Street, Globe

*From Miami continue west on **US 60** for about 17 miles (27km) to Superior.*

Superior, Arizona

3 There is an especially scenic stretch of highway along Queen Creek Canyon and through the tunnel into the major copper-mining town of Superior. At the **Apache Tears Mine**, however, they don't dig for copper but for nodules of beautiful black glassy obsidian, popularly known as Apache tears. Legend has it that these are the tears shed by Apache women when their menfolk leapt from a nearby cliff rather than surrender to US cavalry. A few miles down **US 60** don't miss a tour of the **Boyce Thompson Arboretum**, where you can see excellent displays of desert plants, animals and birds.

ℹ 151 Main Street

*Continue west on **US 60** for 15 miles (24km) to Florence Junction. Turn south on **US 89** for 16 miles (26km) to Florence, then west on **SR 287** for about 10 miles (16km) to Casa Grande Ruins National Monument.*

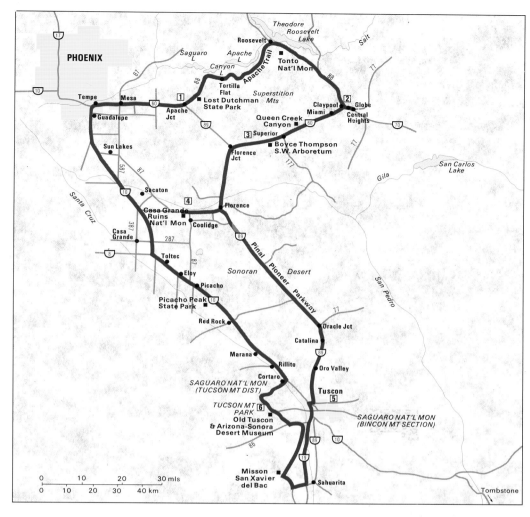

Florence and the Casa Grande Ruins National Monument, Arizona

4 The desert community of Florence, the seat of Pinal County, lies on the old main road **(Highway 89)** between Phoenix and Tucson. Some of its original adobe buildings are preserved in downtown **McFarland State Historic Park**, where the restored **Pinal County Courthouse** (*circa* 1878) serves as a museum of local history and law.

West of Florence, at Coolidge, is **Casa Grande Ruins National Monument**, one of Arizona's most mysterious sites. There has been much speculation about the purpose of this four-story structure, built by Hohokam Indians around 1350 and now protected beneath a steel 'umbrella'. Is it a house, a temple, a watchtower, an astronomical observatory—or something else?

ℹ️ Jacob Souter House, 270 Bailey Street, Florence

*From Florence follow **US 89** for about 72 miles (113km) southeast across the Sonoran*

The morning sun highlights the cacti in Tonto National Forest.

FOR CHILDREN

There is a range of things to see and do along the itinerary which should appeal especially to children. They include a cruise on the steamboat *Dolly* at **Canyon Lake** (1); tours of **Reid Park Zoo** and the **Children's Museum** at Tucson (5); and lots of Wild West fun at Old Tucson (6).

BACK TO NATURE

Of all the desert plants you will learn to identify on this tour of the Sonoran Desert, you cannot mistake the distinctive saguaro cactus. But can you recognize Arizona's state tree, the beautiful palo verde, which splashes the desert with yellow flowers in spring? Keep your eyes open, too, for the desert's special wild creatures, like the cactus wren, exotic hummingbirds, the comical roadrunner and the venomous Gila monster and its potential dinner, the leaping kangaroo rat.

RECOMMENDED WALKS

There are beautiful walking trails through spring wildflowers in **Lost Dutchman State Park**, near Apache Junction (1), and **Picacho Peak State Park**, along **I–10** north of Tucson (5). When visiting the **Boyce Thompson Arboretum**, near Superior (3), don't miss a walk along the 1¼-mile (2km) **Picket Post Trail** into the wilder desert area. There are also enthralling walks along trails in **Saguaro National Monument** (6).

SCENIC ROUTES

Scenic highlights along the itinerary include the Apache Trail **(SR 88)** from Apache Junction to Globe; the Queen Creek Canyon stretch of **US 60** just outside Superior; the Pinal Pioneer Parkway **(US 89)** through the desert from Florence to Oracle Junction; and the gravel roads through the cactus forest in Saguaro National Monument.

SPECIAL TO . . .

5 If there is one place that symbolizes America's Wild West, it is **Tombstone** in southeast Arizona, the site of the famed gunfight at the OK Corral, Boot Hill cemetery and the rollicking Bird Cage Theater. 'The town too tough to die' is now preserved as a National Historic Landmark and is just over an hour's drive east of Tucson via **I-10** and **US 80**. If you have time, don't miss it.

Mission San Xavier del Bac, Tucson, still serving local Indians

Desert through Oracle Junction to Tucson.

Tucson, Arizona

5 Over 700,000 people live in Arizona's second largest city, a sprawling metropolis laid out in a broad desert valley surrounded by mountains. The home of the University of Arizona, Tucson is a vibrant business and cultural center, with many museums, galleries, performing arts events and festivals likely to appeal to visitors. Known affectionately as the 'Old Pueblo', the city grew around the Spanish *presidio* (garrison) established at the foot of Sentinel Peak in 1776. The top of this mountain—popularly known as 'A' Mountain for the huge letter 'A' (for Arizona) whitewashed on its slopes—affords spectacular views of the city and the mountains beyond and is a good place to get your bearings.

The original *presidio* is now gone, but if you take a walking tour around the attractive downtown Presidio Historic District, you will notice many other old adobe structures tucked among the government buildings, offices and shops. Among them are the **Fish House** and the restored 1858 house once used by territorial governor John C Frémont.

If time is limited, you may have to miss the fine **planetarium** and **museums of history, art** and **minerals** on the university campus. But be sure to visit the **Pima Air Museum**, a major attraction in the southeastern part of the city, where you can see an impressive collection of historic aircraft. At the end of your Tucson visit, drive south for 10 miles (16km) on **I-19** to see the **Mission San Xavier del Bac**, a strikingly beautiful building completed in 1797 and often poetically described as the 'White Dove of the Desert'.

ℹ 130 S Scott Avenue

From Mission San Xavier del Bac go north on Mission Road, west on Ajo Way, and north on Kinney Road, a 14-mile (23km) drive, to the desert attractions of Tucson Mountain Park.

Tucson Mountain Park, Arizona

6 Many Western movies, TV series and commercials have been filmed on the permanent set of adobe-and-wood buildings at Old Tucson, a 1939 re-created Old West Town that has been called Arizona's Hollywood in the Desert. Along streets once trodden by stars like John Wayne, you can, if you are lucky, watch scenes being shot or, if not, enjoy medicine shows, make-believe shoot-outs and saloon brawls and ride on a stagecoach or narrow-gauge railroad. It is all part of the fun here.

Not far away you will see desert life at close quarters at the superb **Arizona–Sonora Desert Museum**. It is a sort of combined zoo, aquarium, botanical garden, museum and information center, with fascinating geological exhibits and displays of living animals, birds and plants native to the American Southwest in their natural habitats.

Continuing north, you will then see nature for real: the western section of **Saguaro National Monument**, a protected expanse of the Sonoran Desert that has especially fine stands of saguaro cactus and other desert vegetation, an unforgettable sight at sunset.

ℹ 130 S Scott Avenue, Tucson

*At Cortaro, northeast of Saguaro National Monument, pick up **I-10** northbound for the 92-mile (147km) drive back to Phoenix.*

Phoenix – Apache Junction **31 (50)**
Apache Junction – Globe **76 (122)**
Globe – Superior **23 (37)**
Superior – Casa Grande **41 (66)**
Casa Grande – Tucson **82 (131)**
Tucson – Tucson Mountain Park **48 (77)**
Tucson Mountain Park – Phoenix **102 (163)**

Indian arts are the focus of the annual Indian market each August

ℹ 625 Silver Avenue SW, Albuquerque

*Head east on **I-40** from downtown Albuquerque for about 15 miles (24km) through Tijeras Canyon, and at **Exit 775** turn north onto **SR 14**, the Turquoise Trail, through Cedar Crest.*

Cedar Crest and the Turquoise Trail, New Mexico

1 This fascinating road winds through mesa country east of the Sandia Mountains and is the most scenic route between Albuquerque and Santa Fe. But don't miss the side trip on the Scenic Byway **(SR 536)** which takes you up the wooded slopes past the Sandia Ski Area to Sandia Crest, the area's highest peak. From the 10,678-foot (3,255m) summit there are breathtaking views of Albuquerque and for miles around. Back on **Route 14**, continue north through the old mining towns of Golden (gold), Madrid (coal) and Cerrillos (gold, silver and turquoise), now recovering from decline as artists' communities, with galleries, mining museums, boutiques, fine restaurants and music festivals.

*From Cerrillos continue north on **SR 14** and **I-25** for 24 miles (39km) to Santa Fe.*

Santa Fe, New Mexico

2 New Mexico's old Spanish capital, founded in 1609, lies at 7,000 feet (2,134m) near the southern end of the Sangre de Cristo Mountains. Its Spanish Colonial and Pueblo Indian heritage is plain to see as you wander around its historic center, with its adobe architecture, tree-shaded plaza, narrow, winding alleys and cool courtyards. Be sure to see the historic **Palace of the Governors, Museum of Fine Arts, San Miguel Mission, St Francis Cathedral** and pretty **Loretto Chapel**. Browse through the fine shops and galleries along Canyon Road and, depending on your interests, take a look inside one or more of the museums clustered together south of the downtown area: the **Museum of Indian Arts and Culture, the Museum of International Folk Art** and the **Wheelwright Museum**, which has an especially impressive collection of Navajo sand-paintings. Among the many cultural and other events you might catch on your visit are the colorful Indian Market on the plaza in August and the summer season of the world-renowned **Santa Fe Opera** north of town.

ℹ 1100 St Francis Drive

*From Santa Fe take **US 84-285** north for 24 miles (38km) to Española, then follow the old Camino Alto **(SR 76, 75, 518** and **68)** north for about 46 miles (74km) to Taos.*

Taos, New Mexico

3 Bordering the highway north of Santa Fe near Espanola are several Pueblo Indian settlements, including the San Ildefonso and Santa Clara pueblos, where you will see beautiful

THE ENCHANTED CIRCLE

Albuquerque ● Cedar Crest and the Turquoise Trail ● Santa Fe ● Taos ● Eagle Nest ● Cimarron Springer and Watrous ● Las Vegas and Pecos National Monument ● Albuquerque

Drive north out of Albuquerque and you enter a land that reflects those eternal images of the Old West: gorgeous forest-clad mountains, scrubby mesas gashed by deep river gorges, vast open prairies, ancient Indian pueblos and ruins, historic Spanish towns, old frontier forts and rough mining and ranching communities (cattle and sheep outnumber New Mexico's people two-to-one). It is a scenario where names like Kit Carson, the famous frontiersman, outlaw Billy the Kid and the Santa Fe Trail seem to fit easily. Yet it is also a land for today's four-wheeled traveler, with countless historic sights, cultural attractions, recreational activities and shopping for exquisite Indian crafts.

handmade crafts, colorful dances and various other attractions. On the scenic **Camino Alto**, the high road that winds along the western slopes of the Sangre de Cristo Mountains, you will pass through picturesque old Spanish villages, including Chimayo,

The Santuario of Chimayo: pilgrims come to its chapel for healing

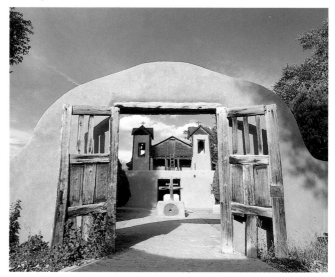

FOR HISTORY BUFFS

5 The fabled **Santa Fe Trail** entered history in 1821, after Mexico declared independence from Spain and trader William Becknell found he could get through unchallenged from Missouri to the old Spanish Colonial capital. Two branches of the trail crossed northeast New Mexico's grasslands, joined at Watrous and followed the route of today's **I-25** to Santa Fe. You can still see old wagon ruts and historic buildings on the trail at Cimarron, Fort Union and Las Vegas.

Cordova, Truchas and Las Trampas, where skilled woodcarvers and weavers practice their craft. Worth a stop along the way are the famous **Santuario** at Chimayo and the sturdy old **mission church** at Ranchos de Taos, a perennially popular subject for New Mexican artists.

Picturesque Taos, founded by the Spaniards around 1617, has been a thriving writers' and artists' colony since the late 1800s. When you have browsed through the boutiques and galleries around the historic little plaza, visit the homes and studios of artists Nicolai Fechin or Ernest L Blumenschein and tour the superb art exhibits at the **Millicent A Rogers Museum** north of town. But don't miss the historic places, like the impressive Colonial **hacienda** of land-owner Don Antonio Severino

Eagle Nest, New Mexico

4 Your only glimpse of the famed Rio Grande on this tour is a spectacular one. Stay on **US 64** as you leave Taos and you will enjoy a breathtaking view of its colossal gorge from the road bridge 660ft (201m) above the turbulent water. Continuing north on **Route 522**, stop briefly at San Cristobal to see writer D H Lawrence's shrine before following the Red River Valley up into the forest-clad mountains. Nestled amid the gorgeous scenery is the old mining community of Red River, now a popular family vacation center and winter ski resort. Summer activities on offer include hiking, fishing, Jeep trips, horseback riding, square dancing and hissing the villain at a Mine Shaft Theater melodrama. The scenic drive over 9,820-foot (2,993m) Bob-

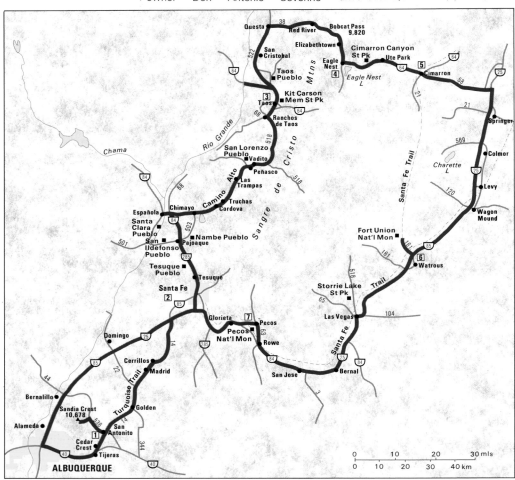

FOR CHILDREN

It is a pretty safe bet that children on this tour will be enthralled by the exciting tales they hear about northeast New Mexico's eventful past. They will also enjoy special attractions like the **Tinkertown Museum**, an animated Old West town hand-carved in miniature, on the Sandia Crest road (1); living history demonstrations at Fort Union (6); Indian dances at the pueblos; and events such as the colorful Rails 'n' Trails Days in late May at Las Vegas (7).

Martinez; the home of New Mexico's first territorial governor, Charles Bent; and the house and grave of the legendary frontiersman Kit Carson.

North of town be sure to visit famed **Taos Pueblo**, the 900-year-old Indian community noted for the multistory adobe architecture that has so impressed artists and visitors over the years. You will also be captivated by the beautiful crafts and the dance ceremonials.

*Follow **US 64** and **SR 522** north for about 24 miles (39km) to Questa, then **SR 38** east for about 29 miles (46km) through Red River and the Sangre de Cristo Mountains to Eagle Nest.*

cat Pass and through the old gold-mining ghost town of Elizabethtown eventually brings you to the all-year recreation center of Eagle Nest, where the beautiful lake is popular for fishing, boating and windsurfing.

*From Eagle Nest follow **US 64** east for about 24 miles (38km) to Cimarron.*

Cimarron, New Mexico

5 The 400-foot (122m) cliffs of Cimarron Canyon are a memorable sight along the scenic drive to Cimarron. This quiet little town, set in verdant ranch country, was once one of the wildest places on the old Santa Fe Trail. Many Old West notables,

Ancient Taos Pueblo: electricity and running water are banned

BACK TO NATURE

With terrain ranging from dry mesas to lush mountain pastures and grasslands, this corner of New Mexico has been blessed with a whole Noah's Ark of wild creatures and plants. Among the wild animals you might see in the mountains are black bear, cougar, elk, bobcat, bighorn sheep and even porcupines. Birds range from ravens and wild turkeys to falcons and exotic hummingbirds. Wildflowers too numerous to list brighten the mountains in summer, while fall splashes the dark-green forests with patches of golden aspen.

RECOMMENDED WALKS

In addition to walking around the various historic towns and other sites on this tour, you can enjoy New Mexico's great outdoors by following off-highway trails in the Sandia and Sangre de Cristo Mountains. Of special interest are scenic trails at Sandia Crest; in the Wild Rivers Recreation Area by the Rio Grande west of Questa around Red River and in Cimarron Canyon State Park.

SCENIC ROUTES

Splendid scenery awaits you all along the Enchanted Circle tour, but special highlights include the sections on the Turquoise Trail **(SR 14)** and Sandia Crest road **(SR 536)**; the Camino Alto between Chimayo and Taos; **Route 38** up the Red River Valley and over Bobcat Pass to Eagle Nest; and **Highway 64** down the eastern slopes of the Sangre de Cristo Mountains to Cimarron.

SPECIAL TO . . .

3 Long before the Spanish explorer Francisco de Coronado wandered through the area in 1540, the many-skilled Pueblo Indians of the Rio Grande valley had become exceptionally adept at making beautiful decorated clay pots and figurines. Among their finest achievements are the polished black pottery developed this century at the San Ildefonso pueblo and the polished red-and-black ware made at the Santa Clara pueblo. Other pueblo crafts include exquisite jewelry, beadwork, wood carvings, woven belts and handmade quilts—all of which, like the pottery, make wonderful souvenirs of a visit to New Mexico.

and gunslingers like Wyatt Earp and Jesse James, checked in at the **St James Hotel**, where bullet holes still ventilate the dining-room ceiling. For more about Cimarron's colorful past, drop by the **Old Mill Museum**. Be sure, too, to visit the **Philmont Scout Ranch**, where you will see a vast herd of buffalo, **Kit Carson's house** and **museum**, the **Villa Philmonte** and the **museum** and **library** of Ernest Thompson Seton, co-founder of the Boy Scouts of America.

*Take **SR 58** east for 19 miles (31km) to join **I-25** southbound for 53 miles (85km) through Springer to Watrous and nearby Fort Union National Monument.*

Springer and Watrous, New Mexico

6 Down on the prairies further east, don't miss the **Santa Fe Trail Museum** in the old courthouse at Springer, with exhibits which depict everyday life of residents at the turn-of-the-century, and the stark ruins of **Fort Union**, near Watrous, which was built in the mid-1800s to protect travelers on the trail from marauding Indians.

*From Watrous continue south on **I-25** for 21 miles (34km) to Las Vegas, then go 44 miles (70km) to Pecos National Monument.*

Las Vegas and Pecos National Monument, New Mexico

7 Settled near hot springs by Spanish families in 1835, the little adobe-built prairie community of Las Vegas

soon found itself hosting not only respectable traders and travelers on the Santa Fe Trail but also less salubrious characters such as Doc Holliday and Billy the Kid. But with the coming of the railroad in 1879, the 'New Town' district sprang up east of town, and Las Vegas blossomed for a time as New Mexico's largest and wealthiest city and a silent film capital. Today, walking tours of the town's nine historic districts take you past hundreds of architectural treasures, from old adobe houses to grand Victorian hotels, like the **Castenada**.

Another sightseeing must along the drive back to Albuquerque is **Pecos National Monument**, with its haunting ruins of an ancient Indian pueblo and two missions built by Spanish Franciscans. Visitors can wander through the ruins on a self-guiding trail.

[i] 727 Grand Avenue, Las Vegas

*From Pecos National Monument continue southwest on **I-25** for about 80 miles (128km) to Albuquerque.*

Albuquerque – Cedar Crest **17 (27)**
Cedar Crest – Santa Fe **54 (86)**
Santa Fe – Taos **70 (112)**
Taos – Eagle Nest **53 (85)**
Eagle Nest – Cimarron **24 (38)**
Cimarron – Springer **72 (115)**
Springer – Pecos National Monument **65 (104)**
Pecos National Monument – Albuquerque **80 (128)**

THE WEST COAST

In 1845 America's western boundary lay along the edge of the Rocky Mountains. But a year later, within months of taking office, President James K Polk had pushed it westward to the Pacific coast by winning Washington and Oregon from Britain and California from Mexico. With the discovery of gold in California's Sierra Nevada in 1848, thousands of people flocked overland or by sea to the Far West to seek their fortune in the new Promised Land—and they have done so ever since.

Today the West Coast is a major vacation destination offering visitors countless sightseeing attractions and outdoor adventures. There are, first of all, the fascinating cities of Seattle, Portland, Oregon City, San Francisco, Sacramento, Los Angeles and San Diego. There are also the region's natural wonders, which include magnificent stretches of shoreline, superb beaches, shimmering bays, fertile valleys, spectacular mountain ranges, thundering waterfalls, impressive forests of redwood and sequoia, and awesome deserts.

The backbone of the region is the north-south mountain barrier formed by the Cascade Range, which separates a mild coastal climate from the interior continental one, and the Sierra Nevada. In the north spectacular snow-capped volcanoes like Mount Rainier and Mount Baker soar above the forested slopes of the Cascades in Washington and Oregon.

Further south, in California's Sierra Nevada, are the majestic granite landscapes of Yosemite National Park, a wilderness of high mountains and deep valleys, and the great sequoia trees (*sequoiadendron giganteum*) of Kings Canyon and Sequoia National Parks. To the east and south are dry plateau and desert regions, which are at their most awesome in the arid expanses of California's Mojave Desert and the blazing cauldron of Death Valley, formed millions of years ago by the folding and faulting of the earth's crust and one of the hottest regions in the world.

West of the flat, cultivated lands of Puget Sound, Oregon's Willamette Valley and the immense Central Valley of California, the Coast Ranges look out over the Pacific Ocean beyond the region's magnificent 1,400-mile (2,250km) shoreline. Here the land meets the sea at the wild headlands and coves of Washington and Oregon, the rugged Big Sur coast and the golden, sun-drenched beaches of southern California.

Seattle:

The futuristic 605-foot (184m) **Space Needle** that dominates Seattle's skyline affords magnificent panoramas of this busy port city's fine waterfront setting beside Puget Sound. At its foot is the Seattle Center, a 74-acre (30-hectare) entertainment and cultural complex that includes the fascinating **Pacific Science Center**. A ride on the Monorail and a short walk will bring you to bustling **Pike Place Market** and the ferry terminals, shops, restaurants and visitor attractions along the waterfront. Among these is the marvelous **Seattle Aquarium** on Pier 59.

Not far away, at historic **Pioneer Square**, there are underground tours of the original downtown district destroyed by fire in 1889 and now lying beneath the boutiques, restaurants and night spots of the restored and raised area. Nearby are the landmark **Kingdome Stadium** and the 48-block Asian neighborhood known as the **International District**. Also worth

The Space Needle, a prominent landmark on the Seattle skyline

visiting are the **Seattle Art Museum** in Volunteer Park and the **Seattle Zoo** in Woodland Park.

San Francisco:

Often shrouded in sea fog, the majestic Golden Gate Bridge sweeps across the entrance to San Francisco Bay, where one of the world's best-loved cities rolls over its hills behind the bustling waterfront. San Francisco's **Embarcadero** is a major visitor attraction, with its bay cruises, maritime museum and shopping complexes, and the seafood restaurants of Fisherman's Wharf. Ferries transport visitors to the grim former **Alcatraz penitentiary** out in the bay, while clanging cable cars hurtle up and down the city's hills to other sightseeing highlights. Most of these are also on the designated 49-mile (79km) **Scenic Drive** recommended for visitors. However you get around, be sure to visit the **Civic Center complex**, **Union Square**, colorful **Chinatown**, **Coit Tower** on Telegraph Hill, lovely **Golden Gate Park** with its excellent museums, the fine city **Zoo**, and **Mission Dolores**, which recalls the founding of the city by Spaniards in 1776. A sophisticated, livable city of around 727,000 people, San Francisco also has an excellent performing arts scene, superb restaurants and lively nightlife.

Los Angeles:

America's second city is part of a vast megalopolis of more than 12 million people that sprawls across the broad plain between the Pacific Ocean beaches and the San Gabriel Mountains. Crisscrossed

Seventh Market Place, Los Angeles—a must for serious shoppers

other visitor attractions, including fine museums, like the **J Paul Getty Museum** in Malibu, performing arts venues, such as the famous **Hollywood Bowl** and the downtown **Music Center**, lively night spots, fine restaurants, and shopping highlights like the famed Rodeo Drive boutiques in Beverly Hills.

San Diego:

California's second largest city, the naval base and port of San Diego nestles beside its magnificent sheltered bay near the Mexican border. With its warm, dry, sunny climate, its superb beaches, its outdoor recreational opportunities and its numerous cultural, entertainment and sightseeing attractions, the city has much to offer visitors. Downtown are the shops, galleries and restaurants of the revitalized 19th-century **Gaslamp Quarter**, the **Seaport Village** shopping complex, and the historic ships of the waterfront **Maritime Museum**. In immense

by a network of busy freeways, this colossal maelstrom of a city is packed with places of interest. Most visitors make straight for **Hollywood**, home of the movies, to see the stars' hand- and footprints and the **Walk of Fame** along Hollywood Boulevard; to tour the make-believe world of **Universal Studios** or the **NBC TV Studios** in nearby Burbank; and to marvel at the palatial homes built by the stars in glamorous **Beverly Hills**.

Los Angeles also has countless

Balboa Park are the impressive **San Diego Zoo**, several fine museums and the prestigious **Old Globe Theater**.

At **Old Town** you can tour the historic Mexican district that grew below the original Spanish hilltop settlement of 1769. The old Spanish mission, **San Diego de Alcalá**, is now relocated further east. Another major city attraction is **Sea World** marine entertainment park in the huge Mission Bay aquatic playground north of town.

OLYMPIC WILDERNESS & PACIFIC SHORELINE

Seattle ● Port Townsend ● Sequim ● Port Angeles and Olympic National Park ● Lake Crescent● Neah Bay ● La Push and the Pacific Shoreline ● Grays Harbor ● Olympia ● Seattle

This challenging tour of the Evergreen State's northwest tip offers a rewarding adventure for everyone but the faint-hearted. It starts with a ferry crossing from Seattle and a pleasant drive through the islands, old fishing ports and logging towns of Puget Sound. But as you cross to the Olympic Peninsula you enter a wilderness world of rugged mountains and glaciers, dense rain forests, rivers teeming with salmon and steelhead, lonely windswept beaches and headlands and remote Indian reservations. A tour of the state capital, Olympia, the starting point of the Olympic Highway, which encircles the Olympic Peninsula, then brings you back to the familiar world of 20th-century civilization.

ⓘ 666 Stewart Street, Seattle

*Take the ferry from Seattle's **Pier 52** across Puget Sound to Winslow. Follow **SR 305** and **SR 3** north for 20 miles (32km) to Port Gamble. Cross the Hood Canal Floating Bridge on **SR 104** and after 16 miles (26km) turn north on **US 101** and **SR 20** for 15 miles (24km) to Port Townsend.*

Port Townsend, Washington

1 This fascinating old seaport at the entrance to Puget Sound is a favorite spot for artists and culture buffs, who throng here to enjoy its many arts festivals. As a National Historic District, Port Townsend boasts it has the best collection of Victorian architecture north of San Francisco. Examples are the **James House** and **Starrett House**, which are open to the public during the semiannual Historic Homes Tour festival in May and September. Don't miss the **Rothschild House**, another gracious 19th-century home, complete with period furnishings, and the

FOR HISTORY BUFFS

1 Port Gamble was founded as a logging village in 1853 and is now a National Historic Site. It is a picturesque town with an old working lumber mill, gas street lamps, many Victorian buildings and a famous **General Store** housing two museums. One of these, the **Pope and Talbot Historical Museum**, features life in a 19th-century lumber town.

The mountains of Olympic National Forest, cloaked in creeping mists

century-old 'Tree of Heaven', said to have been a gift to the town from a Chinese emperor and now its most unusual attraction. Take a stroll by the waterfront, browse through the antique stores, gift shops, and galleries featuring the work of local artists, or just watch the world go by from a sidewalk café. A short drive north out of town will take you to old **Fort Worden**, one of the historic coastal fortresses built in the area to guard the entrance to Puget Sound. Here you will see the restored officers' quarters and the original large, grassy parade ground.

ⓘ 2437 Sims Way

*Return to Discovery Bay on **SR 20**, then turn west on **US 101** for 18 miles (29km) through Gardiner to Sequim.*

Sequim, Washington

2 Pronounced '*Skwim,*' this small town is the gateway to a popular retirement area which lies in irrigated farm country on the sheltered northeast side of the Olympic Mountains and enjoys a dry, mild sunny climate. Recreational activities on offer here include camping, hiking, bicycling, golf, hunting, fishing, boating and windsurfing. Equally varied are the area's attractions, which include the **Neuharth Winery**, open for tours and tastings, and the **Olympic Game Farm**, a 90-acre (36-hectare) preserve for trained lions, bears and other wild animals used in movies and TV programs. If you are lucky you might see a training session or even a scene being shot.

ⓘ 1210 E Washington

*From Sequim continue west on **SR 101** for 17 miles (27km) to Port Angeles and Olympic National Park.*

Port Angeles and Olympic National Park, Washington

3 Port Angeles is the largest town on the Olympic Peninsula, a major fishing port, and a ferry terminal providing a year-round service to Victoria, British Columbia. It is also the entry point to the mountain section of the 1,400-square-mile (3,626 sq km) **Olympic National Park**, a scenic wilderness of snow-capped peaks, great glaciers, rushing torrents and flower-speckled meadows, teeming with wildlife and dominated by 7,965-foot (2,428m) Mount Olympus. The lower slopes are clothed in the vast tracts of coniferous trees that form the **Olympic National Forest**. Follow the popular Heart o' the Hills Highway south for 18 miles (29km) up to 5,228-foot (1,593m) **Hurricane Ridge** or even further to **Obstruction Point**. The viewpoints here offer spectacular panoramas of the mountain peaks and glaciers and of the Strait of Juan de Fuca and distant Vancouver Island

ⓘ 121 East Railroad; also 3002 Mount Angeles Road

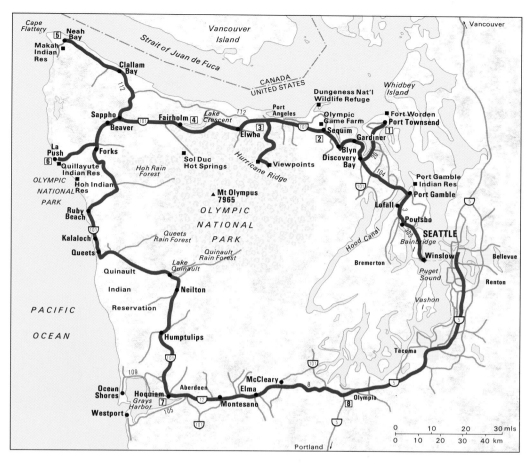

Rejoin **US 101** at Port Angeles and continue west for about 15 miles (24km) to Lake Crescent.

Lake Crescent, Washington

4 Ten miles (16km) long and 1½ miles (2km) wide, this crescent-shaped stretch of deep, ice-cold water is the largest of the three lakes along **US 101** west of Port Angeles. Cradled in a magnificent mountain setting, it is a pleasant spot to stretch your legs and admire the scenery. Just beyond Fairholm, a 16-mile (26km) spur road off **US 101** offers an interesting detour to see (and perhaps make use of) the mineral pools at the old resort at Sol Duc Hot Springs.

ⓘ Storm King, Lake Crescent

*Continue west on **US 101** for about 25 miles (40km) to Sappho. Take the Burnt Mountain Cutoff north for 10 miles (16km) and join **SR 112** westbound along the coast for about 27 miles (43km) through Clallam Bay to Neah Bay.*

The tranquillity of Second Beach at sunrise, Olympic National Park

FOR CHILDREN

There are lots of additional adventures and things to see for kids on this tour. Extra sightseeing treats include the collection of seashells on display at the **Of Sea and Shore Museum** in the General Store at Port Gamble and exhibits of life in the sea at the **Arthur D Feiro Marine Laboratory**, Port Angeles (3). Kids will also enjoy hunting for the famous crabs at Dungeness Bay; beachcombing for driftwood, agates and Japanese glass fishing floats along the Pacific shoreline; and canoeing and riding in Indian dugouts at Lake Quinault.

BACK TO NATURE

3 A paradise for nature lovers, the Olympic Peninsula supports a wide range of flora and fauna, from the rich marine life around its shores to the wild animals and plants of its forests and mountains. On the high slopes of the Olympic National Park you will see colorful wildflower meadows and perhaps deer, elk, mountain goats and marmots and such birds as the majestic bald eagle. In the eerie stillness beneath the giant trees of the rain forests you might also glimpse deer, raccoons, the rare Roosevelt elk and various birds as they flit through the damp undergrowth of moss, ferns and fungi.

RECOMMENDED WALKS

Pleasant walks of varying lengths which are not too strenuous can be found at the wildlife refuge on Dungeness Spit, north of Sequim (2); at Hurricane Ridge, south of Port Angeles (3), where there is a guided nature walk; at Lake Crescent (4), where there is a ¾-mile (1km) trail from Storm King Visitor Center to pretty Marymere Falls; at La Push, where trails through the woods take you to scenic beaches (6); and at the end of the spur roads into the rain forest up the Hoh, Queets and Quinault rivers (7).

SCENIC ROUTES

The most spectacular sections of highway on this scenic tour offer fine views of the Olympic Peninsula's forests, mountains and shoreline. They include the Heart o' the Hills Highway to the mountaintop vistas in Olympic National Park; **US 101** along the shores of Lake Crescent; the spur road through the forest to Sol Duc Hot Springs; the coast road (**SR 112**) between Clallam Bay and Neah Bay; and **US 101** between Ruby Beach and Kalaloch, with its fine ocean views.

SPECIAL TO ...

The Pacific Northwest is famed for the rich harvest of seafood fished from its waters, notably salmon, trout, clams, oysters and the renowned Dungeness crab. Sample Indian-style smoked salmon and the mouthwatering menus served in such famous seafood restaurants as The 3 Crabs at Dungeness.

Neah Bay, Washington

5 This small fishing village, located in the Makah Indian Reservation at the northwest tip of the Olympic Peninsula, provides an opportunity to see the cultural heritage and lifestyle of the area's Indian community, especially if you are here for the annual Makah Days celebration in August. Go and see the exhibits recording their 2,500-year history at the **Makah Cultural and Research Center**, then walk around the town, with its Indian-owned, charter-fishing businesses, retail outlets and motels. Browse through the craft shops for a souvenir of your visit, and sample the Indian-style smoked salmon, a Washington specialty. For a sight-seeing treat take the 7-mile (11km) drive and trail west out of town to **Cape Flattery**, where the cliffs afford

Glacier-clad peaks survey the rest of Olympic National Park

marvelous views of rocky Tatoosh Island and its lighthouse across the pounding surf.

*Retrace the route to Sappho, then follow **US 101** south through Forks and Queets to Lake Quinault, with trips to the Pacific Shoreline starting at La Push, and the Olympic National Forest and Park.*

La Push and the Pacific Shoreline, Washington

6 A narrow 60-mile (96km) strip of the Pacific shoreline between Neah Bay and Queets, in the south, forms a separate, smaller section of Olympic National Park. It is a wild, deserted coastline of rocky headlands, boulder-strewn coves, sandy beaches and rugged offshore islets populated by seabirds and marine animals. But be warned: there is often no escape if you get trapped at the water's edge by the incoming tide. Much safer are the long sandy beaches, where you can take a brisk walk or hunt for driftwood and agates. To get to the shoreline, either take the spur road from **US 101** just north of Forks to the oceanfront village of La Push or stay on **US 101** until you reach the coast at Ruby and Kalaloch beaches.

Drenched in heavy rainfall throughout the year (about 140 inches [350 cm] annually), the western slopes of the Olympic Mountains are covered with a thick blanket of moss-draped rain forest that is unique in North America. Between Forks and Lake Quinault spur roads and trails enter

the forest from **US 101** and follow the Hoh, Queets and Quinault river valleys. The Hoh section of the forest is especially recommended. Its visitor center has informative displays and is a departure point for several nature trails, including the 'Hall of Mosses' trail.

ℹ Hoh Rain Forest, Olympic National Park

*From Lake Quinault continue south on **US 101** for 39 miles (62km) to Grays Harbor.*

Grays Harbor, Washington

7 This immense natural inlet is the location of the twin industrial ports of Hoquiam and Aberdeen, which are often ignored by visitors passing through to the Pacific beaches. Well worth a stop, however, is **Hoquiam Castle**, a turreted 20-room mansion once owned by a lumber magnate and now restored to its former elegance. Another attraction is **Grays Harbor Historical Seaport**, just outside Aberdeen on **US 12**, which features a maritime museum, two full-scale replica 18th-century ships and other exhibits.

ℹ 2109 Sumner Avenue, Suite 202, Aberdeen

*From Aberdeen follow **US 12** for 21 miles (34km) to Elma, then take **SR 8** and **US 101** for 27 miles (43km) to Olympia.*

Olympia, Washington

8 With a population of around 30,000, Washington's capital is small compared to other major cities in the state. But what it lacks in size it makes up for in the grandeur of its public buildings, which are set in magnificent landscaped grounds around the **Legislative Building**. Many, however, are closed at weekends. At the **State Capitol Museum** you will see exhibits relating to Washington's history and government and a gallery with changing displays of art.

ℹ 1000 Plum Street

*From Olympia pick up **I-5** northbound for 62 miles (99km) to downtown Seattle.*

Seabirds search for supper along the beach at Santa Cruz

ℹ️ Hallidie Plaza, Powell and Market Streets, San Francisco

Take either the Bayshore Freeway (US 101) or I-280 south from downtown San Francisco for 45 miles (72km) to Santa Clara, then SR 17 south for about 31 miles (50km) to Santa Cruz.

Santa Cruz, California

1 Just before Santa Cruz take a detour to Felton, where the **Roaring Camp and Big Trees Railroad** has steam train rides, chuck-wagon barbecues and bluegrass music at the 1880s log camp in the redwoods.

A few miles south, the resort town of Santa Cruz fronts onto fine swimming and surfing beaches at the north end of Monterey Bay. Take a stroll along the historic **Boardwalk**, with its 1911 carousel and 1924 rollercoaster, its amusement arcades, eateries and other attractions, and wander around the yacht harbor, the fish market, shops and seafood restaurants on the Municipal Wharf. The present **Mission Santa Cruz** is only a 1931 replica of the original one destroyed in 1857, but the nearby **Casa Adobe** is the genuine article and is Santa Cruz's oldest house. The town's most puzzling visitor attraction is the **Mystery Spot**, a 150-foot (46m) circle where the laws of gravity seem to go crazy.

ℹ️ 105 Cooper Street, Suite 243, Santa Cruz

Follow SR 1 south along Monterey Bay for 46 miles (74km) to Monterey.

Monterey and the 17-Mile Drive, California

2 At the south end of Monterey Bay is the historic town of Monterey, the old Spanish and Mexican capital of Alta California. Collect a map from the Chamber of Commerce and

3 days – Approximately 495 miles (792km)

MONTEREY & BIG SUR

San Francisco ● Santa Cruz ● Monterey and the 17-Mile-Drive ● Big Sur Coast and Morro Bay ● San Luis Obispo ● Paso Robles and the Upper Salinas Valley ● Salinas San Francisco

This tour of superlatives takes you from beautiful San Francisco down one of the most spectacular shorelines in all America. You will gather long-lasting memories of the breathtaking scenery (sometimes shrouded in eerie sea fog), of the quaint art colonies and fishing communities, the teeming marine life, the roar of the surf and the tangy smell of the Pacific breezes. Inland, along the fertile Salinas Valley, you can savor the historic atmosphere of lovely old missions and adobe communities established by Spanish colonists along the Camino Real long ago and visit the home town of writer John Steinbeck, the area's most famous publicist.

follow the self-guided 'Path of History' tour of the old buildings preserved in the **Monterey State Historic Park** and explore the lively

Sunset at Lone Cypress on the scenic 17-Mile Drive

FOR HISTORY BUFFS

6 Just off **US 101**, 19 miles (31km) north of Salinas, the old town of San Juan Bautista spans three centuries of California history. Next to the well-preserved Spanish **mission**, founded in 1797, is the 6-acre (2.5 hectare) section of town designated as the **San Juan Bautista State Historic Park**. It contains a number of restored historic buildings, including the **Plaza Hotel** (1858), the **Castro Adobe** (1840) and the **Zanetta House** (1868).

FOR CHILDREN

Extra treats for children on this long tour might include a trip to see the elephant seals at **Año Nuevo State Reserve** near Santa Cruz and rides and other fun attractions at the **Great America theme park** in Santa Clara (1); a tour of the historic figures at the **Spirit of Monterey Wax Museum** (2); beachcombing for semi-precious stones, shells and driftwood at Cambria (3); a tour of **Helen Moe's Antique Doll Museum**, just north of Paso Robles (5).

BACK TO NATURE

There are few sights on this tour more thrilling than a sea otter lolling on its back in the waves, busily breaking open a clam on a stone carefully placed on its stomach. The Monterey Bay and Peninsula and the coast down to Morro Bay offer more wildlife wonders, with sightings of brown pelicans, cormorants and other seabirds, sealions, elephant seals, dolphins and whales. There are also special seasonal delights, such as the gathering of monarch butterflies at Natural Bridges State Beach near Santa Cruz (1) in March or of eagles at Lake San Antonio near Paso Robles every winter (5). There are also the California poppies, the eternal redwoods and much, much more.

scene down at Fisherman's Wharf. There are fish stands, curio shops and restaurants, boat trips and whale-watching cruises around Monterey Bay. Marine life is also on show at the superb **Monterey Bay Aquarium** at Cannery Row, the waterfront former fish-canning factory area immortalized by the author John Steinbeck.

From nearby Pacific Grove you can follow the famed '17-Mile Drive' around the craggy shoreline of the Monterey Peninsula, with its golf courses, windswept cypresses and white-sand beaches, and its offshore rocks and kelp beds teeming with seabirds and marine mammals. (Some areas of the coast are too dangerous for swimming.) Don't miss the walk to the famous—and much photographed—'Lone Cypress'.

At Carmel, a picturesque artists' and writers' community lying beside a silvery curve of beach, you will be tempted to linger in the smart boutiques, galleries and shops along the pretty tree-shaded streets. But leave enough time to visit beautiful **Mission San Carlos Borromeo**, the last resting place of Father Junípero Serra, the founder of California's chain of missions, and to walk through **Point Lobos State Reserve**, with its grove of cypresses and marine life just south of town.

ⓘ 380 Alvarado Street, Monterey

*From Carmel follow **SR 1** south for about 126 miles (201m) along the Big Sur coast through San Simeon to Morro Bay.*

Big Sur Coast and Morro Bay, California

3 South of Carmel, **Route 1** follows the spectacular Big Sur coast below the Santa Lucia Mountains, a wild shoreline of rugged headlands, rocky bays and crashing surf almost uninhabited except for seabirds, sea-lions and other marine life. At San Simeon you will find the coast's most famous manmade wonder: amazing **Hearst Castle**, officially **Hearst San Simeon State Historical Monument**. Created between 1919 and 1947 by the publishing magnate William Randolph Hearst, this luxurious hilltop mansion—a huge complex in Hispano-Moorish style called La Cuesta Encantada (The Enchanted Hill)—is packed with art treasures and surrounded by opulently landscaped grounds. You will need an advance reservation for a 1¾-hour tour.

South of the quaint art colony of Cambria and the port of Cayucos, a favorite of antique-hunters, the 576-foot (176m) extinct volcanic peak of Morro Rock comes into view, dominating the vast harbor of Morro Bay. Evening dinner cruises around the bay are available aboard the *Tiger's Folly II*. You can also explore the fish markets, tempting seafood restaurants, aquarium and gift shops along the waterfront Embarcadero, and, if you are a chess-player, try a game on the gigantic chessboard below the Centennial Stairway on Harbor Street.

ⓘ 9190 Castillo, San Simeon; also 895 Napa Street, Morro Bay

*From Morro Bay follow **SR 1** inland for 14 miles (22km) to San Luis Obispo.*

San Luis Obispo, California

4 This pleasant old college town and county seat grew by the creek where the Spaniards established Mission San Luis Obispo de Tolosa in 1772. When you have explored the shops and cafés that today line the old **Mission Plaza**, take a short walk to the **San Luis Obispo County Historical Museum**, where you will discover more about the area's history and its original Indian inhabitants. As you wander around the streets you will discover many fine 19th-century homes, such as the restored **Dallidet Adobe** and the Victorian **Jack House and garden**. May is a good time to visit San Luis Obispo, when the town comes to life with parades, a rodeo, a Spanish Market and lots of entertainment during the annual Fiesta.

ⓘ 1041 Chorro Street

*Take **US 101** north for about 28 miles (45km) to Paso Robles.*

Paso Robles and the Upper Salinas Valley, California

5 North of San Luis Obispo, US 101 roughly follows the route of the old Camino Real, or Royal Highway, that linked the missions and towns established by the Spaniards along the Salinas River valley. Around Paso Robles, named for its oak groves, is a large wine-growing region where you can visit wineries for free tastings and tours. In the mountains north of

RECOMMENDED WALKS

You will have plenty of opportunities for bracing walks along miles of unspoiled beaches between Carmel and Morro Bay and for strolls among the art galleries and shops in little oceanside communities like Carmel, Big Sur and Cambria (3). If you prefer something more strenuous, there are rugged trails at **Pinnacles National Monument**, where sturdy shoes are advisable (5).

SCENIC ROUTES

Wherever you are in sight of the Pacific on this tour you will find something interesting to look at. But the most spectacular sections of the itinerary are the **17-Mile Drive off Route 1** around the Monterey Peninsula, with its views of the wildlife along the rugged shoreline, and the Big Sur coast, also on **Route 1**, between Carmel and San Simeon. There is also a beautiful drive through green mountain scenery to Lakes Nacimiento and San Antonio on **Route G14** north of Paso Robles.

The Big Sur coast, south of Monterey, is often shrouded in patchy fog on hot summer days

town via scenic **Route G14**, Lake Nacimiento offers relaxation and recreation with a range of facilities for camping, picnicking, hiking, boating and fishing.

Back on **US 101**, make a stop at San Miguel to see the lovely **Mission San Miguel** of 1797, the restored 1846 **Rios-Caledonia Adobe** and the nearby **Estrella Adobe Church**, built by Protestant pioneers in 1878. At Soledad, a detour east on **Route 146** brings you to **Pinnacles National Monument**, 16,000 rugged acres (6,474 hectares) of volcanic rock spires, cliffs, canyons and caves.

🛈 1113 Spring Street, Paso Robles

*From Paso Robles continue north on **US 101** for 97 miles (155km) to Salinas.*

Salinas, California

6 This manufacturing city, the seat of Monterey County, is the hub of the fertile agricultural region of the lower Salinas Valley. It is also the birthplace of author John Steinbeck. The house, now used as a restaurant and gift shop, is one of many historic buildings preserved in the original downtown shopping district, a nine-block area known as Oldtown. Two other historic buildings, the **Boronda Adobe** and the 1868 **Harvey-Baker House**, now form the Monterey County Historical Museums; their exhibits document the area's history. If you time your visit to Salinas right, you can enjoy the thrills and spills of the big four-day Annual California Rodeo that draws thousands to the town every July.

🛈 119 E Alisal Street

*Continue north on **US 101** for 108 miles (173 km) to San Francisco.*

San Francisco – Santa Cruz **76 (122)**
Santa Cruz – Monterey **46 (74)**
Monterey – Big Sur Coast and Morro Bay **126 (201)**
Big Sur Coast – San Luis Obispo **14 (22)**
San Luis Obispo – Paso Robles **28 (45)**
Paso Robles – Salinas **97 (155)**
Salinas – San Francisco **108 (173)**

SPECIAL TO ...

1 Santa Clara and neighboring San Jose have enough visitor attractions between them to justify a completely separate tour. But try not to miss a guided tour of the weird 160-room **Winchester Mystery House** in San Jose, which has doors opening onto blank walls and stairs that lead nowhere. It is a product of the irrational fears of rifle heiress Sarah Winchester. She thought malevolent spirits would harm her if work on the house stopped, so she kept carpenters busy on it for 38 years.

4 days – Approximately 520 miles (832km)

CALIFORNIA GOLD

San Francisco • Jamestown and the Gold Country • Yosemite National Park • Mariposa • Merced and the San Joaquin Valley • San Francisco

On this tour from San Francisco you will step back in time to the heady days of California's 1849 gold rush as you explore the picturesque and revitalized old mining towns in the foothills of the Sierra Nevada. In these forested mountains you will also discover the awesome grandeur of Yosemite National Park, one of California's greatest scenic gems. The return drive then takes you through the irrigated farmlands of the Central Valley where, in addition to the varied local attractions, you can sample the region's agricultural riches.

FOR HISTORY BUFFS

1 As you cross the bridge over Woods Creek coming into Jamestown on **Route 49**, you are right at the spot where prospectors led by the Reverend James Woods discovered a 75-pound (34kg) gold nugget and sparked off the rush to the area in the summer of 1848. Gold is still being found in Jamestown, but if you are not successful panning for it you can buy souvenir bags of it in local shops.

ℹ️ Hallidie Plaza, Powell and Market Streets, San Francisco

*Cross the Bay Bridge from downtown San Francisco to Oakland and follow **I-580, I-205, SR 120** and **SR 108** east for about 127 miles (203km) via Livermore, Manteca and Oakdale to Jamestown and California's Gold Country.*

Jamestown and the Gold Country, California

1 The wooded foothills of the Sierra Nevada are the scene of the great California gold rush of 1849. Here the highway crosses **Route 49**, the Golden Chain Highway linking the old mining camps on the rich gold-bearing vein, or Mother Lode, that runs north to south along the hills. In

The view from Yosemite's Olmsted Point takes in Tenaya Lake and, beyond, dramatic domes of granite

this southern section, immortalized in the stories of Mark Twain and Bret Harte, are Jamestown, Sonora and Columbia. These picturesque, restored old mining communities now lure visitors with quaint antique stores, restaurants, boutiques, old saloons, historic inns, tours of abandoned mines, gold-panning trips and many other attractions that evoke the gold rush era. A special attraction at Jamestown, the location for hundreds of movies and TV features, is a ride on an old steam train at the **Railtown 1897 State Historic Park**. At Sonora, 'Queen of the Southern Mines', you will see fascinating gold rush artifacts at the **Tuolumne County Museum and History Center**, housed in the old county jail. And at Columbia, so well restored that the entire town is now a designated State Historic Park, there are guided walking tours and stage-coach rides along the tree-shaded streets, and performances of plays at the **Fallon House Theater**.

ℹ️ 55 West Stockton Street, Sonora

*From Jamestown drive south to Chinese Camp. Continue east on **SR 120** for about 50 miles (80km) through Groveland to Yosemite National Park.*

Yosemite National Park, California

2 One of the greatest gems in America's national park system, Yosemite is a natural wonderland of forests, lakes, waterfalls and 10,000-foot (3,048m) peaks covering more than 1,200 square miles (3,108sq km) on the western slopes of the Sierra Nevada. If you have plenty of time, start your visit with the spectacular 80-mile (129km) round-trip drive up the scenic Tioga Pass road (**Route 120**) into the high country to Tuolumne Meadows. Return the same way, then make for Yosemite Valley, the most popular of the park's attractions. This 7-mile (11km) flat-bottomed gorge, carved by glaciers long ago and now drained by the beautiful Merced River, contains Yosemite's most impressive natural wonders. Turn a blind eye to the tourist facilities and the summer traffic congestion and you will be spellbound by the sheer grandeur of its

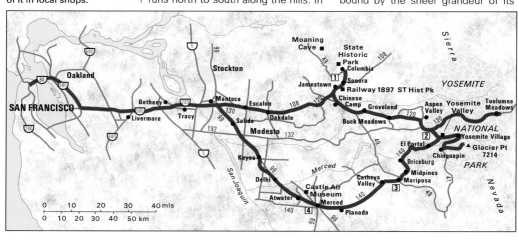

towering rock walls, colossal granite domes and many thundering, snow-fed waterfalls, among them the 2,425-foot (739m) Yosemite Falls, America's highest waterfall.

Another scenic drive, a 32-mile (51km) round-trip, will take you from Chinquapin, south of the valley, past the Badger Pass ski area and up to Glacier Point. Here you will get stunning views of Yosemite Falls and the valley 3,214 feet (980m) below.

ℹ Yosemite Village, in Yosemite National Park

From Yosemite Valley take SR 140 southwest through El Portal for 40 miles (64km) to Mariposa.

Mariposa, California

3 West of Yosemite you pass through the forested Merced River Canyon, a popular spot for white-water rafting and trout fishing, before reaching the old gold-mining town of Mariposa. The main visitor attractions here are the timber **County Court-house** built in 1854, the oldest still in use in California; the **California State Mining and Mineral Exhibit**, which has excellent gold-mining, mineral and gem displays; and the **Mariposa Museum and History Center**, which houses old gold-mining equipment and artifacts of pioneer family life. You can also take a one-hour narrated air tour of the Yosemite area.

ℹ 5158 Highway 140

Continue west on SR 140 for 37 miles (59km) to Merced. Then

Upper and Lower Yosemite Falls in full flow, equal in height to 11 Niagaras

follow **SR 99** *north for about 55 miles (88km) along the San Joaquin Valley via Modesto to Manteca.*

Merced and the San Joaquin Valley, California

4 Merced and Modesto are important processing and distribution centers for the agricultural produce of the San Joaquin Valley. Of interest to visitors at Merced are the fine **county court-house** of 1875, which houses a local history museum, and the **Yosemite Wildlife Museum**, with dioramas of California's wild creatures in their natural habitats.

Other varied attractions then beckon as you follow **Route 99** north. They include the fine displays of historic aircraft at the **Castle Air Museum** near Atwater and tours of the restored 19th-century **McHenry Mansion** and the nearby **McHenry Museum**, with its local history exhibits, at Modesto. And if you want to try some of the area's produce, you can sample the almonds at **Blue Diamond Growers** in Salida and taste the various wines at **Delicato Vineyards** in Manteca.

ℹ 1880 N Street, Merced; also 1114 J Street, Modesto

From Manteca head west to pick up I-205 and I-580 westbound for the 76-mile (122km) drive back to San Francisco via Oakland and the Bay Bridge.

San Francisco – Jamestown **127 (203)**
Jamestown – Yosemite National Park **57 (91)**
Yosemite National Park – Mariposa **168 (269)**
Mariposa – Merced **37 (59)**
Merced – San Francisco **131 (210)**

FOR CHILDREN

There are many attractions kids can enjoy on this tour. Possibilities include a tour of the candy-making process (and samples) at **Hershey Chocolate USA** at Oakdale; a gold-panning bus tour and steam train ride at Jamestown; or a stagecoach ride at Columbia (1); and a visit to **Applegate Park and Zoo** at Merced (4), which has displays of wild animals and birds and rides for the youngsters.

BACK TO NATURE

The High Sierra is home to such wild animals as mountain lion, bighorn sheep and black bear, though you will have to be lucky to catch a glimpse of them. Most likely to catch your eye are the magnificent forest trees, perhaps even giant sequoias and, if it is spring, meadows bright with golden poppies and other wildflowers. For more about California's plants and animals check out the **Yosemite Wildlife Museum** at Merced and the **Great Valley Museum of Natural History** at Modesto (4), which concentrates on the flora and fauna of the Central Valley.

SPECIAL TO . . .

1 A few miles north of Columbia is **Moaning Cave**. It is California's largest public cavern and has a main chamber big enough to hold the Statue of Liberty. Three tours, lasting between 45 minutes and 3 hours, are available, one of them involving a 180-foot (55m) rope descent into the main chamber.

RECOMMENDED WALKS

The guided walking tours of Jamestown, Sonora and Columbia (1) take you around the historic treasures at an easy pace. At Yosemite National Park you can follow more strenuous foot trails through the majestic scenery or enjoy gentler strolls by the Merced River.

SCENIC ROUTES

Many stretches of highway in the Sierras will captivate you with their scenic surroundings, but one of the highlights is certainly the Tioga Pass road (**SR 120**), which affords spectacular views of high-country scenery, with its bare rock expanses, glacial boulders, crystal lakes, pine thickets, twisted junipers and wildflower meadows.

3 days – Approximately 406 miles (650km)

MOUNTAIN RETREATS & DESERT RESORTS

Los Angeles • Riverside • Hemet
Palm Desert • Palm Springs
Joshua Tree National Monument • Indio
Los Angeles

An hour's drive east along the freeway from Los Angeles brings you to the historic heartland of California's famed citrus industry, where you will begin a scenic drive up into the cool pine forests of the San Jacinto Mountains. Below the rugged east face you can explore fabulous Palm Springs, one of the lush, air-conditioned resort communities of the Coachella Valley, where the irrigated desert is patterned with regimented rows of date palms and grapefruit. You will then see the desert as nature intended—hot, dry and hostile—as you drive through the wild grandeur of Joshua Tree National Monument, not without its own hardy residents, of the plant and animal variety.

FOR HISTORY BUFFS

1 If you wish to know more about the development of California's citrus industry, visit the **Riverside Municipal Museum** on Orange Street. Here you will find exhibits documenting the industry's early days in this area. Down the street you can also see the **Japanese Memorial Pavilion**, built in 1987 to commemorate the workers who helped to establish the citrus industry here.

FOR CHILDREN

1 If you linger at all the attractions of interest to children at Riverside, you may not get much further along the itinerary planned. Limit the choice to the fun on offer at **Castle Park**, which includes lots of rides, miniature golf and a video arcade; a tour of the full-size and scale locomotives (with rides some Sundays) at **Hunter Park Live Steamers**; or a visit to the **Earth Science Museum** at the **Jurupa Cultural Center**, where kids can enjoy **Dinosaur Day** and the **Fossil Shack** every Saturday morning.

ⓘ 695 South Figueroa Street, Los Angeles

Follow the Pomona Freeway (SR 60) east from Los Angeles for 56 miles (90km) to Riverside.

Riverside, California

1 An attractive, historic residential city, Riverside is the birthplace of California's billion-dollar citrus industry, which began when two navel orange trees sent from Brazil were planted here in 1873. It is also the site of the Riverside campus of the University of California and is known for its cultural attractions and 19th-century architecture. Driving around, you will see pleasant tree-lined boulevards, Victorian-fronted stores and gracious 19th-century homes, such as the beautifully restored **Heritage House**, built in 1891 on Magnolia Avenue and open some days for tours. A famous city landmark near the center of town is the recently renovated **Mission Inn**, a prestigious, rambling old hotel with patios and gardens, a chapel, 900-bell carillon and Tiffany windows. Its guest list over the decades has included such notables as Theodore Roosevelt, Humphrey Bogart and the honeymooning Reagans.

Other visitor attractions include the mission-style **Art Museum** and the **Botanic Garden**, with its collection of dry-climate plants, on the east side of the university campus. South of

Riverside's Japanese Memorial Pavilion is a tribute to the workers who helped start the citrus industry

town at March Air Force Base, you will see displays of vintage aircraft and other aviation exhibits at the **March Field Museum**.

ⓘ 3443 Orange Street

*From Riverside follow **I-215** south for about 18 miles (29km) through Perris, then take **SR 74** for 14 miles (22km) to Hemet.*

Hemet, California

2 For anyone interested in railroads, there is a worthwhile stop at Perris, off **Highway 215**, to see the railroad equipment and trolleys on display at the free **Orange Empire Railway Museum**. Then drive on to Hemet, on **Route 74**, where a pageant based on Helen Hunt Jackson's 1884 love story *Ramona* is performed every spring in the mountainside amphitheater. About 18 miles (29km) east, make a detour north on **Route 243** into the San Jacinto Mountains to explore the little artists' community of **Idyllwild** and the forested wilderness of **San Jacinto State Park**, where you will find many recreation facilities as well as camp grounds, hiking trails and a variety of wildlife above 5,500 feet (1,676m).

ⓘ 395 East Latham Avenue

*Return to **SR 74** and follow the scenic 36-mile (58km) stretch of highway into Palm Desert and the Coachella Valley.*

Palm Desert, California

3 Palm Desert is one of a cluster of desert resort communities that have developed in the dry, sunny climate of the Coachella Valley.

Palm Springs, named for its mineral springs and towering trees

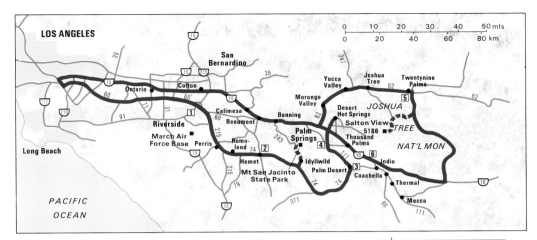

Originally desert, the valley is now a vast irrigated garden producing huge quantities of dates and citrus fruit. To get an idea of the original vegetation, stop by the 1,200-acre (485-hectare) **Living Desert** park when you arrive at Palm Desert. Here you will see not only marvelous displays of desert plants but also the wildlife that inhabits the region. While in town also check out the **McCallum Theater for the Performing Arts** at the prestigious **Bob Hope Cultural Center** on Fred Waring Drive, where you might catch a show, play, movie or other suitable entertainment to round off the day.

ℹ️ 72-990 Highway 111

Follow SR 111 west for about 13 miles (21km) to the center of Palm Springs.

Palm Springs, California

4 The best known of the desert resort communities, Palm Springs grew around the natural hot springs owned by the Agua Caliente Indians at the foot of 10,804-foot (3,293m) Mount San Jacinto. Since the 1920s the town has enjoyed an undiminished reputation as a glamorous

playground retreat for Hollywood stars and the rich. The place is certainly packed with big, gorgeous homes and swimming pools, exclusive shops, fine restaurants, vibrant night spots, dozens of well-manicured golf courses and hundreds of tennis courts. But there are also many other attractions to lure passing visitors, although you may find that some are closed during the hottest summer months.

Apart from hot-air balloon trips, an ever popular attraction is the breath-taking 2½-mile (4km) ride on the **Aerial Tramway** to the cool terraces among the pine trees 8,516 feet (2,596m) up the sheer face of Mount San Jacinto. Drive south on Palm Canyon Drive to visit the **Palm Springs Desert Museum**, a cultural center featuring natural history displays, art exhibits and a theater; to experience the 1930s and '40s shopping atmosphere recaptured at **Ruddy's General Store Museum**; and to see the palm oasis and desert plants at **Moorten's Botanical Garden**. Continue to the spectacular **Indian Canyons** carved into the east face of the San Jacinto Mountains. Here you can walk or ride on horseback along

BACK TO NATURE

Nature adopts various guises on this tour, from cool, forested mountains to searing scrub deserts. Keep your binoculars handy for a sight of soaring birds of prey, though for shy desert creatures you will get better close-up views at the man-made preserves, such as **The Living Desert** at Palm Desert. A special bonus for plant-lovers is the dazzling display of waxy, greenish-white flowers put on by the region's Joshua trees every March and April.

RECOMMENDED WALKS

Places to stretch your legs on the tour include the hilly, 37-acre (15-hectare) **Botanic Garden** at Riverside (1); the little artists' community of Idyllwild; the mountainside forest trails in San Jacinto State Park (2); the Indian Canyons near Palm Springs (4); and the area's commercial nature parks and gardens. Follow sensible precautions when walking trails in Joshua Tree National Monument (5). In particular, don't get too close to the painful spines of the jumping cholla cactus when walking through the **Cholla Cactus Garden**.

SCENIC ROUTES

Once you leave Hemet the road starts to get interesting as you follow the scenic Palms to Pines Highway (**Route 74**) around the San Jacinto Mountains, with its changing views of pine- and oak-covered slopes and painted rock desert and distant panoramas of the Coachella Valley. You will also enjoy the drive through wild desert scenery in Joshua Tree National Monument.

SPECIAL TO . . .

Special attractions that always delight visitors in this part of California are the colorful and unusual annual festivals and events. Highlights include the Easter Sunrise Service atop 1,337-foot (408m) Mt Rubidoux west of Riverside (1); Hemet's springtime *Ramona* pageant (2); January sled-dog races on Mt San Jacinto (2); and even turtle races during the Turtle Days celebration at Joshua Tree in May (5).

trails past bubbling hot springs, spectacular cascades, Indian cliff dwellings and stands of imposing palm trees. Then drive back to town to enjoy some refreshing aquatic fun at the **Oasis Water Resort**.

Twelve miles (19km) north along this road is the old spa town of Desert Hot Springs, with **Cabot's Old Indian Pueblo Museum**, a replica four-story Hopi Indian-style building housing an art gallery.

ℹ 255 N El Cielo Road, Suite 315

Pick up SR 62 west of Desert Hot Springs and continue north and east for about 43 miles (69km) to Twentynine Palms and Joshua Tree National Monument.

Joshua Tree National Monument, California

5 More than 870 square miles (2,253 sq km) of rugged desert and mountain country are encompassed in Joshua Tree National Monument, a spectacular preserve of desert flora and fauna named for its strange-looking Joshua trees. Stop by the Visitor Center at the Twentynine Palms entrance for information and a map before starting your tour. Take plenty of drinking water and plan to leave by the south (Cottonwood Spring) entrance. On the way, don't miss the side trip to Salton View, a 5,185-foot (1,580m) overlook in the Little San Bernardino Mountains affording majestic views of the entire Coachella Valley. Other monument landmarks include the giant **Split Rock** and cave near Pinto Wye, the **Cholla Cactus Garden** and the rock formations at the **Wonderland of Rocks** in Hidden Valley.

ℹ Joshua Tree National Monument, 74485 National Monument Drive, Twentynine Palms

Just beyond the south entrance of Joshua Tree National Monument pick up I-10 westbound for 25 miles (40km) to Indio.

Indio, California

6 If you enjoy dates—the edible kind, that is—this Coachella Valley city has plenty of packing plants and wayside establishments where you can buy them in cookies, cakes, puddings or even just as they are. Indio is, in fact, known as the 'Date Capital of America', a bit of Arabia transported to California. Vast groves, or 'gardens', of date palms and grapefruit trees encircle the town, irrigated by water drawn from the Colorado River. If you are here in mid-February you can watch the unique, zany spectacle of camel and ostrich races during the popular annual National Date Festival.

ℹ 82-503 Highway 111

Follow I-10 westbound for about 125 miles (200km) to downtown Los Angeles.

Los Angeles – Riverside **56 (90)**
Riverside – Hemet **32 (51)**
Hemet – Palm Desert **(55) (88)**
Palm Desert – Palm Springs **13 (21)**
Palm Springs – Joshua Tree National Monument **56 (90)**
Joshua Tree – Indio **69 (110)**
Indio – Los Angeles **125 (200)**

The Joshua Tree, its branches tipped with tufts of leaves and clusters of greenish-white flowers

Mission San Diego de Alcalá, set off by a carpet of floral color

ⓘ Horton Plaza, San Diego

*Take **I-5** north from downtown San Diego for about 10 miles (16km) to the Ardath Road turnoff to La Jolla.*

La Jolla, California

1 Keep for another occasion a tour of Mission Bay's fabulous Sea World marine park and make straight for La Jolla (pronounced '*Hoy-a*'), a sophisticated little seaside town that boasts fine museums, galleries and cultural events. It stands on a rocky promontory below 822-foot (251m) Mount Soledad, from the summit of which there are fine views of the town and its rugged shoreline. Seafront landmarks to explore include Alligator Head, La Jolla Cove (a favorite of scuba divers), Whale Point and the caves in the cliffs below the town. Down by the shore you will also find the **Museum of Contemporary Art**, which displays paintings and sculptures from around the world. Around the bay north of town is another major visitor attraction, the magnificent marine aquarium at the **Scripps Institution of Oceanography**.

*Head north from La Jolla along the coast road **(county road S 21)** or **I-5** for about 28 miles (45km) through the beach communities as far as Oceanside.*

Oceanside and San Diego's North Coast, California

2 Along the shoreline north of La Jolla is a series of pleasant resort communities and flat sandy beaches backed by high, windswept bluffs, marshy lagoons and meandering golf courses. The beaches are ideal not only for swimming but also for surfing and surf fishing. At **Torrey Pines State Park**, named for its unique grove of gnarled Torrey pines, golf and hang gliding are the major activities. Further north, Del Mar is known for hot-air ballooning, the Southern California Exposition (or state fair) in June and July and horseracing at the

Oceanside has national surfing competitions and winter whale-watching

OCEAN BEACHES & DESERT BACK COUNTRY

San Diego ● La Jolla ● Oceanside and San Diego's North Coast ● Pala and Palomar Observatory ● Borrego Springs ● Salton City ● Julian and Mission Santa Ysabel ● Escondido ● San Diego

A kaleidoscope of changing scenes awaits you on this tour of San Diego County's north shoreline and inland back country. After leaving San Diego you will explore the coast's long beaches and delightful resort communities, pass through miles of citrus and avocado groves, climb pine-clad mountains, cross vast expanses of arid desert and descend to an inland sea saltier than the ocean. You will return with memories of old Spanish missions, Indian reservations, a famous mountaintop observatory, an old gold-rush town, a battlefield site, a marvelous wild animal park, and much, much more—Southern California without the glitzy theme parks but every bit as rewarding.

famed **Del Mar Thoroughbred Club** founded by Bing Crosby in 1937. Encinitas has the **Quail Botanical Gardens** and countless acres of commercially grown flowers on the way to Carlsbad, a growing resort town with good beaches and two lagoons. The 1,900-foot (579m) pier jutting into the Pacific is a famous landmark at Oceanside, a popular destination for surfers. There is also a fine harbor with moorings for yachts,

FOR HISTORY BUFFS

7 Along Route 78 between Ramona and Escondido is **San Pasqual Battlefield State Park**, the site of a little-known clash on December 6, 1846, when an American army led by General Stephen Kearny lost a bloody contest with Mexican forces during the Mexican-American War (1846–48). You can see a short video and displays relating to the battle at the Visitor Center.

FOR CHILDREN

Additional things for kids on the tour to see and do include the **Mingei International Museum of World Folk Art** in La Jolla, where toys feature among the many objects on display; and hunting for hermit crabs at La Jolla Cove (1); watching weekend hang gliders at **Torrey Pines State Park** (2); a desert trip from Borrego Springs (4); swimming in the Salton Sea (5); a monorail ride over the enclosures at **San Diego Wild Animal Park**; and rides and other activities at the **Family Fun Center** on Danway at Escondido (7).

BACK TO NATURE

Lagoons and marshes along the ocean beaches are good places to see egrets, herons and many species of waterfowl. With a license you can also go night-hunting for grunion (a type of whitebait) with a torch. Whale Point at La Jolla (1) is obviously the best place to see migrating whales. Spring flowers are a colorful sight in Anza-Borrego Desert State Park (4), where you can also see various cacti, palms, century plants and strange elephant trees and perhaps glimpse animals like the desert bighorn sheep.

pleasure boats and sportfishing boats and waterfront shops and restaurants at Cape Cod Village.

ℹ 550 Via de la Valle, Solana Beach

*From Oceanside turn inland on **SR 76** for 34 miles (54km) through Pala and then turn left (northeast) onto **county road S6** for 11 miles (18km) to Palomar Mountain and Palomar Observatory.*

Pala and Palomar Observatory, California

3 Two interesting places to visit on the route inland from Oceanside are the restored **Mission San Luis Rey**, California's largest and richest mission, founded in 1798, and its much smaller branch **Mission San Antonio de Pala**. Built in 1816, the restored mission at Pala is still being used as a place of worship and school for Indian reservations in the area. It has an unusual freestanding bell tower and a museum housing Indian artifacts.

Further east, **county road S6**, the 'Highway to the Stars', winds up the pine-studded slopes of 6,126-foot (1,867m) Palomar Mountain, where you can walk the forested trails in **Palomar Mountain State Park** before driving on to the famous Palomar Observatory, with its impressive 200-inch (5m) telescope and exhibit of astronomical photographs, at the crest.

*Return to **SR 76** via **county road S7**. South of Lake Henshaw turn left (northeast) on **SR 79** for about 4 miles (6km), right (southeast) on **county road S2** for 4 miles (6km), and left (east) on **county road S22** for about 16 miles (26km) to Borrego Springs.*

Borrego Springs, California

4 The desert resort community of Borrego Springs lies amid the arid wilderness of **Anza-Borrego Desert State Park**, its golf courses kept green by irrigation water from underground sources. The park encompasses some half a million acres (202,350 hectares) of rugged desert and mountain terrain, which supports a variety of wildlife, desert plants and colorful winter- and spring-blooming wildflowers. You can see an audio-

visual presentation and get information on suitable self-guided car trips, Jeep trails and guided walks in the park from the Visitors Center just west of Borrego Springs.

ℹ Anza-Borrego Desert State Park

*Continue east on **county road S22** from Borrego Springs for 30 miles (48km) to Salton City and the Salton Sea.*

Salton City, California

5 East of Borrego Springs **county route S22** offers fine views of the desert as it descends to Salton City and the shores of the Salton Sea, 234 feet (71m) below sea-level. This inland saltwater lake, more than 35 miles (56km) long and up to 15 miles (24km) wide, suddenly came into existence in 1905 when roaring flood-waters of the Colorado River broke through a canal gate and drowned a

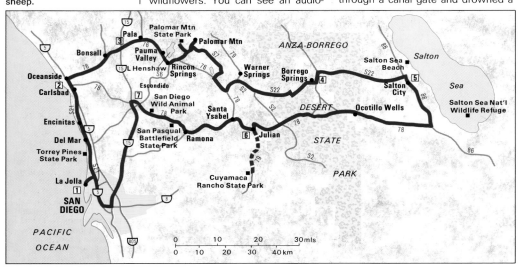

RECOMMENDED WALKS

There are especially enjoyable walks along the rugged shoreline at La Jolla (1), including the Coast Walk by the sea caves; along the pier and through Cape Cod Village at Oceanside (2); along the quiet trails in the area's state parks; down historic Main Street at Julian (6); and along the Kilimanjaro Hiking Trail at the San Diego Wild Animal Park, near Escondido (7).

desert depression. It is now a calm recreational lake used for swimming, boating, water-skiing and fishing. Salton City, halfway along the west shore, is the center for much of this activity. At the southern end of the lake, via **Route 86**, is the **Salton Sea National Wildlife Refuge** frequented by waterfowl.

Follow SR 86 south from Salton City for 13 miles (21km), then turn west on SR 78 for 57 miles (92km) through Ocotillo Wells and Julian to Santa Ysabel.

Julian and Mission Santa Ysabel, California

6 The flavor of the Old West lingers on at the picturesque little town of Julian, an old mining community that sprang to life following a gold strike back in 1870. You can recall those colorful days as you walk down Main Street, with its old false-fronted stores, and tour the now-abandoned **Eagle** and **Highpeak mines**. These days Julian is the center of a lush orchard and farming area, and you can buy apples and other produce along the main road and taste the local wines on a tour of the **Menghini Winery** at weekends.

South of town via **Route 79** you can enjoy a pleasant side trip to **Cuyamaca Rancho State Park**, on the forested slopes of the Laguna Mountains. Northwest of town, on **Route 78**, you can visit Mission Santa Ysabel, founded in 1818, where there are a small **museum** and an **Indian burial ground**.

ⓘ Main and Washington Streets, Julian

From Santa Ysabel continue west on SR 78 for 34 miles (55km) through Ramona to Escondido.

Spring bursts into life at Anza-Borrego Desert State Park

Escondido, California

7 Along the San Pasqual Valley Road (SR 78) beyond the poultry-raising town of Ramona, you will find one of Southern California's major visitor attractions. It is the 1,800-acre (728-hectare) **San Diego Wild Animal Park**, where more than 2,500 animals roam free in re-created natural habitat enclosures, although some are performers in animal shows. The park also features a giant aviary, small mammal exhibits, petting area, monorail ride, hiking trail and behind-the-scenes tours.

Escondido lies in rolling hill country surrounded by groves of lemons and avocados, golf courses and wineries that are open for tours and tastings. One of these is the **Deer Park Winery** on Champagne Boulevard, where there is also an interesting **vintage car museum**. Another area attraction is the little **museum** housing memorabilia of the band leader Lawrence Welk at the theater of the **Lawrence Welk Resort**. And for history buffs, there is **Heritage Walk**, featuring a collection of 19th-century buildings at **Grape Day Park**.

ⓘ 720 N Broadway

From Escondido take I-15 south for 25 miles (40km) to downtown San Diego.

San Diego – La Jolla	**10 (16)**
La Jolla – Oceanside	**28 (45)**
Oceanside – Pala	**45 (72)**
Pala – Borrego Springs	**45 (72)**
Borrego Springs – Salton City	**30 (48)**
Salton City – Julian	**63 (101)**
Julian – Escondido	**41 (66)**
Escondido – San Diego	**25 (40)**

SCENIC ROUTES

The coast road (**county road S21**) through the beach communities north of La Jolla offers constantly changing views of the windswept southern California shoreline. Inland, the most scenically rewarding stretches of road include the tree-lined 'Highway to the Stars' **(S6)** up to Palomar Observatory small mammal exhibits, and the winding section of **SR 78** between Ocotillo Wells and Julian, with its fine views of the desert and forested mountains.

SPECIAL TO ...

On the drive back to San Diego, turn off **I-15** at Mission Valley to visit **Mission San Diego de Alcalá**, known as the 'Mother of the Missions'. Founded in 1769, it was the first in the chain of 21 missions begun by the Franciscan Father Junípero Serra along the California coast during the period of Spanish colonization. During your tour you will see records in his handwriting and other historic relics.

INDEX

References to captions are in italic.

ACKNOWLEDGEMENTS

The Automobile Association would like to thank the following photographers, libraries and associations for their help in the preparation of this book:

J ALLAN CASH PHOTOLIBRARY   92 Death Valley, 93 Scotty's Castle, 114 Joshua Tree, 115 Harbourside Reflections.

CHICAGO OFFICE OF TOURISM   58 Chicago.

GALENA/JO DAVIS COUN CONVENTION & VISITORS BUREAU 56 U S Grant House, Galena.

GEORGIA DEPT OF INDUSTRY & TRADE   35 Milledgeville, 39 Madison.

E INGLEFIELD   12 Breakers, 61 Festival, 62 Minnihaha Falls, 63 Hastings.

D NOBLE   Cover Yosemite National Park.

ROCKFORD AREA CONV & VISITORS BUREAU   55 Tinker Swiss Cottage Rockford.

ST CHARLES CONV & VISITORS BUREAU   57 St Charles.

S ILLINOIS REG TOURIST COUNCIL   66 St Louis Iron Mountain Railway, 66 Garden of the Gods, 68 Old St Vincent's Church.

SPECTRUM COLOUR LIBRARY   22 Virginia site of Battlefield, 31 Virginia Tobacco Drying, 86 Central City Mining Town, 89 Farm Pastures, 90 Echo Valley.

SPRINGFIELD CONV & VISITORS BUREAU   59 Lincoln's Home.

TEXAS DEPT OF COMMERCE   74 Texas State RR Rusk, 75 Caddo Lake State Park, 76 Jefferson House of the Seasons, 78 Big Thicket Nat Reserve.

THE STOCK MARKET   1 Centrest Tower, Miami, 2 J F K Library, Boston, 3 Amish, 4 Rocky Mountains, 6 Whale Show San Diego, 8/9 John Hancock Tower, Boston, 9 Trinity Church Boston, 10 Cape Cod Highland Light, 11 North Bridge Concord, 13 Thanksgiving Meal, 14 Tarrytown, 15 Hudson River, 16 Westpoint, 17 Long Island Lighthouse, 18 Long Island South Fork, 19 Greenport, 20 Sign Williamsburg, 21 Washington, 23 Blue Ridge Mountains, 24 Fredericksburg, 27 Virg Memorial, 28 Winterthur, 29 Amish, 30 Valley Forge, 31 Jamestown, 32 Williamsburg, 34/5 Charlotte, 36 Charlatter, 37 Biltmore Ashville, 38 Blue Ridge Mountains, 40 Northbrook, Chicago, 40 Cannonball House, Macon, 43 Miami, 43 Miami Beach, 44 Key West, Florida, 44 Everglades, 46 Seven Mile Bridge, 47 Cinderella Magic Castle, 48 Pier, St Petersburg, 49 Marina Sarasota, 50/1 Cincinnati, 52 Jefferson County Court House, 53 Mammouth Cave Park, 54 Lexington, 60 Illinois State Cap Building, 64/5 St Louis Arch, 69 Avery Island, 70/1 Shadows on the Teche, 71 Mardi Gras N Orleans, 72/3 Dallas, 77 Galveston, The Coonel Steamboat, 79 River Taxi San Antonio, 80 Austin, 81 LBJ's Home, 82/3 Denver WTC, 84 Estes Park, Rocky Mountains, 87 Salt Lake City, 88 Mt Timpanagos, 95 Phoenix, 96 Red Hot Peppers, 97 Tanto Nat Forest, 98 Mission San Xavier Del Bac, 99 Santa Fe Market, Santario de Chimayo, 101 Indian Pueblo, 102/3 Seattle, 103 7th Market, Los Angeles, 104 Olympic Nat Forest, 105/6 Olympic Nat Park, 107 Santa Crus birds, 109 Big Sur, 110 Yosemite Nat Park, 111 Yosemite Upper Falls, 112 Jap Mem Riverside, 115 Mission St Diego.

VIRGINIA DIV IF TOURISM   25 Oatlands, 26 Great Falls, Potomac Park.

ZEFA PICTURE LIBRARY (UK) LTD   5 Chicago, 91 Las Vegas, 112/3 Palm Springs, 116/7 Barrego State Park.